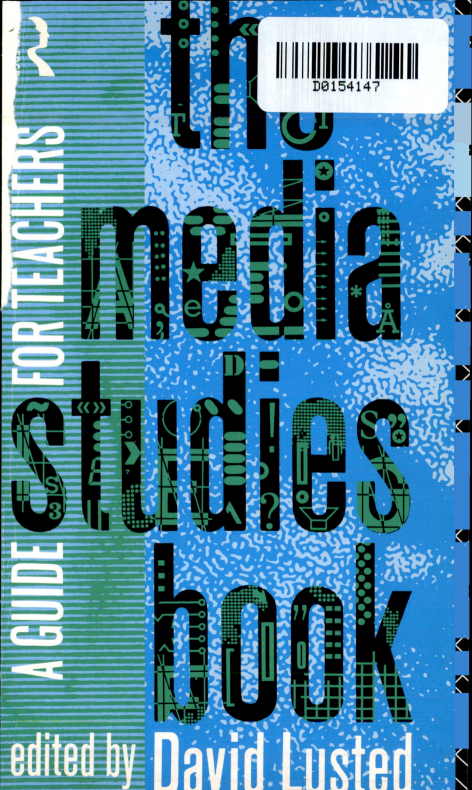

FOR TEACHERS

A GUIDE

the
media
studies
book

edited by David Lusted

The Media Studies Book

A guide for teachers

Edited by David Lusted

A Comedia book
Published by Routledge
London and New York

First published 1991
by Routledge
11 New Fetter Lane, London EC4P 4EE

Simultaneously published in the USA and Canada
by Routledge
29 West 35th Street, New York, NY 10001

Reprinted 1992, 1994

This collection © 1991 Routledge; individual contributions

© 1991 individual contributors

Typeset by J & L Composition Ltd, Filey, North Yorkshire
Printed and bound in Great Britain by T J Press Ltd, Padstow, Cornwall

British Library Cataloguing in Publication Data
A catalogue record for this book is available from the British Library

Library of Congress Cataloging in Publication Data
A catalog record for this book is available from the Library of Congress

ISBN 0-415-01460-3 (hbk)   ISBN 0-415-01461-1 (pbk)

Contents

Illustrations

The authors and publishers would like to thank the following for their kindness in supplying and giving permission for the use of photographic and other illustrative material: the International Wool Secretariat for Figure 1.1; the British Film Institute for Figures 2.1 and 6.4; UIP for Figure 3.1; Columbia Picture Industries Ltd for Figure 3.2; News International plc for Figure 4.1 (photo of Rupert Murdoch taken by Brian Aris); Channel 4 for Figure 4.2; the Central Electricity Generating Board for Figure 5.1; the Broadcaster's Audience Research Board Ltd for Figure 5.2; London Weekend Television for Figure 5.3; Jill Fermanovsky Associates for Figure 6.2; Granada Television for Figure 6.3; Montague Primary School, Newcastle-upon-Tyne, for Figure 8.1; Amber Films, Newcastle-upon-Tyne, for Figure 8.2.

Notes on contributors

Tim Blanchard has been involved with media education for a number of years. His publications include: *The Music Business: A Teaching Pack, Media Studies at 16+* (1989), *Media Studies and the GCSE* (1986) and *Media Studies and the CPVE* (1985). He currently works as an education officer for a local education authority.

Gill Branston works as a Senior Lecturer in Film and Media Studies at West Glamorgan Institute of Higher Education, Swansea. Among her previous publications are *Teaching Media Institutions* (1989) and *Mapping the Media* (reprinted in the BFI's Secondary Media Education Statement, and revised as part of the Open University's forthcoming course on media education).

David Buckingham is a Lecturer in Media Education at the Institute of Education, London University. He is currently Director of an ERCS-funded research project on 'The development of television literacy'. He has published on aspects of media education in a wide range of journals, including *The Times Educational Supplement*, *Radical Philosophy*, *Cultural Studies* and *Screen*. He is the author of an Open University Course Unit on *Media Education* and also of the book *Public Secrets: 'EastEnders' and its Audience* (1987). He recently edited *Watching Media Learning: Making Sense of Media Education* (1990).

Jenny Grahame is Advisory Teacher for Media Education at the English and Media Centre, London (formerly the ILEA English Centre). She was formerly an English and Media teacher and youth worker in Inner London comprehensive schools, and subsequently an ILEA Advisory Teacher for Media Education. She is an examiner for City and Guilds and LEAG GCSE Media Studies courses, secretary of Teaching Media in London, and teaches a wide range of INSET and adult education courses for the BFI, Birkbeck College and other institutions. She is author of *The English Curriculum: Media 1 Years 7–9* (1991), and co-author of *Criminal Records* (1986); she contributes regularly to *The English Magazine* and has also written for *Media Education Initiatives* and *Teachers Weekly*.

David Lusted is a freelance lecturer, writer and organizer of the Media Education Agency. He has taught in all sectors of the education system and is currently teaching Film and Drama for the University of Reading. He is Chief Examiner for the Cambridge 'A' Level in Media Studies. Published work includes *Raymond Williams: Film TV Culture* (1989) and *TV and Schooling* (1985) for the BFI, and for journals such as *Screen* and *Screen Education*.

Karen Manzi is a trainee psychotherapist and sociology graduate from North London Polytechnic. She is an occasional worker in the catering industry.

Ben Moore is Advisory Teacher for Media Education in Newcastle-upon-Tyne. He was formerly a Lecturer in Media and Communication at Huddersfield College of Further Education. He has published articles in *The Times Educational Supplement* and was a contributor to *Primary Media Education* (1989), edited by Cary Bazalgette. He is a moderator for NEA GCSE Media Studies, and the NREB representative on the NEA Subject Committee for Media Studies. In addition, he is coordinator of the Newspapers in Education Project for the Newcastle Chronicle and Journal Ltd.

Allan Rowe is Director of Studies at Epping Forest Tertiary College, where he teaches Film and Media Studies. He is an Assistant Examiner for Film Studies 'A' Level.

Gillian Swanson taught Film and Media Studies in London until 1987. She now lives in Brisbane, Australia, where she teaches Cultural Studies and Women's Studies at Griffith University. She is working on a study of public controversies over sexuality for Routledge and co-editing, with Christine Gledhill, an anthology on the history and representation of women in World War II. She has previously published articles in *Undercut*, *Framework*, *Continuum* and *Screen* and is a member of the Editorial Advisory Board for *Screen*.

Adrian Tilley has been involved in Media Education since the early seventies. He is currently Advisory Teacher for English in Devon and Assistant Chief Moderator for GCSE Media Studies (NEA).

Tana Wollen taught English and Media Studies in two London secondary schools and co-authored *Learning the Media* (1985) with Manuel Alvarado and Robin Gutch. She joined the British Film Institute in 1986, and is now Head of the BFI's Television and Projects Unit.

Acknowledgements

Many people have been part of this book before and during its production. Specifically, there are the teachers who have contributed to the British Film Institute (BFI) Education Easter Schools since the first in 1981 – David Buckingham's essay originated from a presentation at the 1986 meeting – and to the media seminars organized in London by BFI Education since 1986, from which evolved some of the contributions on core concepts in this book. Generally, there are events and activities organized around Britain by or through BFI Education, the regional Media Education Initiative (MEI) groups (associated with the Society for Education in Film and Television before it was wound up in 1989), regionally based DES Media Education groups, the Association for Media Education in Scotland (AMES) and many other agencies – such as advisors to local education authorities (LEAs) – all of whom have contributed ideas and practices to a developing media education movement of which this book is part.

Thanks also to the skills of Giuliana Baracco, David Morley, Julie Maher, Mary Slater, Diane Bailey, Maxine Elliott, Lynne Thompson, Gina Yiangou, Rachel Marks, Sarah Loveless and those who worked on drafts and other matters related to the production of the book.

David Lusted

Introduction

David Lusted

This book is a guide to the most common concepts in Media Studies, to assist with thinking and teaching about the media in the classrooms of secondary and tertiary education, in particular for teachers of the 14–18 age range. It is intended as an *introductory* handbook for teachers new to Media Studies and also as a *critical* reference work for teachers feeling any measure of familiarity with the history of debates and teaching about the media.

The recent increase of interest and activity in teaching about media is at least surprising if not extraordinary. When government policy leads, as now, to a narrowing of the curriculum frame, it is surprising to discover evidence of considerable growth in a focus of knowledge on the periphery of proposed cores and foundations. Evidence is discernible from 'A' Level and GCSE syllabuses, TVEI modules, DES and other INSET courses,[1] and the proliferation of agencies and conferences whose object is to promote and extend education in the media. As little as five years ago, the range of activity was no more than could be comfortably referenced in the memory and a single bibliography. Today, it is hard to keep track of each new book and classroom resource as it emerges. Consequently, it is harder to chart overall provision.

All this suggests that teaching the media is now a growth industry. But what kind of industry is that? What are the ideas that constitute its 'raw material'? How can they be organized for the 'production' of knowledge about media in the classroom? And what are the aims, assumptions, organizing principles and working practices that constitute *informed* teaching about media: the proper 'conditions of service'? In answer to these questions, we will note the speed of changes and advancing quality of practices in recent years.

Teachers have been using films and television programmes, photographs, music and posters as stimuli or aids to learning for many years. Classroom talk about the products of cinema, broadcasting or the record business is also a longstanding feature of English teaching and forms of liberal education. It is only more recently that these media have become objects of study in themselves for more than a few committed teachers. The interest now has changed in degree but also in kind.

No longer does it seem strange for a Geography teacher to analyse as well as display posters from commercial companies or tourist boards, or for an English teacher to note the recurrent gender and racial types as well as the written language of advertising, or for any teacher to situate a schools broadcast programme in the spectrum of daily scheduling. This development has come about with greater awareness of the idea that posters, ads and TV programmes are media products and hence study objects as well as study aids.

Similarly, the social sciences have increasingly included approaches to analysing products of the media in their study of media institutions. This development occurs as a reaction to the idea that the meaning of media products can be 'read off' from the nature and practices of the organizations producing them. Increasingly, then, the idea that all media make meaning through *language* has gained prominence right across the curriculum, forcing attention to the non-verbal languages alongside the written and spoken word.

Interdisciplinary teaching also makes for hazier boundaries between traditional subjects. Teaching workloads have increased under new government initiatives and from changes in working conditions as a result of GCSE and TVEI. But it would be sad if the burdens arising from these initiatives obscured the opportunities they afford teachers to question well tried and familiar educational practices, and to develop new ones. In particular, when subject doors are forced open, the unaccustomed exchange between subject specialists can establish more common pedagogic ground than expected on which to develop interdisciplinary and cross-curriculum work.

If central government opinion is pulling – albeit in inconsistent and contradictory ways – towards rigid divisions between subjects and proscription in subject definition, classroom practices pull in different directions, towards greater flexibility in combinations of subjects and realignments of knowledge. Traditionally, teachers have been formed by the specific characteristics of their subject specialisms. But as new understandings emerge – especially among teachers in the arts, humanities and social sciences – of connections between subject specialisms, so teacher formations shift, too. We note, then, the changing practices of teaching that result from developments in knowledge and the curriculum. These changes also arise, though, from pressures within the cultural context in which teachers and their students work, the 'real conditions' of their daily labours rather than the ideals of government reforms.

The new educational concern with media appears to be connected with this context, borne of a convergence of ideas and changes. There is a sense that conventional educational uses of media materials and technology have been adjusted in response to debates about media products and organizations. Prime time television magazines, 'pop' music and high street videos, the tabloid press and paperbacks are among media *forms* that have penetrated the rhythms and routines of living, the social relations and activities of many teachers and students alike.

The range of alternative and overlapping sources of information and entertainment, instruction and art is more extensive, perhaps, than ever before. Newspapers, broadcast radio and TV, Prestel and Ceefax compete for news attention; multi-channel broadcasting, time-switching and video rentals compete with multi-unit music provision for our leisure time in domestic settings. Cinemas, theatres, galleries and sporting events continue to offer sites for more public pleasures. So hot, indeed, is the competition for our time that new generations appear to have adapted to their surroundings by evolving the ability to read, watch, listen and attend to any combination of media without loss to – and at the same time as engaging in – homework, housework and social exchange.[2]

This cultural revolution, brought about by new technologies and changing social and leisure patterns, takes on a particular force in schooling. New generations of teachers share experience of these features of a swiftly changing culture most directly with their students. This process narrows the culture gap between largely middle-class teachers and especially working-class students, with many more shared cultural experiences, expectations and pleasures than heretofor. It is harder now to ignore *EastEnders*, *The Face*, rock revivals and bestsellers as once *Coronation Street*, *The Beano*, chart-toppers and pulp novels had been. Of course, teachers were never able to exclude media cultures from the playground as they could from the classroom, but signs are that there are fewer 'No

Entry' signs and a few more 'Welcome' mats at classroom doors these days.

Changes in cultural provision and their penetration into all realms of social activity have tested some well-worn divisions; between information and entertainment, for instance, and between art and escapism, work and leisure. Teachers recognize that an interest in children's culture need not threaten literary or art objects and may well indeed change attitudes to them for the better. Worries about 'declining standards' in the media and suspicion of popular forms, whilst still common to moral panics,[3] are losing their force in education. One reason for this lies in new patterns of leisure for children. Far from frustrating the objectives of schooling – a common assumption until recently – there is increasing acknowledgement that comics, magazines, videos, etc. interact in quite complex ways with what is made on offer from the institutions of schooling and the media. A rich range of media are produced for educational purposes by companies with a clear eye on developments in design and fiction in the mainstream media. What constitutes these educational media now – whether it is subject textbooks or visual aids, a schools or Open University TV programme, *Horizon* or *The Singing Detective* – is more various and looks more attractive than ever before. They are distinctive in content and tone, but their forms connect as much with overt entertainment forms like children's television and comics, game shows, soaps and the rest, as with other didactic forms like DES circulars and annual company reports.

There is a greater sense of the ubiquity of the media forming a part of educational as much as cultural life, and a sense of connection between the media cultures of teachers and the taught. But if there are less clearcut distinctions generally between the media inside and outside school, another reason for a decline in suspicion lies in an increasing disposition to educational enquiry into the nature and role of the media. For a very long time, schools have been the central cultural agency charged with responsibility for education. Without threat to the mandatory nature of that function, there are arguably grounds for dispute over the centrality of that role. To the extent that media institutions have replaced universities as the central definers of the nation's intellectual agenda[4] – or, at the very least, have co-opted its agents into their own structures – so have they contested the place conventionally allocated to schooling in the lives of children alongside family, home and friendship relations. The notion that children spend more time in front of a television set than they do at school need not be the cause of shock and scandal that it still too frequently is. It is enough to acknowledge the primary role of television and the media generally in social and cultural life to register their importance, rather than their threat, to schooling. Children in schools are as much educated, albeit informally, through their everyday and casual media experiences as they are through the more formal structures and practices of the education system. Indeed, so bound up are the media with our sense of identity – who we are and how we think of ourselves and others – that it is arguable which has greater claim to our attention: the education system, for its face-to-face power of exchange, or the media, for the superiority of their resources, technologies and forms of spectacle.

What an educational concern with media can offer is a new site to engage with this and the many other features of the new relation between education and the media mentioned earlier. The case for greater consideration of the media in schooling is as good as that for a greater indivisibility between media use and media study in schools. All education practices are concerned with media as means of expression and communication, of pleasure and challenge, as well as with the media as institutions at least as important and powerful as the education system itself.

Every time a poster is displayed, a book read or a film screened in school, every time there is a public controversy about a banned television programme or half the nation's population watches prime time Christmas day TV, teacher and taught alike are engaged in the process of making sense of cultural phenomena, an experience of making meaning from media. It is but a short step to formalize the study of this process in media teaching. It is for these reasons and in these senses that so many teachers are now turning to ways of organizing teaching about the media into the textures of their own teaching, whatever its subject, sector or focus. This is the educational space Media Studies inhabits.

What is it that fills this space called Media Studies?

Judging from syllabuses at GCSE and 'A' levels, courses in Media Studies seem to share a basic consistency of approach.[5] All have their content organized through the teaching of concepts. Teaching conceptually is a common approach to Media Studies and one that frequently puzzles teachers coming new to the subject area, even though the concepts may have been formed by the very disciplines through which media studies have most developed: namely, literary and film theory and criticism on the one hand, the social sciences on the other.

The term 'media studies' is used in two senses here. First, there is *Media Studies*, a curriculum subject or topic within another subject. This organizes the many *media studies* in the second sense of the term: studies from theory, criticism and debate about the media. So, it can be said that Media Studies increasingly organizes media studies through a conceptual approach. Even modules within the framework of TVEI and units of work developed within the primary and early secondary sectors bear witness to a developing consensus that this is the most appropriate strategy for organizing teaching about the media.[6] The reasons for this are perhaps most to do with the logic of media systems and the classroom economy of schooling at the turn of the 1990s.

The media themselves, in their patterns of ownership and consumption, are increasingly interdependent in historically quite novel ways. More and more, they are organized on global lines, breaking national boundaries and mixing cultural expectations. Rupert Murdoch's communications empire typifies trends in the international expansion of companies with fingers in multi-media and other industrial pies. Aided by new technologies like cable and satellite, words and images spread across many broadcast and print media. Likewise, social and leisure patterns have changed to accommodate symptoms of these changes as the growing number of media forms enter into the routines of everyday life in varying ways and with varying degrees of accessibility. If the media are everywhere, even more ubiquitous must be the ways in which they are *used* and structured into the textures of work and play, thinking and being. Those uses in turn affect the direction of the media industries and the next generation of products they produce; the wheel keeps turning.

If the logic of the new media systems is one reason for developing ways of teaching about them that confront rather than artificially separate their interconnectedness, the current condition of the education system presents another. Government policies for education have led to new organizations and new initiatives in the practices of schooling. Curriculum developments, particularly in the move to establish a national core and foundation of compulsory subjects for state schools; the intervention of the MSC in new forms of pre-vocational education like the TVEI scheme; the contradictions between these two drives, born as they are of competing wings of recent conservative ideology; shifts in the terms and conditions of service for teachers; changes in funding and access for pre- and in-service training: all this risks a narrow or instrumental idea of teacher roles and skills.

Yet, from an entirely different direction and set of impulses comes a challenging sense of curriculum change as many disciplines quite independently 'look in' on the construction of knowledge offered through subject teaching. Professional subject organizations hold conferences and write in journals about the 'crisis' of English or Religious Education or Science or whatever, with an unexpected openness in the process of such self-enquiry. As a result, teachers of traditional curriculum subjects move closer toward sharing knowledge with subjects around them. In this climate, Media Studies has developed as a product of many education interests and disciplines, being genuinely interdisciplinary rather than multidisciplinary. Consequently, Media Studies finds itself – alongside or perhaps within English – part of turbulent winds of curriculum change, with a share in altering the landscape of humanities teaching and developing teaching approaches that spread across the curriculum to play a part in the reformation of subject teaching. As syllabuses bear out, the development of concepts has been a key activity in this scenario, making connections across a vast choice of potential content within and across subject knowledge.

Directly, a conceptual approach within Media Studies finds a way to teach about the media that refuses a simple linear sequence in which one media is taught after another. Indeed, a concept like *language* enables attention to be given to all media products and the meanings produced across the full range of media – whether video and television, newspapers and the press, fiction and literature, film and cinema, photographs and photography, advertisements and advertising, records and the music industry, and so on. *Language* is one of several concepts which have been developed precisely for this purpose of explaining and exploring what is general to a range of media whilst remaining sensitive to what is specific to any medium, focusing on differences between them as well as on their similarities.

The core concepts chosen for this book are *language*, *narrative*, *institution*, *audience* and *representation*. In addition, and more controversially, the idea of practical work that leads to the *production* of media artefacts is here offered as a concept rather than just a practice, a classroom activity or a learning process.

Each concept is taken as the subject of an essay by teachers with long experience of organizing and teaching for secondary school students and their teachers in-service. Their brief has been to provide a guide to the concept in ways that pay attention to three related concerns. The first concern is to indicate the origins and development of the concept, to describe its full meaning as well as how and why it developed. The second concern is to demonstrate ways of putting the concept to work in the classroom, to show how it can organize a course, module or unit of work. The object here is to attend to matters of where to begin; how to sequence exercises logically and in order to explore the full potential of the concept; how to maximize learning, to indicate where orders of diffi-culty in the concept might suggest difficulties for certain age groups; and to propose where the potential of the concept ends or gives way to other concepts and other questions. The third concern is to chart the battery of teaching materials, most significant publications and other resources tried and tested in the teaching of the concept.

This brief has proved a tall order and each writer has found a method of their own to meet it. It has come as a revelation to discover that there can be so many pathways through the core Media Studies concepts; that there are indeed approaches rather than a model approach. The essays therefore offer individual approaches to the tasks of conceptual teaching, evidence that teaching is as much a creative activity as the researching, writing, planning and organizing that accompanies it.

Essays on the core concepts also form the core of this book. Karen Manzi and Allan Rowe describe ways of rendering the products of the media as study objects for analysis in the classroom. Their emphasis is upon image analysis: how the still picture, then moving images in sequence, can be understood as making sense through the concept of *language* in ways which are comparable to, if different from, the coded sign system of the written and spoken word.

Adrian Tilley draws on studies of fictional forms to analyse the *narrative* structure of all media products, including those like newspapers and news programmes whose nature as non-fiction does not immediately appear amenable to analysis as 'stories'. He offers a detailed procedure for working through the many ideas about how narrative works to organize understanding of media forms.

The concepts of language and narrative offer refined procedures of textual analysis, there to understand how meaning is made of media products. This emphasis on the production of meaning is characteristic of modern Media Studies and does not stop with these textual approaches. With the concept of *institution*, Tana Wollen attends to the contexts for media products, to the organizations, routine practices and histories of the various media. She offers ways of thinking about media institutions, together with classroom materials and exercises, that can shape an otherwise overwhelming complex of information and analysis – in statistics, reports, research and histories – into a coherent course for the secondary school classroom.

Gill Branston continues this contextual study but brings the wheel full circle back to understanding the full potential of textual studies in her account of the concept of *audience*. Accounting for the various critical constructions of those who come into contact with evidence of the media, either as unknowing or willing subjects, Gill Branston argues against teachers falling into the trap that snares so many elite social groups, of thinking of their students as passive respondents of the media. Instead, she demonstrates the *activity* of interacting with the media, taking up their multivarious uses, 'reading' and 'making' rather than 'consuming' possible meanings. These ideas are offered through the concept of *audience* which, moreover, identifies a pedagogy, a set of attitudes to, and practices in, learning as well as teaching.

A concern with a developed pedagogy for Media Studies is central to the treatment of the final conventional core concept. The concept of *representation* functions in sophisticated ways that interact between media texts and contexts. Crucially it is a concept which puts our sense of ourselves and our sense of others at the centre of media studies through the way it seeks to ask not only what is being represented by and in the media but also what representations *we make* of the media. In Gillian Swanson's account, the concept also extends beyond mainstream media forms, to render alternative and often otherwise remote media forms accessible to secondary classroom study.

An addition to this core of concepts is made by Jenny Grahame in her account of *the production process*. For most teaching, transforming ideas about the media into classroom practice requires more than analysis of study objects in the form of texts and evidence of their institutional contexts. Here, practical exercises and activities

in the form of storyboarding or simulations become crucial ingre-
dients of the Media Studies store-cupboard. But the place of own-
production (of making images, narratives, etc. through the media
of television and photographic cameras, say) within study and
practice is not self-evident. How is it possible to arrange for
production within the strict limitations of finance and technology
typical to under-funded and under-resourced schools? What can be
done with products when produced? How does own-production
relate to the ideas and methods of analysis of other conceptual
approaches? Jenny Grahame imaginatively argues that thinking of
the production process conceptually enables these and other difficult
questions about classroom study and practice to be thought anew.

Surrounding these essays on core concepts for Media Studies are
two situating essays. In 'Teaching about the media', an essay
especially useful to readers new to the field of Media Studies, David
Buckingham offers a background to the many strands of history in
teaching about the media, and describes the nature of contemporary
Media Studies. Ben Moore accounts for the recent arrival on the
educational scene of the term *media education*, an integration of ideas
and strategies from concepts in Media Studies into the web and
weft of all subject teaching. He offers tentative and preliminary
ideas for how humanities and science subjects, as well as other
curriculum topics and initiatives, may put the core concepts of
Media Studies to work in the interests of their own teaching.

The book concludes with a select and rigorous listing of the
central publications and resources for Media Studies teaching.
Bibliographies already exist,[7] some quite extensive, so attention
has been given here to the ways in which a new bibliography can
fill gaps and meet needs. In the same way that core concepts have
been selected, the Listings, compiled by Tim Blanchard, aims for a
balance between breadth and depth. In his judgement, and that of
many Media Studies teachers whose contributions lie buried in the
lines of this book, the listings include all the basic material that
teachers of Media Studies should be aware of. It is organized in
ways hopefully most convenient for quick reference by teachers.

The pace of change in the politics of education in recent years has
been rapid, especially in the administration and examination of
schooling, and in particular with government plans for the national
curriculum. Advances in the constitution of media studies have also
occurred during the production cycle of this book. Every effort has
been made to deal with such changes and predicted changes.

NOTES

1 The acronyms stand for: GCSE: General Certificate of Secondary Education, the new 15+ examination replacing GCE, the General Certificate of Education; TVEI: Technical and Vocational Education Initiative, modular courses originated by the Manpower Services Commission providing a supplementary pre-vocational curriculum for about 5 per cent of selected secondary school students at 13+; DES: the Department of Education and Science, the central governing body for the education system; INSET: courses of training for teachers 'in-service'.

2 See the many examples in Philip Simpson, *Parents Talking Television*, (London: Comedia, 1987) and more theorized evidence in David Morley, *Family Television: Cultural Power and Domestic Leisure* (London: Comedia, 1986).

3 For an extended exploration of the term see Stuart Hall, 'Reformism and the legislation of consent' in *Permissiveness and Control: the Fate of 60's Legislation*, National Deviancy Conference (London: Macmillan, 1980).

4 As is argued by Regis Debray in *Teachers, Writers and Celebrities: the Intelligentsia of Modern France* (London: Verso, 1981).

5 There are currently five GCSE syllabuses: two NEA (one of these in modular form) and one each SEC, WJEC and SEG. The syllabuses are critically appraised in Tim Blanchard, *Media Studies at 16+* (London: BFI, 1989). A more extensive account can be found in Tim Blanchard, *Media Studies and the GCSE* (London: SEFT, 1986) and in a special 1987 supplement. There are three 'A' Level syllabuses; two Cambridge and one WJEC.

6 See Tim Blanchard, *Media Studies at 16+* (London: BFI, 1989) and *Primary Media Education: A Curriculum Statement* (London: BFI, 1989).

7 See Lez Cooke, *Media Studies Bibliography* (London: BFI, 1988) and the bibliographies in other general books on teaching the media in *Listings*, Section 1(a) (p. 192) to which this book should be seen as a complement and companion.

Chapter 1

Teaching about the media

David Buckingham

INTRODUCTION

Why teach about the media? There are a number of possible answers to this question, which derive from quite different views of the media and of young people. Yet most arguments for Media Studies begin with two significant assertions. The first concerns the *amount of time* children spend with the media. Statistics on television viewing, for example, suggest that children today spend more time watching television than they spend in school. If we add to this the amount of time spent watching films, reading comics and magazines, and listening to records, we arrive at figures which typically provoke a mixture of surprise and horror – particularly, perhaps, among teachers, who are likely to feel that their students' time would be far better spent on activities they themselves consider more edifying. The second assertion appears to follow inexorably from the first. If the media are such a major element in children's lives, it seems self-evident that they must exert a very powerful *influence* on their ways of thinking about the world – and as such, teachers simply cannot afford to ignore them.

These assertions are certainly very persuasive. Teachers who have sought to establish a place for Media Studies in the school curriculum, often in the face of considerable opposition, have used them to great effect. This may well be because this view of the power of the media has an appeal to most shades of political opinion. Many people on the Right regard the media as agents of moral depravity, while many on the Left see them as carriers of objectionable ideologies: yet they are united in a view of the media as a powerful and predominantly negative influence – an influence which schools have a responsibility to resist.

While these assertions may therefore appear quite convincing, in devising effective approaches to teaching about the media, it is necessary to look beyond them, and in certain ways to qualify them. In this respect, it is important to make a distinction between the simpler, more rhetorical arguments which may be of use in *promoting* Media Studies, and the more complex understandings which should inform classroom practice. Media Studies teaching clearly needs to be grounded in a thorough understanding of children's experience of the media – an experience which the more simplistic notions of 'influence' do not adequately explain. In particular, I shall argue here that teaching about the media should be based on the view that children are *active producers of meaning*, and that this production of meaning is fundamentally a *social* activity.

PERSPECTIVES ON CHILDREN AND THE MEDIA

Concern about the influence of the media on young people has a very long history.[1] Perhaps the earliest recorded example is Plato's *Republic*, written four hundred years before Christ, which warns its readers about the dangerous effects of the theatre on Greek youth. In more recent times, this attention has focused particularly on those mass-produced media forms which have been especially popular with a working-class audience. There have been successive waves of public concern and outrage about popular literature (in the nineteenth century), the cinema (notably in the 1920s and 1930s), children's comics (in the 1950s) and, most recently, television and video. In this section, I shall briefly identify three popular contemporary perspectives on children and television. Despite significant differences between them, there are important underlying continuities; and it is these continuities, this 'common-sense wisdom' about the media, which often seems to inform the work of teachers and schools.

'Moral panics'

For many writers, and particularly for many politicians, questions about children and television are almost inevitably questions about children and television *violence*. Although researchers have experienced considerable difficulty, to say the least, in establishing causal connections between television violence and violent behaviour,[2] the belief that such connections do exist is extremely widely held.

Indeed, such a belief is often asserted as 'simple common sense' which no rational person could possibly dispute.

This concern about the effects of television violence may usefully be seen as part of a broader anxiety about the collapse of social order. For example, the most recent wave of debate – the moral panic around so-called 'Video Nasties' – can be traced back to the aftermath of the inner city disturbances of 1981. Politicians keen to present these disturbances as instances of a general decline in respect for law and order argued that the media were a central causal factor. Thus, we had the alleged 'copycat' riots: young people in Handsworth took to the streets after watching TV reports of violence in Soweto, people in Tottenham then imitated the TV reports of Handsworth, and so on.[3] Less directly, it was also argued that television violence, and in particular 'Video Nasties', were contributing to a general rise in violent crime among young people. The debates around the Video Recordings Act of 1984, and subsequently Winston Churchill's Bill to extend the Obscene Publications Act to television in 1986, focused particularly on the dangers to young people, and on the failure of parents (significantly working-class parents) to exert adequate control over their children's viewing.[4]

One of the main problems with such arguments is that they are typically based on very inadequate evidence, not merely about the scale of the phenomenon but also about its presumed effects. The 'Video Nasties' research,[5] for example, signally fails to prove any causal connection between viewing and violent behaviour – in fact, all it proves, in painstaking detail, is that many 'experts' *believe* there to be such a connection! As a result, it inevitably fails to account for the complexity of children's understanding and the *pleasures* they may derive from viewing such material. In this way, the moral panic about television violence may deflect attention away from other possible causes of social unrest, and sets a very limited agenda for public debate, which effectively excludes any more sophisticated understanding of the relationship between children and television.

'The plug-in drug'

A second major area of concern about children and television focuses on its effects, not so much on children's behaviour, as on their thought processes. The emphasis here is not primarily on the *content* of television, but on the nature of the activity of viewing itself. Marie Winn's symptomatically-titled *The Plug-in Drug* is a representative example of this approach.[6] It provides a barrage of research evidence to support the view that television undermines family life and destroys children's capacity for intelligent thought. Thus, we are told that watching television retards the development of the brain, blunts the senses and encourages mental laziness. It impairs children's sense of their own identity, their linguistic abilities and their attention span. Furthermore, because of their addiction to television, children are deprived of play and of the opportunity to participate in the interpersonal rituals of family life. The metaphor of television-as-a-drug recurs throughout Winn's book: TV is 'an insidious narcotic', children are 'TV Zombies' who watch in a 'trance-like state' which 'blots out' the real world, and parents are urged to help their children 'kick the TV habit'. Reading (which, as a more private activity, could be seen to induce an even greater sense of social isolation) is regarded as an inherently superior form of mental training, which develops powers of concentration and imagination stunted by television – although, according to Winn, this is only the case with *real* books, not newspapers or the kind of popular fictions she disparagingly terms 'non-books'.

Neil Postman, in a similarly polemical account, argues that television is primarily responsible for the 'disappearance of childhood'.[7] He describes television as a 'total disclosure medium' which has led to a blurring of the distinction between adulthood and childhood: because of television, adults can no longer keep 'secrets' from children and 'protect' them from adult ways. As a result, children have begun to dress like adults (and vice-versa), use bad language, have sex earlier and are generally more ill-mannered than they used to be. As in Marie Winn's book, television is also seen as a primary cause of social unrest, rising crime rates and the kind of discontent among young people which surfaced in the 1960s, with the coming of age of the first 'television generation'.

Here again, the family is enjoined to resist television, although its ability to do so has been progressively undermined by its enemy. Likewise, for both writers, the school is seen as the last bastion of a dying print culture: the use of television within education is described by Winn as 'an act of true desperation', and a dangerous distraction from the primary aim of *eliminating* television.

It would be easy to mock the barely restrained hysteria of such arguments and to demonstrate their contradictions. In the case of Marie Winn, the evidence she adduces to support her case is extremely partial, and in many instances highly impressionistic; and Neil Postman is ultimately unable to prove a *causal* connection between television and the broad social developments he describes. Yet perhaps the major omission from both accounts is of any consideration of the *pleasures* which lead children to watch television in the first place. According to Winn, watching television derives from a pathological inadequacy on the part of children, which is encouraged by the weakness and irresponsibility of their parents. Children are merely victims of a dangerous addiction which they are powerless to resist.

'The consciousness industry'

Where the previous two perspectives were concerned primarily with the influence of television on children's behaviour and on their cognitive development, a third view – of the media as 'consciousness industries' – is more explicitly concerned with their influence on attitudes and beliefs. The media are seen here as a primary means whereby the ruling class maintains its ideological domination of subordinate classes. A series of fairly direct causal connections are drawn between the capitalist ownership of media industries, the ideologies contained within media output, and the acceptance of such ideologies by audiences.

Media research has increasingly come to question and to qualify this approach: indeed, it is probably fair to say that much of the best work in the field has developed through an implicit debate with and against what is often described as 'economic determinism'.[8] Nevertheless, the simplicities of a 'conspiracy theory' do retain an undeniable attraction, very similar to the attractiveness of the commonsense beliefs already outlined. As Ian Connell[9] has argued, the tendency to blame the media has become almost routine for many on the Left. Yet, as he suggests, it is based on a view of audiences as the innocent victims of a powerful 'propaganda machine': the idea that the media are able to *impose* particular 'biased' attitudes on audiences is an oversimplification which ignores the active participation of viewers in making meaning.

'Blaming the media' has its parallels in attitudes towards children and television, and in particular on the question of stereotyping. Analyses of media content – often statistical analyses which, for example, quantify the numbers of men and women appearing in particular occupational roles – have typically been used as evidence to support broad rhetorical assertions about the role of the media in forming stereotyped beliefs.[10] The media are regarded as a direct source of undesirable attitudes which children adopt, often 'unconsciously'. There is little sense here that children may compare their experience of television with their experience of the social world, or that they may question or distance themselves from the representations it provides. Here again, the concentration on the media as the primary source of influence may deflect attention away from other, perhaps more direct, and therefore more powerful, sources. Finally, this perspective also seeks to discount or invalidate the pleasures which children derive from watching television. Pleasure is regarded as the sugar for the ideological pill, as a distraction which enables television to exert its unpleasant effects on children's minds. Pleasure is something to be deeply suspected, and which we must encourage children to 'own up' to if we are to free them from it.

Continuities

Despite the significant differences between these three approaches, both in terms of their areas of concern and their political perspectives, there is a remarkable continuity between them. In different ways, they all provide a reassuringly simple account of the relationship between children and television; and it is perhaps this very simplicity which accounts for their undeniable attraction, particularly for those of us who have been educated into a respect for the authority and superiority of print. Yet it is precisely this simple 'commonsense' view which I am seeking to question here.

First, each of these approaches regards the media as an extremely powerful and almost exclusively harmful influence. In each case, the media are defined as a primary cause of undesirable social changes. For the Right, the media are responsible for various forms of moral decline and degeneracy; for the Left, they are often blamed for the failure of socialism to win the hearts and minds of the masses. In each case, blaming the media may relieve us of the painful necessity of looking for other possible reasons for such decline or failure – on the one hand, for example, in the inequalities and contradictions within the social fabric or within the institution of the family or, on the other hand, in the relationship between the official organizations of the Left (political parties and trade unions) and those on whose behalf they claim to operate.

Second, each approach implicitly regards media audiences as made up of passive consumers. Children, in particular, are seen as innocent and vulnerable targets for media manipulation, largely incapable of resisting its seductive and beguiling messages. This is even more true of children whose family background may be 'pathologized', as in some sense providing them with inadequate protection – and here, of course, these writers are particularly referring to working-class families. Studies of the history of childhood[11] indicate that this view of children as 'impressionable', and therefore in need of adult protection and control, is a relatively recent phenomenon, largely confined to Western industrialized societies. In this sense, the notion of children as innocent can hardly be regarded as a straightforward reflection of some timeless 'essence' of childhood: and if children are to be regarded as active producers of meaning from the media, it is a view which must inevitably be questioned.

Third, insofar as any of these perspectives is concerned with teaching about the media (and some at least would reject the very idea as a symptom of the kind of degeneracy they wish to oppose), the basic aim of such teaching is seen to be one of *inoculation*. Teachers need to arm their students, to help them resist the negative influence of the media, and to see through the falsehoods and pseudo-satisfactions they provide. The history of Media Studies in Britain, and in many other countries, is essentially the history of the evolution of this perspective.[12] From the work of the literary critics F. R. Leavis and Denys Thompson, with their emphasis on *discrimination* between the spiritually and morally superior products of high culture and the shoddy, debased forms of popular culture, through to the more recent emphasis on *demystification*, encouraging students to 'see through' the ideologies of media output, this view of Media Studies as inoculation has remained the dominant approach.[13]

In criticizing this view, I do not wish to imply the contrary, that the media have very little influence on young people – although this is in fact a contention which the vast bulk of research into media effects would broadly support.[14] Even research which has sought to identify the effects of directly persuasive communications – for example, the influence of political campaigns on voting, or that of advertising on consumer behaviour – has repeatedly concluded with 'null findings'. In general, however, such research has found considerable difficulty in identifying *longer-term* effects, as opposed to short-term changes in attitudes or behaviour: and it is perhaps the former that educationalists would regard as most important.

Nevertheless, the major problem with much of this research, and with the 'commonsense wisdom' I have identified, is that it implicitly defines the relationship between children and the media in very limited terms. Notions of influence (literally, a one-way flow) and cause-and-effect are themselves inadequate ways of defining the nature of that relationship, and thus form an equally inadequate basis for teaching. To establish a more effective approach, it is necessary to ask more fundamental questions.

UNDERSTANDING THE MEDIA

What do we mean by the term 'media'? In studying a given medium, we may choose to focus on a whole variety of different aspects. In the case of television, for example, we might look at any or all of the following:

- the *programmes* themselves: the ways in which they represent the world, their characteristic narrative forms, the rules and conventions of specific genres, and so on;
- the *contexts* in which the programmes are transmitted: their place within the flow of television, their location in the schedules, and the way in which they are 'framed' or mediated by television journalism, and by everyday conversation;
- the *organizations* which produce them: the patterns of ownership and control within broadcasting, the professional practices of television production, and the ways in which producers regard their audiences;
- the *technologies* of production, distribution and reception;
- and finally, the different ways in which *audiences* respond to, and use, television.

This is certainly a list which could be extended. Yet while it is fairly straightforward to enumerate possible areas of study, it is far more difficult to connect and organize them. Each of these areas is obviously intimately related with the others. For instance, it is difficult to talk about 'the programmes themselves' independent of the ways in which different audiences may make sense of them, and yet we can hardly talk about audiences without taking account of how audiences themselves are targeted, for example through scheduling, and of how producers' implicit assumptions about their audiences are manifested in programmes. Some critics[15] have even questioned the extent to which we can talk about programmes as self-contained objects, given the rather haphazard conditions in which television is often viewed, and the tendency (at least in commercial television) for the distinctions between programmes and the surrounding commercials, previews and continuity announcements to become increasingly blurred.

Thus while it may be necessary to break down the field of study when designing a sequence of lessons, it is important in teaching to strive to make connections between the different elements and to avoid the kind of fragmentation represented by the listing above. This is equally true of the ways in which we deal with different media. Just as it may prove difficult to make distinctions between different 'elements' of a particular medium, so too it may be misleading to separate, say, television and radio, or (particularly with the advent of video) television and film. As Len Masterman has argued,[16] Media Studies courses often run the risk of in-coherence by asking different questions of different media and failing to develop a consistent line of enquiry.

Models of communication

How, then, are we to connect these areas of study into a more coherent approach? One commonsense solution would be to organize them into what is often termed a 'flow' model of communication, in which messages are seen to flow in one direction, from producers, via media, to audiences. We might represent this schematically thus:

Producer → Text → Audience
(Message → Medium)

(The word 'text' is used here to include written, visual and audio-visual forms. Likewise, the term 'reader' applies to readers of all kinds of texts.)

Insofar as teaching is able to intervene in this process, it can mediate between the text and the audience. Thus, literature teach-ing is traditionally seen to be concerned with the work of individual geniuses, whose personal vision is conveyed via the text to individual readers. The aim of such teaching, as writers like I. A.

Richards, the founder of 'practical criticism', conceived of it,[17] is to increase the *receptiveness* of readers: students of literature learn to shed 'stock responses' and to hone their sensibilities in order to be as sensitive as possible to the author's intentions. The 'inoculation' approach to Media Studies seeks to intervene for quite different ends. Here, the teacher aims to develop, not receptiveness, but *resistance* to the messages texts are seen to contain.

However, there would seem to be two major problems with this model, and hence with the teaching strategies which are based upon it: both stem from the fact that communication is seen to flow only in one direction. First, as in the approaches outlined in the previous section, audiences are regarded here as passive receivers – who may, perhaps, be 'activated' by the intervention of teachers. The problem here is of course that audiences 'read' – that is, make sense of – media texts in a whole variety of different ways, according to their social position, their prior knowledge and their particular interests and concerns. Furthermore, the meanings they make may well not correspond to the intentions of the text's producers. Some theorists would see this diversity as evidence of a *failure* in communication, as a result of 'noise' in the system. Yet this is clearly an oversimplification. In a very basic sense, texts do not have meanings without readers. It is readers who *produce* meanings from texts, and the meanings they produce depend not merely on the instructions or invitations given by the text, but also on the meanings (and strategies for producing meaning) which readers bring with them. In this sense, meaning should be seen not as something which texts impose on readers, but as something which readers negotiate with texts. Reading, or producing meaning from, a text is thus a more complex and uncertain process than the one-way flow model would suggest.

Second, the model implicitly sees the production of texts as a neutral process, as a matter of fitting a pre-existing message into an empty vehicle, the medium. To use a different terminology, the model separates 'form' and 'content', and implicitly regards form as secondary, or even irrelevant. The problem here is that the 'form' or medium used cannot be seen as neutral. To draw a parallel with language, individual speakers clearly do not invent language anew each time they speak. Verbal statements only make sense insofar as they use a shared system of language. Yet in certain ways this language system determines or limits what can and cannot be said and, insofar as language and thought are intimately related, what can and cannot be thought.

Furthermore, as feminist work on language has indicated, it may do this in ways which tend to serve the interests of powerful groups in society. In this sense, there may be systematic 'biases' in the system itself – for example, the way in which the pronoun 'he' is often used to refer to both men and women, or the word 'mankind' to mean the human race. However, this is not to suggest that these groups have absolute power over language, or that these 'biases' are simply imposed on language users. To extend the example, it may well be the case that women readers fail to identify themselves with 'mankind' in the same way or to the same degree as men. Furthermore, these 'biases' can be directly contested: feminists have certainly struggled to change language in this way.

These arguments about language apply equally to the language of the media. Media language – the sets of codes and conventions which are shared between producers and audiences, and which enable meaning to be produced – cannot be seen as merely neutral. Just as with verbal language, we can identify institutions which have sought to control language, and thereby to define the ways in which the world is talked about and represented. By promoting certain meanings and excluding others, language may come to embody and maintain existing power-relationships, by presenting them as natural and inevitable: it becomes difficult to talk (or think) about things in any other way. Nevertheless, this power is rarely absolute or uncontested: because it relies upon the active participation of audiences, it is constantly being re-negotiated.

To sum up, and to restate the central points made in my introduction, reading the media should be seen as both an *active* and a *social* process. In the following section, I shall illustrate and develop this argument by means of the analysis of a single advertisement.

Making meaning

Consider the advertisement reproduced in Figure 1.1: it is part of a recent campaign for 'pure new wool' which appeared in many fashion magazines and colour supplements.

The image on the right-hand side, which is perhaps what catches the reader's eye first, raises a number of questions. For instance, we might surmise that the man is being chased and is jumping to save

Figure 1.1

his life. But we don't know why his pursuers seem so intent on killing him, and in such an extravagant way, or whether he will survive by catching hold of the street-lamp which conveniently lies in his path. In this way, the image invites us to construct a *narrative*, to fill in its past and predict its future: and given the type of image it is, we are perhaps more likely to do this with reference to other texts (for example, urban crime or action-adventure films) than to personal experience.

The image and the caption on the left-hand side, far from providing a way to explain or fix the meaning, merely compound the enigma. Although there is a visual link between the two images – the sheep are leaping over a fence, just as the man presumably has done – the ironic contrast between the cosy innocence of the child's picture book and the jarring modernity of the action photograph is quite disconcerting. The writing in the book could provide one possible explanation – that the right-hand image is, as it were, a still frame taken from a dream – although this may be too simple an answer to put us fully at our ease.

Finally, the caption, which is in very small print and thus likely (along with the wool trademark) to be one of the last things we see, partly contributes to our insecurity by urging us to 'beware'. Yet at the same time, once we have noticed the trademark, the pun becomes clear – the woollen suit is the 'sheep's clothing' and the man is presumably the wolf. There is perhaps an implicit reference here to children's fairy tales; in stories like *Little Red Riding-Hood*, the wolf is seen as a dangerous threat to the safety of the young girl. According to certain modern interpretations,[18] the wolf symbolizes the power of male sexuality: and in this sense the image on the right could be seen as offering a modern version of this myth.

Yet it is also far from immediately obvious what, if anything, is being advertised here: and it is only when we discover the *name of the product* that at least some of our uncertainties are resolved. We might say that the advertisement has a kind of *internal narrative* in which we are led to participate. As well as inviting us to generate questions and look for answers regarding the meaning of the two images, and the relationship between them, we also *expect* the product to be named, and therefore attempt to seek it out. This moment at which the narrative ends is thus the moment of *naming* – the point at which we 'get' the joke (and the product). The feeling of satisfaction which this generates is what advertisers call 'product warmth'.

Of course, this advertisement will not have the same meaning for all readers. You may well have perceived completely different processes at work, or indeed found the advertisement as a whole incomprehensible. It has not been my intention here to produce a single, definitive reading, but rather to draw attention to some of the ways in which the advertisement invites us to read it. The important question here is not so much 'What does it mean?' but 'How does it come to have a meaning?'

As I have indicated, the meaning of this advertisement derives from the *active participation* of the reader. It invites us to construct a narrative, to ask questions, to generate hypotheses and to seek for answers. It invokes expectations and plays with them in a teasing and ultimately pleasurable way. These expectations, the meanings and strategies for producing meaning, which we bring to the advertisement, derive from our prior knowledge.

Two types of prior knowledge might be identified here. First, there is the *cultural* knowledge drawn from our general social experience: in this instance, a set of stereotyped notions about masculinity and male sexuality is being invoked. Second, there is the more specific *intertextual* knowledge, derived from our experience of other texts – in other words, our knowledge of the ways in which meaning may be produced. In certain instances, this is highly localized, as in the oblique reference to *Little Red Riding-Hood* or the action–adventure image, which may invoke some quite elaborate sets of associations. In others, it is more general: for example, our past experience of *narrative* leads us to expect and to attempt to supply an ending which explains and thus resolves the enigmas; and our past experience of *advertising* leads us to expect and to predict the name of the product.

It is important to emphasize, however, that these expectations are not merely confirmed: rather, there is a complex interplay between similarity and difference – between having our expectations confirmed, and having them subverted in new, and possibly surprising, ways. For example, the advertisement certainly invokes stereotyped notions of masculinity, but it also plays with them (or encourages us to play with them) in an enigmatic and potentially pleasurable manner.

Clearly, the prior knowledge which informs these expectations will differ for different readers, and therefore the meanings they produce will also be different. Yet certain significant aspects of it are likely to be shared, since it is, crucially, *social* knowledge. To return to my analogy with language, the advertisement 'works' (enables us to produce meaning) insofar as it uses a language with which we are all, to a greater or lesser extent, familiar. Although in theory it would be possible for different individuals to produce an infinite variety of meanings, in practice, within a given community of language users, these meanings are likely to be rather more limited in range.

My choice of the wool advertisement as a basis for this analysis was obviously not a random one. It is certainly more complex than most advertisements, although it could be seen as representative of an increasingly popular style of modern advertising (of which the famous Benson & Hedges 'gold' campaign is probably the best-known example). Nevertheless, I would assert that my general arguments here are more broadly applicable, not merely to advertising, but also to other media forms.

To summarize: meaning cannot be seen as something which is contained within the text, and which has been placed there by the author. Rather, it is readers who actively produce meaning by drawing on their prior knowledge, which is itself derived both from their social experience and from their experience of other texts. Although this knowledge will be different for different readers, it is *socially produced*, and will tend in certain crucial ways to be shared. This final point will be developed at greater length in the next section.

The social production of meaning

If, as I have argued, the production of meaning from media texts depends upon knowledge which is shared by a community of language users, one major aspect of teaching about the media must be to identify where that knowledge comes from, and how it is constituted.

Media Studies therefore aims to demonstrate that the language of the media is not natural or neutral, and to investigate the ways in which it is socially and historically produced. In order to achieve this, the relationship between media language and the realities it seeks to represent or construct needs in various ways to be 'made strange'. Furthermore, the complex and contested ways in which this language embodies broader relationships of power, and the ways in which language users are themselves inevitably implicated in these relationships, need to be carefully addressed.

Learning about the media is thus fundamentally a matter of questioning one's own use of language, both as a producer and as a reader of media texts. Students involved in the practical *production of texts*, for example on videotape, will inevitably have to make a series of choices about the way they use the camera, the way they combine sequences of images, and juxtapose images and sound – in short, about the language they use. The danger which many critics have identified in such work[19] is that these choices will be made unthinkingly, and that students will merely imitate dominant professional practices because they see them as the *only* language available. The teacher's role here is to enable students to understand that choices *are* being made, to ask questions about their potential meaning for audiences and to suggest that alternatives are possible.

Similarly, making available to students material which in various ways draws attention to the limitations of dominant media language, or seeks to develop alternative forms, may also lead them to question the language they take for granted. Media texts from other cultures, or those produced in this country outside the mainstream, may well prove unfamiliar, if not unpleasurable, at first, but may enable students to perceive the socially relative nature of media forms and conventions.[20] More positively, they may also indicate that new forms of language make possible new, and hitherto excluded, meanings; and this may in turn encourage students' efforts to use different forms of media language for their own purposes.

A further strategy, which I would like to discuss in more detail here, is to study the *historical* evolution of media language, and the role of the *institutions* that have sought to control it. If we study the early history of cinema, for example, it is possible to see how all the things we now take for granted – our notions of what the cinema is and is not – in fact evolved gradually through a complex interaction of social, economic, technological and aesthetic factors. On a very basic level, for example, we might investigate why the dominant form of commercial cinema is the fictional feature film lasting around ninety minutes. The early cinema typically took the form of shorter films, interspersed with live acts, and freely mixed fantasy and documentary elements. The feature film evolved at least partly because film distributors wished to reach a more middle-class audience in order to increase their profitability. They therefore sought to bring cinema more into line with the forms favoured by that audience, particularly the novel and theatre. Studies of the evolution of film language through the early part of this century have demonstrated that the 'classical Hollywood style', which we now take for granted, was far from being a natural or inevitable development.[21]

Similarly, if we study the early history of radio in this country, we can perceive a conflict between a view of radio as a 'narrowcast' medium (with small cable stations serving specific local communities) and the notion of 'broadcasting' (with a single source serving the whole country, using 'wireless' technology). The fact that the latter definition was the one ultimately adopted was due in no small part to the way in which its major advocate, John Reith, used the BBC to support the Government during the General Strike of 1926. Yet it was Reith's view of broadcasting as a means of disseminating middle-class culture and moral values which was severely contested with the advent of commercial television in the 1950s, and its genuine popularity with a working-class audience largely alienated by the BBC's paternalistic approach. More recently, the advent of 'new' technologies like cable and satellite have been seen by many to pose a major threat to the present broadcasting duopoly. According to their more enthusiastic proponents, they may make possible a greater degree of decentralization and 'consumer sovereignty', while for their critics they herald the end of social responsibility in broadcasting.[22]

What is fundamentally at stake in this history is the right of small elites to speak to, or on behalf of, a mass audience – what one writer has aptly termed 'the battle between television and its audience'.[23] Although the broadcasting organizations clearly do possess a significant power to control who can speak to whom and the language in which they can do so, their power is far from absolute, and is in fact continually contested by politicians and pressure groups of various kinds. Furthermore, that power is itself highly precarious, based as it is on the approval of audiences: ultimately, the claim of broadcasters to speak on behalf of the public depends on how far the public is willing to accept that claim. Although broadcasters may address their audiences in certain ways, and thereby seek to define their interests and values, audiences may not recognize themselves in, and may indeed refuse, these definitions.

So-called 'access' programmes are one arena where these definitions are both constructed and contested, and where the power-relationship between broadcasters and their audience is negotiated.

Thus, on the one hand, a programme like the BBC's *Points of View* seeks to disclaim responsibility, by representing television as something fundamentally trivial; yet it also reinforces the idea that, since the audience is made up of capricious and often eccentric individuals, it is only fair and reasonable that broadcasters should have the right to arbitrate between them and thereby decide what they should receive. On the other hand, Channel Four's *Right to Reply* presents this relationship in terms which are often close to gladiatorial combat; and while the ritualistic half-hour slot may often merely defuse conflict, it can also provoke it in ways which seriously challenge the authority of broadcasting institutions.

Ultimately, then, the relationship between media institutions and media audiences is an unequal, and yet a contested, one. However, this inequality is not merely a question of access (who is allowed to speak?) but, more crucially, one of language (*how* are they allowed to speak?). Insofar as the ability to control language, and thereby to define the terms in which the world may be talked about and represented, can be seen to reside with certain powerful groups in society, language itself may inevitably function to maintain existing inequalities.

In order to question the 'naturalness', even the invisibility, of this process, Media Studies must concentrate not so much on *what* texts may appear to say, but on *how* they work. This should be the case, I would argue, even where the primary function of the text would appear to be one of providing information. Considerable energy has been expended, for example, on quantifying instances of 'bias' within television news, largely through enumerating examples of misrepresentation or clearly partial uses of language.[24] Yet audience research suggests that viewers remember very little of the informational content of the news: much of their pleasure, and their reasons for watching, derive from the *form* of the news, the general sense it conveys of being 'up to the minute', and its tendency to assure viewers that 'all's well with the world'.[25] In this sense, the particular 'biased' attitudes which television news has been accused of promoting may be less significant than its more powerful ideological role as a means of reassurance. As Robert Stam[26] argues, the form of television news seeks to flatter the viewer by creating the illusion that he or she is a privileged witness, the audio-visual master of the world. The 'bias' of television news, he suggests, may derive less from deliberate manipulation than from a desire to avoid disturbing or challenging the viewer.

As I have implied here, teaching about the media is inevitably a political process, which is centrally concerned with the relationship between power and knowledge. At the same time, it is important not to oversimplify the process. The media cannot adequately be seen as mere purveyors of propaganda and lies; and teaching about the media should therefore not be regarded as a process of 'demystification', in which the veils of illusion are torn from students' eyes and the truth revealed. If the media are indeed powerful, then this power cannot be seen as something which producers impose on audiences: rather, it is a power which depends upon the active participation of audiences. The 'power of the media' is thus not a *possession* of producers but an unstable and contradictory *relationship* between producers, texts and audiences.[27]

IMPLICATIONS FOR PEDAGOGY

The view of children as active producers of meaning has a number of implications in terms of *how* we teach about the media. As I have argued, an 'inoculation' approach to Media Studies, which is based on a view of children as passive and uncritical consumers, or even victims, of media influence, and which attempts to render them 'active' and 'critical', tends to ignore the complexity of children's experience of the media. Much recent research on children and television,[28] for example, indicates that even very young children are far more active, critical and sophisticated viewers than is often assumed. Likewise, accounts of the social context of television viewing[29] suggest that the view of children as 'television zombies', 'glued to the box' for twenty-five hours a week, is highly inaccurate. This research suggests that in making sense of television children are employing a wide range of abilities, in processing, interpreting and evaluating information: there is a complex interaction between the meanings children bring to television (what I have termed their prior knowledge) and the meanings they construct from it. One of the main weaknesses of past research into children's use of the media, and, I would argue, one of the main dangers in teaching, is to assume that the meanings researchers (or teachers) construct from the media are necessarily the same as those constructed by children.

At the very least, this implies that as teachers we need to understand more about what our students *already* know before we start trying to teach them what we think they ought to know. Yet it also points to the need for a more open, questioning style of teaching. As Richard Dyer[30] has argued, teachers should aim to understand the nature of their students' experience of the media, rather than assume that they already know about it. 'To take popular television seriously', he suggests, 'is to get inside the experience of it, to grant a legitimacy to the pleasures it offers and *then* to ask questions of value, social responsibility and politics.'

Clearly, this approach means abandoning the notion of the text having a single, definitive meaning. Rather than seeking to impose consensus, teachers will need to acknowledge the *differences*, both between their own readings and those of their students, and between those of different students. As I have argued, these differences arise from the different forms and degrees of prior knowledge which readers bring to texts. Yet this is not to suggest that there is an infinite plurality of readings, all of which are equally valid. Rather, different forms of prior knowledge are available to different groups in society. Women and men, for example, have different 'cultural competencies', which predispose them to read texts in different ways.[31] It is important to be aware of these differences in teaching, and to acknowledge that we cannot read for others. For example, the way in which I, as a white teacher, may identify the 'racism' of a programme like *No Problem!* may well ignore the complex ways in which my black students may seek to identify positive images of themselves within it. Likewise, in teaching about gender representation, it is important to acknowledge the complex pleasures which young women may derive from media forms which may appear in many respects demeaning to them.

As teachers, we need to be sensitive to the ways in which meaning is negotiated and in which, for young people in particular, the media may be appropriated to produce new and potentially subversive meanings and pleasures. Perhaps the most spectacular example of this is 'Youth Culture' itself. It is often argued that young people are simply manipulated by the purveyors of popular music and fashion, and thereby lulled into a superficial consumerism. Yet it is clear that they may at times appropriate these commodities in ways which are seen as highly threatening by the established social order.[32] While it would be naive merely to celebrate the manifestations of 'Youth Culture', they can certainly be regarded as processes of *negotiation* which may have quite contradictory effects.

This process is perhaps less visible with other media forms – although the *Grange Hill* phenomenon provides an interesting example of a television programme whose extraordinary popularity with young people was regarded by many adults as potentially dangerous, precisely because (at least in the early series) it was seen by many as undermining the authority of teachers. Particularly when teaching about media forms which are very popular with young people, it is important to avoid imposing one's own readings. Teenage magazines, for example, are often condemned by teachers as stereotyped and trivial on the basis of what is generally a very superficial knowledge. Students are assumed to accept the 'values' of romantic fiction or of violent adventure stories uncritically. Yet if one takes the time to listen, it becomes clear that the process is far more complex: such material may be popular not because it allows an easy escape into fantasy but, on the contrary, because it provides a space which young people can use to negotiate their own identities. This is clearly a process which teachers ignore at their peril, and which they must learn to respect.

Yet at the same time, as I have indicated, Media Studies seeks to identify the ways in which meaning is socially produced, and the relationship between language and power. In other words, we cannot merely *validate* the meanings students produce: we must also encourage them to analyse *how* they are produced, and thereby to question them. In a sense, this is a matter of moving from the question 'What does it mean?' to the question 'How does it come to have a meaning?' Studying the social production of meaning implicitly involves recognizing the role of the *institutions* which have historically sought the power to define and control it.

As well as asking us to discover, or rediscover, what we already know, Media Studies also requires us to consider *how* we know it. Yet this movement from validating to analysing is inevitably fraught with difficulties. Clearly, classrooms are also places where meanings are produced and negotiated: yet they are typically places in which teachers have greater power to set agendas and impose meanings. By virtue of its subject content alone, Media Studies implicitly challenges this traditional relationship between teacher and taught: the teacher can no longer be seen as the sole source of knowledge, or as the only person who has the right to ask questions. To regard students as active producers of meaning poses a further challenge to the view of teaching as a one-way process of transmission. If Media Studies is concerned to investigate the production of meaning from media texts, it thus also inevitably raises questions about the production of meaning within classrooms themselves. In this sense, the argument for Media Studies is not merely for changing the content of the curriculum: it is also implicitly an argument for developing new approaches to teaching and learning.[33]

NOTES

This chapter was written in 1986.

1 David Lusted, 'A history of suspicion: educational attitudes to television', in David Lusted and Phillip Drummond (eds), *TV and Schooling* (London: BFI, 1985), and Geoffrey Pearson, 'Falling standards: a short, sharp history of moral decline' in Martin Barker (ed.), *The Video Nasties* (London: Pluto Press, 1985) provide useful overviews.

2 For a thorough critique, see Graham Murdock and Robin McCron, 'The TV and delinquency debate', *Screen Education*, no. 30, 1979, pp. 51–68. Aimée Dorr, *Television and Children* (Beverly Hills: Sage, 1986), Chapter 4, and Cedric Cullingford, *Children and Television* (Aldershot: Gower, 1984), Chapter 8, provide brief summaries of research. See also David Buckingham, 'Children and television: an overview of the research' (available from British Film Institute Education Department).

3 See Howard Tumber, *Television and the Riots: a Report for the Broadcasting Research Unit* (London: Broadcasting Research Unit, 1982).

4 Martin Barker, 'Nasty politics or video nasties?' in M. Barker (ed.), *The Video Nasties* (London: Pluto Press, 1984); Julian Petley, 'A nasty story', *Screen*, vol. 25, no. 2, 1984, pp. 68–75.

5 Geoffrey Barlow and Alison Hill (eds), *Video Violence and Children* (London: Hodder & Stoughton, 1985).

6 Marie Winn, *The Plug-In Drug* (Harmondsworth, Penguin, revised edn 1985). For a similar example, see Martin Large, *Who's Bringing Them Up?* (Martin Large for the TV Action Group, 1980).

7 Neil Postman, *The Disappearance of Childhood* (London: W. H. Allen, 1983).

8 Particularly in the work of the Birmingham University Centre for Contemporary Cultural Studies: for example, Stuart Hall *et al.* (eds), *Culture, Media, Language* (London: Hutchinson, 1980). Also Michele Barrett *et al.* (eds), *Ideology and Cultural Production* (London: Croom Helm, 1979). Recent American examples of the 'consciousness industry' approach include Dallas Smythe, *Dependency Road* (Norwood, New Jersey: Ablex, 1981) and Herbert Schiller, *Who Knows? Information in the Age of the Fortune 500* (Norwood, New Jersey: Ablex, 1981).

9 Ian Connell, 'Fabulous powers: blaming the media', in Len Masterman (ed.), *Television Mythologies* (London: Comedia, 1985).

10 For example, Maureen Lalor, 'The hidden curriculum', in Rick Rogers (ed.), *Television and the Family* (UK Association for the International Year of the Child, London: University of London Department of

Extra-Mural Studies, 1980). Kevin Durkin, *Television, Sex Roles and Children* (Milton Keynes: Open University Press, 1985) summarizes several such studies, and provides a useful counter-argument.

11 See Lloyd de Mause (ed.), *The History of Childhood* (New York: Souvenir Press, 1974) and Philippe Aries, *Centuries of Childhood* (Harmondsworth: Penguin 1973).

12 See Len Masterman, *Teaching About Television* (London: Macmillan, 1980) and Jim Cook and Jim Hillier, *The Growth of Film and Television Studies, 1960–1975* (London: BFI, revised edn 1982), for useful outline histories.

13 F. R. Leavis and Denys Thompson, *Culture and Environment* (London: Chatto & Windus, 1948; first published 1933) represents the earliest Media Studies 'textbook' for schools. See Francis Mulhern, *The Moment of 'Scrutiny'* (London: New Left Books, 1979) for a thorough and balanced reappraisal of the Leavises and their colleagues.

   On 'demystification', see David Buckingham, 'Against demystification: *Teaching the Media*', *Screen*, vol. 27, no. 5, 1986, pp. 80–95. Len Masterman's response appears in the same issue, pp. 96–100.

14 For overviews, see Joseph Klapper, *The Effects of Mass Communication* (New York: Glencoe Press, 1960) and Shearon Lowery and Melvin L. DeFleur, *Milestones in Mass Communications Research: Media Effects* (London: Longman, 1983). David Morley in Chapter 1 of *The 'Nationwide' Audience* (London: BFI, 1980) provides a useful critique of this tradition. See also Cedric Cullingford, op. cit. (note 2) for an example of this argument specifically in relation to children.

15 For example, John Hartley, 'Encouraging signs: the power of dirt, speech and scandalous categories', in W. D. Rowland and B. Watkins (eds), *Interpreting Television: Current Research Perspectives* (Beverly Hills: Sage, 1984); also Raymond Williams, *Television, Technology and Cultural Form* (London: Fontana, 1974).

16 Len Masterman, *Teaching About Television* (London: Macmillan, 1980), pp. 3–7.

17 I. A. Richards, *Practical Criticism* (London: Routledge & Kegan Paul, 1929).

18 Angela Carter, 'The company of wolves', in *The Bloody Chamber and other stories* (Harmondsworth: Penguin, 1981), and Neil Jordan's film based upon it.

19 For example, Bob Ferguson, 'Practical work and pedagogy', *Screen Education*, no. 38, 1981, pp. 42–55; Len Masterman, op. cit., Chapter 8. See also David Buckingham, *Unit 27: Media Education* (E207: *Communication and Education*, Milton Keynes: Open University Press, 1987), Section 4.

20 Gill Swanson, 'Independent media and media education', *Screen*, vol. 27, no. 5, 1986, pp. 62–8.

21 See Michael Chanan, *The Dream that Kicks* (London: Routledge & Kegan Paul, 1980); Noel Burch, 'Porter, or ambivalence', *Screen*, vol. 19, no. 4, 1979, pp. 91–106; David Bordwell, Janet Staiger and Kristin Thompson, *The Classical Hollywood Cinema* (London: Routledge & Kegan Paul, 1985).

22 See Mark Pegg, *Broadcasting and Society 1918–1939* (London: Croom Helm, 1983); Timothy Hollins, *Beyond Broadcasting: Into the Cable Age* (London: BFI, 1984); Raymond Williams, op. cit. (note 15).

23 Ien Ang, 'The battle between television and its audiences: the politics of watching television', in Phillip Drummond and Richard Paterson (eds), *Television in Transition* (London: BFI, 1985).

24 For example, in the work of the Glasgow University Media Group, *Bad News* (London: Routledge & Kegan Paul, 1976), *More Bad News* (London: Routledge & Kegan Paul, 1980), *Really Bad News* (London: Writers and Readers, 1982), *War and Peace News* (Milton Keynes: Open University Press, 1985). See Martin Harrison, *TV News: Whose Bias?* (London: Polity Press, 1985), for a counter-argument using the same approach.

25 For example, Peter Dahlgren, 'The modes of reception: for a hermeneutics of TV news', in Phillip Drummond and Richard Paterson (eds), *Television in Transition* (London: BFI, 1985); Kaarle Nordenstreng, 'Policy for news transmission', in Denis McQuail (ed.), *Sociology of Mass Communications* (Harmondsworth: Penguin, 1972).

26 Robert Stam, 'Television news and its spectator', in E. Ann Kaplan (ed.), *Regarding Television* (Frederick, MD: University Publications of America, 1983).

27 This distinction derives from the work of Michel Foucault. For an introduction, see M. Foucault, *Power/Knowledge* (Brighton: Harvester Press, 1980).

28 Particularly Bob Hodge and David Tripp, *Children and Television* (Cambridge: Polity Press, 1986); Aimée Dorr, *Television and Children* (Beverly Hills: Sage, 1986); Kevin Durkin, *Television, Sex Roles and Children* (Milton Keynes: Open University Press, 1985); David Buckingham, *Public Secrets: 'EastEnders' and its Audience* (London: BFI, 1987).

29 David Morley, *Family Television: Cultural Power and Domestic Leisure* (London: Comedia, 1986); Patricia Palmer, *The Lively Audience* (Sydney: Allen & Unwin, 1986).

30 Richard Dyer, 'Taking popular television seriously', in David Lusted and Phillip Drummond (eds), *TV and Schooling* (London: BFI, 1985).

31 The term 'cultural competence' derives from the work of the sociologist Pierre Bourdieu. See David Morley, *The 'Nationwide' Audience* (London: BFI, 1980) and Dorothy Hobson, *'Crossroads': The Drama of a Soap Opera* (London: Methuen, 1982), for research on media audiences which illustrates this argument.

32 See Elizabeth Wilson, *Adorned in Dreams* (London: Virago, 1985), for a valuable recent discussion of this issue.

33 The *Screen* special issue on *Pedagogy: Critical Accounts of Media Education*, vol. 27, no. 5, September–October 1986, provides a number of valuable contributions to this developing area of debate within Media Studies.

Concepts in Media Studies

Chapter 2

Language

Karen Manzi and Allan Rowe

In his book about the 1950s campaign against the American horror comic, Martin Barker[1] analyses a comic story called *The Orphan* which at the time was the target of moral crusaders for its alleged depravity. Barker suggests that *The Orphan* possesses aesthetic qualities that convey a complex and insightful exploration of childhood overlooked by the moralists in their rush to condemn.

How can conflicts in interpretation like this one be explained? Is it possible for texts to be read in many different ways? Or is it something in the assumptions of the readers that leads to different readings? Could there be even more interpretations? What might children at the time – those for whom the comic was intended – have understood it to be about? What sense would children in classrooms today make of it as an object of study?

Questions like these are often posed in disputes about the media and its effects. What is at issue is *meaning*, the sense made of media texts and *how* sense is made. Classroom work on the media often starts with making media products into study texts, learning skills of textual analysis and discovering the many ways that meaning is made of texts.

The media, and particularly visual media, are often thought of as communicating directly. Meaning is often seen as a matter of subjective perception: like beauty, it lies 'in the eye of the beholder'. These common views of the media as transparent can be tested by introducing *procedures* for textual analysis into the classroom.

Some principles and a little of the history of teaching the language of the media follow here. Most approaches study texts in ways that 'make strange' our experience of reading and viewing. Despite differences of emphasis, the aim of the activity is to slow down the *process* of reading to see how meaning is produced in texts and what meanings are actually taken up.

TALKING ABOUT THE MEDIA

The history of media teaching moves from views of the transparency of texts – that their meaning is obvious and no effort is required to understand it – to analytical, structured and self-questioning approaches. Typical of early approaches is an influential book on film education called *Talking About Cinema*.[2] It places stress on studying films linked together by their themes, like 'youth' or 'war'. The choice of films is significant: in form, they are mainly social realist and the choice of issues for defining themes are humanist ones.

The approach was and remains important for the emphasis it places on *talk*, for providing students with opportunities to exchange their own understandings and experiences. As such, it is a worthy corrective to the idea that 'official' readings of texts, often through teachers' accounts, are the most (or only) legitimate ones. Nonetheless, talk can become aimless unless structured and a considerable weakness in this approach is its lack of concern with analysis. Too easily, media texts can become mere reflections of society; fictional events and characters are talked about as if they have lives separate from the page or image; factual events and figures are treated as if they are directly accessible, rather than being in some sense 'reported about'.

The temptation to talk about *EastEnders*, say, as if it were like life in its London setting can easily become debate (and possibly dispute) about its 'realism' – whether life in the East End is really like *EastEnders*. To avoid this, some attention needs to be given to the *form* of texts, how their images and words or dialogue are organized to *make* meaning. Procedures for analysis are required which demonstrate that it is *language* which is producing meaning rather than the real expressing itself. The advantage of being sensitive to this idea of the language of the media is that it delays a familiar rush to judgement. It gives opportunity to see what is being said, how and with what effects. Returning to the example of *EastEnders*, it then becomes possible to ask what sense audiences make of what the programme is saying about life in the East End (and many other issues) and how it says it.

POPULAR ART AND SOCIOLOGY

Analysis of media texts in education commonly takes one of two forms. In literature, an emphasis on close reading means coming to recognize the artistic worth of a text in the literary canon. The aesthetic approach can also find expression in forms of media studies that discriminate within popular forms, celebrating the songs of Frank Sinatra or The Beatles, effective and economical writing in the *Daily Mirror* or the quality of the central relationship in *Steptoe and Son* over other types of popular music, tabloid newspapers or television sitcoms.[3]

Another form of textual analysis is in media sociology[4] which sees the text as the product – in a very literal sense – of the organizations that produce them. Here, the art of the medium is of little concern compared to its function as the product of the commercial or political tendencies of its producers. Texts become less the object of analysis than the economic conditions and the organizational practices and personnel that produce them.

Approaches to textual analysis in art and sociology share assumptions about the single, immanent meaning of the text even though their methods and evaluations differ. Transferred into classroom practices, they can pose problems for the likely differences in reading and differences between teachers and students as readers, especially where the study objective is the search for 'correct', authorized interpretations.

SEMIOLOGY

Dissatisfaction with these approaches is now widespread among media educationists. In their place, methods of analysis have grown that pay attention to the formal production of meaning and deal with a *polysemy* – a range of possible interpretations – of readings.

Work in linguistics introduced into Britain from the early 1970s is significant in this context. Termed *semiology*, this work treats all acts and forms of communication – whether written, spoken or visual – as *signs*. Meaning arises from a particular combination of signs and their place in a language *system*. The semiologist offers a method of analysis of any artefact as text, whatever its cultural status. Original hopes for founding a *science of signification* have become greatly moderated over time into claims for a *systematic approach* to textual analysis.

As might be expected from a discipline with its roots in linguistics, much literary analysis adopts semiotic approaches. But more than works of literature have been the objects of analysis. In the work of Roland Barthes in particular, films, television programmes, even all–in wrestling have been studied alongside texts of greater cultural status like Balzac's novella, *Sarrazine*.[5] Indeed, prompted by Barthes, even more surprising phenomena have become legitimate media study objects: official speech, youth cultures, dress and fashion, etc. This development has given space for integrated cultural and social analyses, for instance, in the work of Paul Willis on school culture[6] and Dick Hebdige on youth sub-cultures.[7] Semiology, then, marks a movement beyond traditional aesthetics and aligns textual and social analyses of media products.

Part of this movement includes the development of a specialist vocabulary for exploring the processes of thought through which meaning is constructed. From this language of analysis, many useful teaching strategies emerge. A key example is a procedure arising from the distinction between denotation and connotation. *Denotation* refers to the act of *describing* the components of a text, naming this colour as red or that shape as a face. It enables us to *recognize* a text as a news photograph, a display advertisement, a TV news item or a scene from a fiction film. *Connotation* is the second stage of analysis. Here the reader *interprets* the denoted elements. Drawing upon a shared cultural knowledge, the reader recognizes that a particular configuration of red, white and blue *denotes* a flag called the Union Jack and *connotes* wider meanings of nation and patriotism.

In the classroom, it may not be possible for a group to agree on aspects of denotation and connotation. Where this happens, the *reasons* for differences of view can be established and discussed. The object of the exercise is to draw attention to the process of reading and the (causes of) disagreements, uncertainties and ambiguities that go with it, rather than to reach an agreed interpretation.

By this procedure, students can establish a basic relation between what semiology calls the *signifier* (a written word, sound pattern or arrangement of light and dark) and the *signified* (the object or concept to which the signifier refers). The separation of the sign into these two levels of signification demonstrates that meaning resides neither in the intention of the producer of an artefact nor in the formal composition of the artefact but, rather, from the *work* done by the reader to make sense of both. Meaning depends on the cultural understandings and the emotions of the reader which are themselves a product of the society – with its particular history, culture and values – within which the signs are produced and the reader reads. Where producer and reader share cultural backgrounds, there is likely to be a greater congruity of intention and reading. Where the background is not shared, little congruity is likely.

ADVERTISEMENT ANALYSIS

A semiotic analysis reveals the process of reading, how we make sense and are able to make sense of what we read. For many teachers, advertisements offer clearest evidence of this approach. Their attention is known and much useful work has been done on them.[8] To study images through photographic slides offers a common and controlled experience for a class. Good teaching material is available to aid study in this area, including the slide pack, *The Semiology of the Image*,[9] containing late 1960s adverts, magazine covers and news photographs largely from American, French and German sources. Such culturally strange material often provides a useful unfamiliarity from which to start.

To demonstrate the semiotic approach, we choose the third slide of the set, an advertisement for Old Nick Rum (Figure 2.1). This can be used to show how a range of signifiers – objects, gesture, colour, lighting – constructs a particular image. The recommended strategy is to show the slide briefly and to ask the class to record what they remember. The idea of denotation enables us to note the use of objects like the straw hat with its connotations of leisure and naturalness. The predominant use of a warm colour, brown, and a gesture, the raised glass, suggest welcome and friendship. There is a physical intimacy between us and the man constructed by an extreme close-up and direct eye contact. The formal arrangement centres attention on the mouth of the man – positioned between bottle and glass, with fingers and cigar pointing to it – assisted by the tonal differences of the bright white teeth among otherwise muted colours. Apart, these elements could have a range of meanings, but in this particular configuration their meaning is *anchored* in connotations of pleasure, connecting warmth, leisure and health to the attraction of the product.

In our own use of the slides we have experienced an ambiguity,

Figure 2.1   Old Nick Rum advertisement.

only touched upon by Gauthier, to do with our reading of the man's status. Is he the 'colonialist' or 'weekender' Gauthier suggests or a dark-skinned, local/Third World figure? If the latter, is the image a tourist's dream, accepted by the locals – if only temporarily – as one of them? This kind of discussion raises issues about the politics of image-making and its connection to a more familiar kind of politics; here, those concerning the production of rum in the Third World and its consumption in the First World. The activity also centrally concerns ideological questions: about how, for instance, a dark tan and well (cosmetically?) preserved teeth can come to connote 'naturalness'.

   Matters of the political and ideological nature of the image can seem contentious and volatile in the abstract, especially when initiated or developed by teachers, but one of the strengths of the semiotic method is its systematic procedure for breaking down the image through collective analysis. Groups can work out between themselves where meanings come from and how meanings are produced. Across a range of images, the matter can be raised too of who has the power to construct and maintain a certain pattern of meanings and with what effects.

CODES AND FORMS

To understand the form of any media text is to understand the signifying codes or conventions that construct it. This approach shifts attention away from the individual psychology of the producer ('Why did she do that?') to the rules that govern the readings of those who use the code ('How come it means that to me?'). Meaning may be clear in the operation of relatively simple codes, such as those governing the colour of traffic lights – the classic example of a consenting code – and even in advertisements – where intentions are known. For more complex forms, understanding lies in the relation and organization of codes; for example, in combining one form of editing with a particular tempo of background music to produce excitement and in another to produce sentiment. It is valuable to work out exercises which identify particular codes at work in any text and to discover the effects of particular combinations. There are even materials that deliberately play with the conventions of coding such as the programme on gender in the *Viewpoint 2*[10] TV series when the reversal of male and female voices in a romantic story produces a disruptive effect.

Most media forms are immediately recognizable to us. We recognize the codes and conventions of genres like the western or television news through regular contact. Such forms become enclosed, self-referential systems, like right and wrong in the western or relevance and news values in TV news. These genres present regular, coherent worlds, so convention-bound that they risk occasional moments of code-breaking; sending up the hero in a comedy western such as *Blazing Saddles* or the news reader interrupting a report to joke about his own slip of the tongue. Code-breaking can go beyond jokey self-references however. It has been argued that some genres such as melodrama[11] or soap operas[12] reveal their own conventions as they attempt to maintain coherence and produce logical resolutions. Thus they may expose the ideological operation of, say, the family, far more effectively than other equally rule-governed – and seemingly more serious – forms such as documentary or drama-documentary. The film *Mildred Pierce*,[13] for instance, tells two stories: one a personal account told by the eponymous heroine in a melodrama, the other a male-dominated detective story. At the end of the film the male code seems to triumph as the detective opens the window to 'let in the truth' of the heroine's innocence and Mildred returns to her estranged husband. Yet this triumph is hard won. Our own experience with students is that, with a collective groan, they refuse to accept the film's attempt to resolve its ideological tensions in a conventional resolution.

READING THE MEDIA

A concern with language is a concern with the act of reading. There are different bodies of opinion about how this relationship between text and reader is to be understood.[14] According to one, texts *construct* their readers. In conventional language, our sense of self is created through the use of the pronoun 'I'. As we use language, we may feel like free agents making choices about what we say. With the media we do not have such a direct sense of creating our own language. The language used by the media can nevertheless be seen as creating us as *ideal spectators*. In particular, the language of film and TV present the reader with a position both inside and outside the text. Through devices of identification, in particular those constructed by the point of view shot (Figure 2.2), we relate to certain characters. Yet rarely do the media present a person or position to identify the origins of what we see, read or hear. Fiction

Figure 2.2   Point of view shot, from Frank to Morton (*Once Upon a Time in the West*).

films and dramas appear to come from nowhere. The voice-over narrator of a fiction or documentary can appear to be the objective authority of 'that which we see'. Even the TV news reader or programme presenter can seem to be part of the television furniture.

The idea of readers as subjects positioned by texts has some explanatory power. It explains how we sometimes feel in thrall to the text, gaining considerable pleasure from our abandonment to it, slumped in front of the TV screen, or unable to put a 'good book' down. The process by which we identify our position in the text is inevitably and necessarily invisible to us; the power of media language is overlooked.

In the light of such arguments, questioning the relation of our position to the text is a useful pedagogic device. 'Why do you feel like that about these characters at this particular point in time? What do you expect to happen next and what informs your expectations? What are we being told to think and feel? How do you know that? Who does this text think we are?' Such questions can help to explore assumptions ingrained or deeply structured in previous experience of texts. Operating such a classroom strategy involves fragmentation of experience and possibly denial of pleasure, both in the classroom ('Can't we see how it ends?') and also outside ('I can't watch a programme now without doing a shot count!'). Although the purpose of media studies is not to deny pleasure but to explore its causes, care is required particularly when the text in question is felt by the students to be part of 'their' culture and when the pleasure challenged is their pleasure.

This approach to media stresses the work done by the text to produce an *ideal* reader, as if *inscribed* by the text, who correspondingly produces a *preferred* reading, according to a *dominant* code. However much this work on subject positioning provides the possibility of exploring the relationship of text and reader, its weakness does lie in constructing the teacher, as in the earlier literary approach, as one who offers a preferred reading. The rigid tendencies of this approach have been recently contested by new developments in ethnographic studies of media audiences.

DIFFERENT READINGS

More recent work on audiences has stressed the possibility of negotiated or oppositional readings. David Morley, in his study of the *Nationwide* audiences,[15] distinguishes between *dominant* readings (where the readers/viewers decode the intended message), *negotiated* readings (where the readers/viewers broadly accept the messages, but modify them in part on the basis of their own experiences) and *oppositional* readings (where the readers/viewers recognize the dominant reading, but interpret the material in a different way). In some instances, the message is seen as so far outside the experiences of readers/viewers that there is a refusal to read.

Such a different idea of the reader arises from attention paid to the differing social and cultural experiences of actual readers, rather than ideal readers positioned by texts. It also understands readers as bringing differing prior textual experiences to the reading of new texts or the conscious adoption of alternative frameworks for understanding texts. Exploring alternative readings, organizing and making sense of them, and holding them in tension with analyses of dominant readings, are important classroom activities.

There are methodological problems involved with any study of readers but the phenomenon of alternative readings recognizable to any teacher using any media in the classroom, can be used as a point of entry. The teacher listens to a range of possible readings and interpretations in the classroom. Although many of the questions posed of texts will remain the same ('What do you expect to happen next? Why? What do you feel about that?'), the basis for the answers will extend beyond the text on view to previous textual and other cultural experiences. There will be fewer calls for and assumptions about 'correct' answers, even though some answers may find more consensus than others. Variations in response need to be dealt with, understood and discussed in terms of the range of cultural, social and biographical experiences of the students.

DOMINANT TEXTS

The most common texts for study in the classroom are usually those whose *form* is most familiar – Hollywood films, broadcast TV programmes, national newspapers, etc. These are immediately recognizable and distinguishable. Study focuses on those textual characteristics of image, copy and their design through which we recognize and name any text.

These texts are termed *dominant* not only by their familiarity but also by their centrality. They appear to produce their meanings easily and coherently but study will demonstrate the work they have to do to produce meaning at all. Dominant texts are as contradictory and confused in meaning as any other, however, and it is valuable to choose exemplary texts which best enable that idea to be explored.

Many media are available for study by purchase across shop counters or on order from specialist suppliers. Fiction films and TV dramas, to be legally studied, have for the most part to be hired. Of these, some titles are available for hire in extract form and make good study texts.

Once Upon a Time in the West[16] is used here as an example of analysing a complex dominant text. The film is the work of a highly stylized director, Sergio Leone, in a distinctive sub-genre known as the Spaghetti (Italian) Western and dealing with American history and its social structure.[17] At the denotative level, the extract from the film features a confrontation between Morton, a railway entrepreneur, and Frank, a gunfighter. We see the two competing for control of a chair using their respective symbols of power – a wad of dollars and a gun – which they 'draw' on each other as in a gunfight. The connotations concern tensions between the restrictions of institutional compromise on one hand, and principles of freedom, honour and integrity on the other.

However, aspects of the visual form of the scene confound any simple rendering of this opposition and complicate its meaning (Figure 2.3). The camera makes Morton the dominant figure of the two, with low-angled shots, and in the 'point of view' shot (Figure

Figure 2.3 'It's almost like holding a gun ... but much more powerful' (*Once Upon a Time in the West*).

2.2) following him across the space of his railway carriage. Yet, as he hauls his crippled body under a bizarre bamboo frame and is thrown about by the action of the train, he is clearly not in control of even his own physical movements. The contradiction over Morton's power is there in the dialogue, too, as his claims to represent a modernizing power in the West are mocked by Frank's metaphors of sickness.

As the visual and aural codes of the film make it difficult to identify Morton as hero, so too are there codes that deny Frank the role. Despite being played by a film star, Henry Fonda, the character has confounded expectations of heroism by ruthlessly killing a child early in the film. Our distance from both characters confuses any simple responses to what they represent and hence any clearcut identification with individualism or collectivism, civilization or barbarism, etc. As in our earlier example of *Mildred Pierce*, the climax of the film will not resolve the contradictions and complexity of this scene. Both characters will die ignobly and the tensions they set off can only be magically resolved through the action of a third character at the end of the film.

ALTERNATIVE TEXTS

Procedures of close textual analysis identified so far presume that students will be familiar with the types of products and the forms offered for study. There are many examples of formally-experimental media made by alternative groups and voices outside the mainstream institutions, especially in film and video workshops and in marginal artistic practices, which are important to study.[18] Not only do they work on alternative forms of media language but they also bear on the way we understand more conventional texts. Films which experiment with form, like *Wavelength* or *Gold*, draw attention to their own textual procedures and the way they are constructed quite self-consciously.

They invite a spirit of enquiry, to interpret what we see, since 'It must make sense, mustn't it?' There may be initial rejection by some students if an experience is so different as to be alienating so thorough preparation, re-organizing expectations that will have arisen from study of dominant texts, is essential. This may include reducing the length of extracts for screening, stopping frequently for discussion and responding sensitively to calls to 'make sense of' the experiences until students become more familiar with them and the adjustments in analytical procedures they demand.

CONCLUSION

All forms of textual analysis are in one sense 'practical' work but clearly any interest in media language needs to incorporate students' own production of images, videos, etc. Hand in hand with developing facility in analysing texts produced outside the classroom should go the opportunity for exercises in production inside the classroom, using practical exercises arising from criticism.

In outlining a history of textual analysis in media studies we have tried to offer some procedures for studying the language of the media. Skills of textual analysis are the key to the careful and considered study necessary for understanding the way we read the media and are influenced by it, and indeed the way the media creates its artefacts. However the media are social as well as cultural phenomena, and their languages are wrought and interpreted in real material circumstances. The understandings available through semiotics and subsequent developments are central but no more than a starting-point for textual analysis and studying the media in general.

NOTES

This chapter was written in 1986 and updated in 1989.

1 Martin Barker, *A Haunt of Fears* (London: Pluto, 1984).
2 E. Ann Kaplan and Jim Kitses, *Talking About Cinema* (London: BFI, 1964).
3 This more liberal approach to the media is well demonstrated by Stuart Hall and Paddy Whannel, *The Popular Arts* (London: Hutchinson, 1964).
4 David Barratt, *Media Sociology* (London: Methuen, 1986).
5 Roland Barthes, *Elements of Semiology* (London: Jonathan Cape, 1967); *Mythologies* (Boulder, CO: Paladin, 1973); *S/Z* (London: Jonathan Cape, 1975).
6 Paul Willis, *Learning to Labour* (London: Saxon House, 1978).
7 Dick Hebdige, *Subculture, The Meaning of Style* (London: Methuen, 1979).
8 John Fiske, *Introduction to Communication Studies* (London: Methuen, 1982); Roland Barthes, 'The rhetoric of the image' in *Image-Music-Text* (London: Fontana, 1977); Gillian Dyer, *Advertising as Communication* (London: Methuen, 1982); Judith Williamson, *Decoding Advertisements* (London: Marion Boyars, 1978).
9 Guy Gauthier, *The Semiology of the Image* (London: BFI Education, 1976).

See also *Reading Pictures* and *Selling Pictures* (London: BFI Education); Andrew Bethell, *Eyeopeners* (Cambridge: Cambridge University Press, 1981); Mike Clarke and Peter Baker, *Talking Pictures* (London: Mary Glasgow, 1981).

10 *Viewpoint 2* (London: Thames TV Schools Broadcasting).

11 Christine Gledhill, 'Melodrama', in Pam Cook (ed.), *The Cinema Book*, (London: BFI, 1985); Ien Ang, *Watching 'Dallas'* (London: Methuen, 1985).

12 Richard Dyer *et al.* (ed.), *Coronation Street* (London: BFI monograph 13, 1981).

13 Pam Cook, 'Duplicity in *Mildred Pierce*', in E. Ann Kaplan, *Women in Film Noir* (London: BFI, 1978).

14 Perhaps the most accessible introduction to this area is Terry Eagleton, *Literary Theory: An Introduction* (Oxford: Blackwell, 1983).

15 David Morley, *The 'Nationwide' Audience* (London: BFI, 1980).

16 *Once Upon a Time in the West*, film study extract, one of over 400 available from the BFI Film and Video Library.

17 Christopher Frayling, *Spaghetti Westerns* (London: Routledge & Kegan Paul, 1981).

18 Christopher Rodrigues and Rod Stoneman, 'The use of independent film in education', in *BFI Production Catalogue 1979/80*.

Chapter 3

Narrative

Adrian Tilley

Scheherazade told her stories through Arabian nights to keep death at bay. In everyday life, however, we seem to need no threats to prompt yet another tale to unwind. Indeed, so commonplace and natural does story-telling appear that it may seem invisible to study. Yet story-telling is a complex process with important implications.

What seems so natural is actually learned from our earliest moments and becomes part of our social experience. Children quickly learn patterns of story-telling from story books, advertisements, cartoon chases and pop songs. As their vocabulary increases, they acquire skills of story-telling, peppering their talk with 'and then' to sequence events logically. They learn to recognize conventions that signal the start and close of a narrative, to predict what will happen in between and to make connections between different stories. They build a stock of expectations and make judgements about characters by distinguishing roles, for instance between heroes and villains.

More, we are socialized through narrative forms which offer stories to moderate behaviour ('Don't do that or . . .'), to develop language ('Mary, Mary, quite contrary . . .'), to engage the imagination ('Beware the wolf in the forest . . .') or to make us laugh ('This little piggy went to market . . .').

Becoming competent in recognizing, predicting and using stories is something we learn. Recognizing our knowledge of *narrative* and putting it to use is another matter, however, to be learned more formally.

To *study* narrative, then, is to pick apart story-telling, our own and that of others around us, in our personal interaction and in our relations to other agencies who are in the business of 'telling tales'.

The media are in the forefront of narrative production and offer ripe pickings. They produce, circulate and present a vast range of narratives that share certain similarities and can be distinguished by important differences. Some characteristics they share with our own acts of story-telling but others are very different. There are differences in *forms* of narrative and differences in the *situations* in which narratives are met; between 'story time' at school and in television's *Jackanory*, between writing a newsbook in school and being asked what we did at school today when we get home.

The nature of media narratives and their relations to our social situations is the object of narrative study.

NARRATIVE STUDY

The term 'narrative' refers to the coherent sequencing of events across time and space. The process of narration – acts of story-telling – is termed 'narrativity'.

Narrative is a central concept in Media Studies for three main reasons. First, the notion of narrative shifts attention from the *content* of stories to the *structure* and *process* of their telling. This avoids, not least, a hasty rush to judgement about the worth or value of any act of narration.

The story is a prominent feature of education. Cast as 'fiction', its study has been central to English Literature where the stress has been on evaluation of a canon of classic writers and in the essentially moral search for abiding truths about human nature. To study narrative, rather than just fiction, the novel or the 'great novel', is to rejig the 'Lit. crit.' emphasis on authors and their intentions, on texts and their meaning.[1] These become, instead, factors in the process of story-telling, part of the stock contributing to *how* as well as *what* sense is being made.

Some traditions of History teaching have also been story-based. Like authors in Literature teaching, History has its litany of 'the great and the good', historical moments and movements seen through the activities of individuals, 'authors of destiny', in a grand sweep of progress over time. Like the moral tales of Literature, some practices in History teaching offer stories as evidence rather than as accounts of the past.

Through the idea of narrative, these issues of taste and discrimination, of the past and point-of-view, can be made amenable to study rather than assumed or in other ways made invisible.

Second, since narratives take a multiplicity of forms – fictional and non-fictional, across a range of media (print, visual, oral, aural) – an equally ubiquitous range of media can be organized for study through the concept of narrative *similarity* and *difference*. The news, whether in print or image, shares certain features of narrative with historical evidence, photographic records, paintings, song, etc. To discover formal similarities through comparative study can be surprising and revealing. But *different* narrative forms are discernible too: the nature and implications of those differences can also be revealed.

Third, by studying currently popular or central media forms like tabloid newspapers or soap operas, students can discover how the meanings and pleasures of these narrative forms relate to the wider disposition of social power. Work on *EastEnders*, for instance, can reveal how its narratives interweave ideas about marriage, parenthood, ageing, race, and so on, that recur over the longevity and frequency of continuing serials. The popularity of such serials suggests that these ideas relate to many of our own – and perhaps predominant – attitudes and values. They become narrative *discourses* spanning the media and social life, weaving powerful ways of understanding the social world and our place in it.

NARRATIVE MODELS

How to study narrative? What follows is a possible course outline, beginning with three different models of analysis.

Structure and problems

All stories can be seen to be similar in *structure*; they share a movement across a series of three 'problems':

ESTABLISHING A PROBLEM	ELABORATION OF PROBLEM	RESOLUTION OF PROBLEM

In a crime story the central problem may be to solve a crime. There are likely to be various elaborations of this problem as the investigation proceeds, perhaps confusing or surprising the reader with other problems, involving many characters as suspects in different settings or even at different moments in time, as in the film flashback. Ultimately the problem will be resolved or neutralized with the apprehension or death of the law-breaker. That resolution will also settle for the reader the elaborations which have become less important in narrative significance.

The nature of the narrative problem and how it is resolved may depend upon the *genre* of the story. Most problems are solved through some ritualized violence: the western is famous for its gunfight (*3.10 to Yuma*, *My Darling Clementine*, *The Wild Bunch*), the crime thriller for street assassinations (*Little Caesar*, *The Godfather*) and the horror genre for the conflagration (*Frankenstein*, *The Fall of the House of Usher*, *Carrie*). Other genres are resolved by other forms of action: a disaster epic may be resolved through a supreme act of sacrifice (*Earthquake*), whereas, in a musical, resolution may be reached through a song and dance routine (*Top Hat*).

The problem formula is well suited to the study of extracts from the opening or climax of films; asking what narrative problems are being established and resolved, and how we know, can reveal patterns and variations of the formula. Applied to whole texts, the formula can reveal the core structure beneath the apparent shapelessness, complexity or confusion of narratives.

Equilibria

This basic formula is developed from, and can give way to, exploring the model offered by Todorov[2] where a narrative consists of a fictional world in which an *initial equilibrium* is then *disrupted*, with a different and *new equilibrium* produced at the end. The initial equilibrium may be a balance of social, psychological or moral elements according to the story genre: the harmonious social and family grouping in the opening scenes of *Klute* or *The Godfather*; Josey Wales in *The Outlaw Josey Wales* tilling the soil of his land in a dappled sunlight; the rocket launch – a pinnacle of technological achievement – in the opening of *The Quatermass Experiment*. Even non-fiction titles such as *The Nine O'Clock News* begin with an initial equilibrium – the safety and reliability of reports from the world of news – soon to be disrupted by that 'other world' of violence, death and politics. After a series of accounts of an event, interpretations are made by 'experts' on our behalf, resolution and order are re-established by a final, often lighthearted story offering relief and release in a new equilibrium.

The notion of equilibrium raises questions about how social order is represented and how it functions to effect *closure* within stories.

We leave the news world as we found it, with the readers at their desks as the credits roll and the music plays once more; the 'other world' has been dealt with for the time being and we can proceed safely onwards. At the end of *The Outlaw Josey Wales* a new community has been created – a sharing and stable community of male and female, young and old, white and red. Threat and disruptions of that new order have been dealt with violently – in the case of the marauding Redlegs – and by negotiation – with the local Indian community. The utopian resolution of many fictions and news programmes contrasts with the more ambiguous resolutions of other examples. In the final sequence of *Klute*, Bree Daniels, a call girl who has been the victim of a psychopath's brutal campaign of fear, leaves her flat – and, apparently, her independent city existence – to share a small-town life with John Klute, the detective who has 'saved' her. *The Godfather* ends with the initially sympathetic Michael Corleone, the only surviving son of the mafia family, avenging himself on the rival gangs and asserting a new, harsh order on the criminal world. In *The Quatermass Experiment* London (and therefore the human race?) is saved by the joint efforts of a doctor, a policeman, a scientist – and a television company.

Comparing the initial social order with the final social order is always revealing. Key questions will be: What has changed in the world of the story? What has been transformed? What has been added or lost in the process? How have the characters' relative positions of power and status changed?

Across a range of narratives, patterns emerge. Positions of dominance or submission are taken up by certain characters depending on their gender, race, class or position in a family. So, in *The Quatermass Experiment*, whilst medicine, law and order, science and the media co-operate together to prevent catastrophe, it is science which asserts its dominance and independence at the end as the Professor marches into the night towards a technological future. The film has a familiar and powerful discourse on the primacy of science as saviour of the world's troubles. Narrative analysis like this can deal with the way narratives speak *ideologically*, about organizations and relations of power.

Character as function

The advantage of the problem and equilibrium formula is that it is revealing and accessible but it operates at such a general level that many details of narrative are ignored.

A more complex model lies in Vladimir Propp's proposal[3] that any narrative consists of thirty-one categories of event and character. These categories, which Propp calls *functions*, organize the progression of a narrative. Characters are understood not for who they are or what they are like but for the structural role they play in the story. Thus, characters are rendered as hero, villain, donor (of gifts or help) or magical agent. Events function similarly in a cause-and-effect relation of action and reaction.

It is useful to first classify *characters* according to their minimal types and functions. A diagram like this might help:

Character Types	Function	Example
The hero/subject	s/he who seeks	
The object	who/what is sought	
The donor	who sends the object	
The receiver	where it is sent	
The helper	who aids the action	
The villain/opposer	who blocks the action	

This simple exercise can establish a method of analysis and introduce the Propp model with its more extensive list of functions. Since it was at first based on Russian fairy tales, many of its categories have been rendered from their frequent fantasy setting to more modern ones. A simplified version of the character/event typology, drawing out the key elements of the model, is offered here for use in the classroom:

Functions	Example
An initial situation: a family, a community, a kingdom	
A warning is offered and disregarded	
A serious problem develops	
An act of villainy creates a lack or loss	
Agreement to take action	
The hero leaves	
A character acts as a donor/magical helper (person or object)	

Functions	Example
The action moves to a special setting	
A struggle	
The hero is marked or branded	
The villain is defeated	
The serious problem or lack is resolved	
The hero returns	
A pursuit and/or rescue	
An arrival	
A false hero makes claims	
Recognition and exposure of the false hero	
A new order signalled by a marriage	
An 'enthronement' (acquisition of power and status) or ritual	

The Propp model presents pupils with a wide range of narrative *forms* in many different media, across fiction and non-fiction. They can produce a typology of their own, listing specific *character* types and connecting them to their narrative *functions*: what they cause to happen.

The Proppian model can be applied to any narrative and not just fiction; to the study of newspapers, for instance, to trace how character types and events function in news reporting. News stories feature heroes, who are seen as supporting and defending the social order, and villains seeking to disrupt and destroy it. This is at its starkest in news coverage of terrorist acts,[4] strike pickets and moments of civil disorder. Historical figures, too, can be seen as functions, according to how they appear in historical narratives.

Study involves testing out typologies and character groupings on various media texts. When they are applied to the reporting of news, significant questions arise: Who are the villains, heroes, donors and so on in the reporting of strikes, social unrest, deprivation, war? How do news stories narrate like fictions? By re-writing television news commentaries or articles in newspapers so that 'heroes' become 'villains', 'opposer' becomes 'helper', etc., students can see how non-fiction forms use many of the devices of narrative.

What literary approaches render as complexity of character – the psychological realism of conflict and contradiction within a character – can be perceived in this account as the function of stories grouping characters in contrasting or complementary ways. In *The Taking of Pelham 123*, two groups compete for the 'prize' of a captured train – hi-jackers and transport police. Each group is represented by patterns of psychological traits: single-mindedness, vengefulness, cynicism, doubt. The way these traits are blended suggests possibilities of future conflict or crisis. Can the hi-jack leader, Mr Blue, control the psychopath in their group? Can Garber, the transport police chief, control the transport system? Narrative movement here depends upon how these characteristics are grouped to create conflicts.

There are three broad ways in which characters advance narratives. The first is through the process of *character change* where the hero is engaged in a search for identity, a search which brings about changes of attitude, response and belief. Second, the character is defined in terms of its *role within a hierarchy* (such as a son or mother in a family) where challenges to the role produce conflict. The third element involves *the search or task* undertaken by the hero. Usually such action involves breaking social codes of conduct, the 'law'. The private eye transgresses legal rules and the avenger seeks justice outside the law in westerns and gangster films. Persistent acts of selfishness recur in sub-plots of continuing 'soap opera' serials to drive the narrative on; as once Den in *EastEnders* offended the familial roles of father and husband, so Mrs Mangle in *Neighbours* offended against the community ethos. Resolution for the hero corresponds to the establishment of new social orders in the earlier narrative models; a new state of equilibrium is brought about by the disruption of other existing orders of family and society.

How order is re-established is a crucial element of study. The functions of punishment, marriage and 'enthronement' within a narrative may work at a symbolic level and require interpretation. They may serve to efface inherent contradictions in the re-establishment of order. How is it that through these events characters can suddenly find happiness and peaceful security despite the deaths and deprivations often experienced immediately before? What we may find is the dominance of certain values and ideas over others with justice, marriage and family creating a stable social hierarchy in a final order free from threat, doubt or contradiction. Such an approach takes much of the mystery out of story-making, demonstrating that what has gone unnoticed or passed as natural can be revealed as highly constructed, organizing thinking about social orders in particular ways.

These models of narrative analysis make apparent the relationship between texts and the notion of social order. Narratives are about the survival of *particular* social orders rather than their transformation. They suggest that certain systems of values can transcend social unrest and instability by making a particular notion of 'order out of chaos'. This may be regarded as the ideological work of narrative. Narrative analysis can make the 'natural' relations between narratives and social orders not only less natural but possibly even open to change.

NARRATIVE CODES

The narrative models of Todorov and Propp offer valuable textual analyses of narrative but they are not much concerned with the reader. We need to look elsewhere than these *formalist* models for a mode of analysis disposed towards the reader.

One way of understanding the text/reader relation is to see a story as a set of intended meanings expressed by the narrator in particular ways that are interpreted by the reader. The intended meanings and the interpreted meanings will differ unless the mode of expression is commonly understood by sender and receiver. To guarantee that agreement, the mode of expression takes the form of *codes* working to make meanings and reproduce those meanings. In other words, meanings will be *en*coded by the narrator, transmitted through a medium and *de*coded by the narratee. This 'ideal' model rather mechanistically expresses the social nature of reading, however. Rather than a model of an active text and a passive 'receiver' of its meanings, the idea of *cultural codes* can make claims for *active* reading. In this more sophisticated model, the reader *produces* meaning from a text, whether intended or not, from their own cultural experience and identity. Thus, the pleasures of *Minder*, for instance, can be activated by a reader who recognizes the subtleties of a subterranean world suggested by a Ford Capri, a pork pie hat and a fast line in street slang; pleasure comes then from the meanings made by readers as they interact with the pleasures offered by the text.

Work on the *codes* of narrative and the *activity* of reading is provided by Roland Barthes in a model which offers an account of how the reader is enticed by and transported through the narrative.

Barthes[5] proposes five codes of meaning or signification. Three (the Semic, Referential and Symbolic) refer to the form and style of a narrative, cutting 'vertically' through a narrative. Two (the Proiaretic and the Hermeneutic) are concerned with the sequencing of a narrative and therefore function 'horizontally'. The Proiaretic is the Action code and the Hermeneutic the Enigma code; both are concerned with narrative *development*. They determine the other three codes which organize the 'texture' of the narrative. The Semic code is the descriptive code especially applied to characters. The Referential code refers outwards from the word/image to the 'real world'. The Symbolic code embodies the metaphoric – the substitution of one small or concrete thing for a larger, abstract one.

Barthes' analysis was applied to the literary text of Balzac's short story *Sarrasine*, so care needs to be taken in applying it to visual texts like films and television programmes. However, the action and enigma codes, because they deal with the linear structure of stories, are clearly transferable.

Enigma codes generate and control what and how much we know in a narrative. They also engage and hold the interest of the reader. The tap of Blind Pugh's stick along the street in *Treasure Island*; Mr Bingley's arrival as a single, marriageable man at Netherfield Park in *Pride and Prejudice*; Marnie's long walk along the station platform in the film *Marnie*; a news headline announcing an economic crisis – all are presented as enticing enigmas, puzzles which demand to be solved. Answers to the questions posed by the enigmas are provided in a sequence according to their narrative significance. In the course of the story, the enigmas will multiply and interweave. The less important will be forgotten or readily solved while central ones will be held over to the end of the story before they are resolved; Blind Pugh will soon be forgotten in favour of Long John Silver, Mr Bingley's initial importance will recede as Darcy becomes the heroine's favourite, and Marnie's importance will grow as she becomes the film's central enigma.

The enigma code is discernible in a wide range of media: the tantalizing build-up to a new TV series through previews, the *TV Times* and *Radio Times*, and in newspaper articles; the release of a major film with a campaign of posters, trailers and television appearances by its star; the birth of a new daily newspaper; the publication of a devastating exposé novel; an advertisement for a new car with a new braking system; the release of a government report on nuclear waste. All use enigma codes to stimulate maximum

Figure 3.1   Five shots from the opening of *Mildred Pierce*. (a) Title card and the first enigma – who is the woman of the title?

(b) A darkened house – the site of the narrative events?

(c) A murder. An aggregation of enigmas – who is the victim? the murderer? why the killing?

(d) The victim murmurs Mildred's name as he dies. Is she the murderer?

(e) A car leaves the house – shifting our attention from victim to a murderer whose identity is withheld.

public interest and, at the same time, contain and limit what we are to know.

The series of enigmas shown in Figure 3.1 establish the narrative and drive it pleasurably towards disclosure.

Action codes makes complex ideas and feelings immediately recognizable, at the same time ordering their significance in the narrative. In a western, the buckling on of a gun belt signifies a set of possible intentions of character – decisiveness and determination – and action – to solve a problem through violence. In other situations, the simple action of packing a suitcase can connote determination, despair or duplicity. In both examples, the action, however coded, will forward the narrative. If enigma codes build a story through (lack of) knowledge, action codes explain the significance of moments in the story. We know (because we have learned from other stories) that the gun belt being buckled on heralds a showdown, and we know (from other stories, but also, perhaps, from our social experience) that the packed suitcase will lead to a confrontation or escape.

How puzzles arise within a story – how they can be delayed, extended, and resolved – can be made into open-ended discovery activities for students. Central enigmas can be charted through a story and distinguished from delays, complications and minor resolutions.

The following diagram charts in this way the story of *Coma*, a film about a doctor's investigation of a series of unexplained deaths at her hospital:

Central enigma resolution	Delay event/ sequence	Minor event/ sequence	Complication event/ sequence	Final resolution
Why are there so many coma cases in the Boston Hospital?	Doctor is reassured by the Head of the hospital.	Doctor takes an enforced holiday.	Doctor discovers where coma patients are taken.	Head of the hospital revealed as villain.

The enigmas of any narrative can be charted like this. Comparing three or four formally different texts can reveal some suggestive similarities and differences between genres and between fictions and non-fictions; list action codes in a narrative, relate each to similar examples in other texts, predict their possible narrative effect (i.e. what *might* happen as a result) and compare their actual narrative effect.

This form of narrative analysis considers the nature of the pleasures of the text and how they 'call up' its audiences. It may be the pleasure of being 'in the know', recognizing, understanding and re-experiencing the familiar. To be able to predict what will happen is as pleasurable as having those predictions and expectations confounded by a new twist or shock in the narrative. Ultimately, it is that desire for knowledge and the drive to know which is stimulated by the narrative form.

GENRE

Once familiarity with the codes of narrative is established, genre – how stories are grouped into types like thrillers, melodramas and so on – can be studied with more substance. Certain genres draw more freely on enigma codes than others.

The crime thriller conventionally features a number of enigmas – some based on characters, others on events. The central enigma may be about an event such as a murder or robbery. Character-based enigmas (a series of suspects) will work toward the resolution of that central enigma. In melodrama, the narrative puzzles will be character-based, generating event-based enigmas concerned with family relationships, sexual behaviour, class background and consequent conflict. The horror genre, in a more limited way, employs enigma codes around identification and concealment. The threatening monster or maniac seeks to gain a place within society (through its desire or deviousness) in order to escape being identified. That identification only becomes possible through the discovery of specific knowledge which can bring about its defeat.

Genres like the western or war story depend far more upon action codes: the search, the chase, the trek, the task. In the musical the action codes are expressed, and problems are ultimately solved or at least controlled, by a song or dance. Here the individual character's problems develop alongside the group's problems: Lydia and Leroy in *Fame* have professional and personal problems to solve whilst the members of the School are faced with the problem of producing the show; the personal problems of the central characters played by Powell and Rogers in *Forty-Second Street* run parallel with the rest of the theatre company's problem of survival; Maria's individual problems in *The Sound of Music* are linked to the problems of the Trapp family. In all these examples individual and group problems are resolved by the final musical *action* sequence.

Analysis of enigma and action codes can make it possible to study the text and also the social *context* in which those texts are produced and consumed. How codes are differently patterned reveals much about how notions of maleness and femaleness are represented in media products, for instance. Often enigma codes will be organized around the central female figure; overtly, as in *The French Lieutenant's Woman*, *Mildred Pierce* or *Vertigo*, among other fictions, or even covertly, as is often the case in non-fiction. The media account of 'Margaret Thatcher', for instance, developed through enigmas of her corner-shop origins, her role as wife and mother, her propensity for work and 'bossiness', all part of an underlying enigma of 'What makes Maggie tick?' It is an enquiry into the female subject as much as the political individual. In the same way, and more indirectly, what can begin as an investigation into a crime evolves into an investigation of the female subject. In *Klute* the audience is quickly shifted from an interest in the disappearance of a businessman to an interest in the relative freedoms and constraints in the life of a call-girl. Many of the 1940s 'films noir' exemplify the same displacement of narrative interest from the criminal to the female. Within the horror genre, a similar displacement occurs where the source of the threat shifts from the supernatural to the secular female: the mother (*Rosemary's Baby*, *It's Alive*) and the girl-child (*The Exorcist*, *Carrie*). The enigmas are here transferred from a concern with general threats to the social order, on the one hand, to the specific 'threats' of maternity and female child sexuality on the other.

Conversely, action codes tend to collect around the male character. Surveillance – the various acts of looking and observing – is frequently presented as male activity (often with the female as the object observed) as is questioning, confrontation and violent action. A useful contrast can be made to those fictions where 'male' codes are appropriated by female figures as in *Coma* or *Cagney and Lacey*.

These genre relations to action and enigma codes explain the different pleasures we get most evidently. But they can also explain the different ways we are invited by codes to respond to narratives as male or female readers.

THE NARRATOR

From the balladeer to the raconteur, the narrator has enjoyed status and privilege. In the Hans Andersen story *The Elfin Mount*, a bride is selected, not for her beauty, but for her ability to tell entrancing stories. Othello wins Desdemona through his story-telling prowess. Many television news presenters become stars with their own programmes. The voice-over for a documentary carries the credit 'Narrator'. The central events of the Falklands War were communicated less as journalistic accounts and more as personal testaments by commentators like Brian Hanrahan.

The narrator not only tells us about the events of a story but *evaluates* them for us, indicating what is important in what is being told and how we should think about it. When recounting personal stories, students tell not only of the events they experienced

('We went on a trip to Blackpool') but offer evaluations ('It were great, weren't it?' 'Ace it was.') to engage the listener.

The narrator also seems to guarantee truth, acting as a voice from within the narrative against which we can test other 'voices'. The narrator has knowledge which we will possess ultimately, but we entrust the truthful expression of that knowledge to the narrator. It is a convention rarely broken.

The narrator establishes a relationship with an audience that offers an implied role or position to 'receive' the story. It may feature as an appeal to certain dispositions on the part of the reader. In the address of the Victorian novelist or the contemporary 'Agony Aunt' to her 'Dear Reader' the appeal is to specific class values, learning and sympathies. The crime detective assumes the reader to be a city person, knowing and cynical, able to understand the language of urban cultures. Similarly, the news reader assumes that the audience shares a view of what political, social and human stories in circulation make for 'news'. The narrator in a documentary generally places the audience in a position from which they will accept not only the knowledge offered but the authority of the position to offer it. Thus particular voices are selected which are familiar and trusted (Anthony Quayle in the Conservative Party political broadcasts) or of a specific class (Kenneth Clarke, Jacob Bronowski).

Narration comes from one of two positions: either *third person* where the narrator tells the story from outside it or *first person* where the narrator is a character in the story. Literary narratives commonly use either form of narration as do documentaries – the voice-over narrator or the on-screen presenter. But fiction films and television prorammes are rarely narrated in the first person. Each *Star Trek* episode is instigated by Captain Kirk's voice narrating from the Star Log and establishing the dramatized events that continue the television series. More often, characters may narrate their stories which are then dramatized in the form of flashbacks. A playful example is the opening segment of Hammer Films' *Dracula*. A narrator, Jonathan Harker, appears to be telling his own story to us through his diary entries which record the events of his arrival at Castle Dracula. The film twists this convention as we discover that he is already dead and that the diary is actually being read by someone else. In effect the film shifts from a first-person to a third–person narration, affording much pleasure as the audience realizes it has 'mis–read' the narrator of Harker's story.

Through consideration of the status of the narrator, it is possible to tease out some of the sources of pleasure in any narrative. Expectations created by the narrator's tale can be confounded quite delightfully. In *Kind Hearts and Coronets*, the villainous multi-murderer played by Dennis Price narrates his crimes from what transpires to be the solitude of a prison cell, only to leave behind the incriminating memoirs on his release; the narrator of *Sunset Boulevard* is gradually revealed to be a *dead body*; the hero of *Lady in the Lake* narrates his story from 'behind' the camera in a sublime act of film subjectivity.

There are many possibilities for practical work to explore these ideas about the role of the narrator and its variations. Students can dub a narrator's voice over a silent visual sequence – initially a series of still images recorded on video, then a segment of a film or TV programme on video – to discover the variety in arising sets of interpretations. Students can offer alternative narrations to the news programmes or documentaries with voice-over narrations, exploring the possibilities and limitations of changing the meaning of the narration. A lot can be revealed about how an audience perceives the truth and worth of a narrator by working on the tone and 'quality' of the narrator's voice. A female voice can be substituted for a male voice, a child's for an adult's; regional accents, colloquial or slang forms can take the place of standard English. How these substitutions affect the 'reading' of the segments can reveal audience assumptions about the race, gender, class and age of 'proper' narrators.

NARRATION

The role of the narrator is one clear device of narration – the act of telling – and occurs regularly in some form in nearly every medium. But *how* stories are told differs from one medium and type of text to another; there are very significant differences between a five-hundred page novel, a ninety-minute feature film, a TV soap opera episode, a radio play and a newspaper report, etc. Though they may share features of narrative *structure*, they differ in their narrative *form*.

Narration organizes events according to its use of *time* and, in visual narratives especially, *space*. We understand events through a wide variety of conventions, like flashbacks, diaries and discovered letters. Visual conventions connect one scene to another and one camera shot to another in cause and effect sequences according to familiar principles of editing.[6] These conventions are so familiar that they may seem obvious or plain common sense. Exercises can be set up that reveal the highly *constructed* nature of this process of narration – *deconstructing* the shot composition of a few minutes of a film, calling out the cuts and camera-changes by number as a TV programme starts, planning and story-boarding own productions.

The visual narrative, like films or TV programmes, develops through a series of shots edited together. Conventional narratives are based on a principle of continuity, 'matching' shots in a variety of ways that constitute a *system*. Exercises like the following one on a fragment of the film *The Big Heat* enable students to see how narratives are composed, the extent to which any one conforms to or deviates from the continuity system, and how active that makes a film audience in the process of making narrative sense of any film experience.

1 Time

Events in a narrative are experienced on two time scales: *story time* is the time it takes for the events of the story to happen and *narrative time* is the time it takes to tell the story. The two are rarely the same. There has to be compression or, more rarely, extension of story time. A novel's story may span decades whilst the reading time is several hours. In cinema, a journey which might take months, as in *The Searchers*, is edited into a few minutes of screen time. Conversely, an event which takes only moments to happen may take hours to read as in William Golding's *Free Fall* where the moment of death of the main character is the substance of the story. Similarly, in the film *Incident at Owl Creek*, the few seconds in which a soldier is hanged becomes twenty minutes of film time through slow motion, cross-cutting and repetition.

To convey the passing of time in a radio play, a range of aural conventions are used: voice-over, fade-out, mixes, musical cues or sound effects. In newspaper reporting, the language of journalism compresses a range of events into shortened narratives with an economy of expression. The compound word ('riot-torn', 'banner-waving') and word combinations ('Mr Big', 'drug swoop') evoke familiar narratives. The story time of those narratives is then compressed by the repeated specifics of time and place (Beirut,

Figure 3.2   Sequence from *The Big Heat*. (a) The detective hero enters the bar. A commotion audible off-screen right draws his attention. As he looks . . .

(b) . . . we see what he is looking at, a group at the far end of the bar. This sequence is called a shot/reverse shot; this is an elementary way of cutting on action, through a character's look off-screen, to advance the narrative.

(c) The camera moves in close on the action and dialogue. As the villain moves from left to right to attack a woman, so the heroine reaches in the same direction to pull him off. The camera cuts on that movement to ...

(d) ... the woman running into a new space. This is a cut on action but not a matching cut. The narrative is confused for a moment, echoing the shock we experience at the act of villainy. Another cut to ...

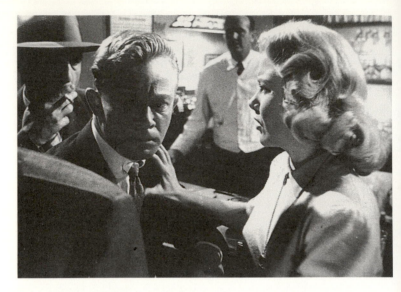

(e) ... another surprise. A man expresses his (and our) shock to his friend. Where is he? Where are we?

(f) Cut to another space, another character. Again, confusion. Where are we now, who is this man?

(g) Cut to the character in (f) as he rises from his chair, entering this frame from right to left and confronting the pair previously met in (e).

Now we get our bearings again as all these minor characters are seen in the same space, and in a familiar arrangement at the bar in a 180 per cent change of camera position from (b).

Despite our momentary disorientations, we quickly learn about new characters in a developing situation, through economic and exciting methods of visual narrative development such as these.

6.40 a.m.) and constant references to the act of narration ('as reported yesterday ...', 'here is an up-date on ...').

Soap operas can use a different relation of story time to narrative time. In *Coronation Street* story time and narrative time are closer. Within a segment of an episode, not only may these times be equal, but the time within the story may parallel the time of the viewing. Events are signalled as 'happening' on the day of viewing. The fictional world and the audience are thus more tightly bound together, a process especially important to the success of any on-going serial.

Much work has been done on the development of codes of film narration. Early cinema filmed story events as an unbroken temporal sequence. Story time and real time were identical. Subsequently, cuts in time were clearly labelled by the caption ('Three days later ...') or by a change of shot, a fade (the screen darkening) or an iris-in (the shape of the screen imploding to black). Narratives become more complicated with the notion of parallel action; two events happening at the same time could be juxtaposed by cross-cutting. The flashback re-ordered the chronology of time.

Students can explore these conventions practically. A sequence from a modern film can be re-worked on video, using the original dialogue if necessary, within the visual conventions of early films. Students learn to work largely in medium and long shot, and to adapt acting styles. Similar work can be carried out for television by comparing the early coverage of football (usually one camera in a grandstand position accompanied by a detailed commentary) with the modern multi-camera, multi-commentary version. Simulations of the two styles can be worked around the video recording of an indoor game like draughts or snakes and ladders.

Narrative time can be further explored according to the categories of *order*, *duration* and *frequency*. Events may occur in one order but are narrated in a different order, as in *Citizen Kane*. Narration can begin with the end of the story and progress as we are led backward in time.

Duration – the amount of real time it takes for an event to happen – may be varied from event to event. An ellipsis cuts out redundant action and collapses time (the breakfast scene between Kane and his wife Susan is exemplary) whereas in a scene which contains mostly dialogue, story time and narrative time are equal. Scene-setting may even require longer in narrative time than story time. A summary, as used in chapter headings ('Chapter ten in which our heroine . . .') or television serials ('Debbie has crashed in the Andes . . .'), has a variable tempo, using both ellipsis and scene.

With these three elements, students can chart the time structure of any narrative, breaking segments down into narrative sequences of different duration. They can find patterns, repetitions and differences of duration not only within texts but also across texts, often according to their genre form. It may be found, for instance, that melodrama relies more on scenes, TV news on summary and scenes, cartoons on ellipsis, etc.

With *frequency*, a narrative may recount one event repeatedly, as in the reconstruction of a murder by Hercule Poirot, or may recount once that which happened frequently. In a crime thriller or western, one robbery shown will often represent a series of robberies. In the news media, one image of a football 'pitch invasion' may be used to illustrate a news item on all 'pitch invasions'.

Study of the various operations of time within narrative can realize practical work. The sequence of images from *Mildred Pierce* (Figure 3.1) offers a study exercise to explore how an audience makes sense of the relation between one image in a sequence and the next. After investigating how a particular order or sequencing suggests, for instance, that the killing (c) happens in the house (b), or that the car (e) bears the unidentified killer, students can create additional shots to find out what happens when more time is given to the murder, and then the getaway. The object of the exercise is to see how meanings change with elisions in time and shifts in point of view.

Students might re-order the events of a story so that knowledge of what happens becomes different with different effects. The task may be to re-work part of a conventional chronological story into a series of flashbacks. Alternatively it might be to produce a summary sequence of parts of a story. This is straightforward enough in literature but involves a sophisticated set of choices in film and television. This exercise is different from the construction of a trailer which usually offers a series of narrative enigmas or 'hooks'. The summary entails a sequencing of setting, characterization and narrative development.

2   Space

In literature, 'a man walks into a room' is a statement with a high level of generality. In film and television, 'man' and 'room' must be shown, made concrete and specific. Students' own work needs to consider questions of scale and size; positioning of objects within a frame, in relation to each other, in relation to the camera, lighting and focus. Formal matters like these are the subject of many teaching packs[7] and film slide sets.[8] Students can explore how the audience's attention is directed to that which is significant to the narrative, how matters of form construct narrative *space*.

A film or TV segment may be chosen as 'base material' for work on characters, dialogue, action. Students can then re-work the same base material by video-recording their own versions of that sequence but organizing the story space differently. Through different camera angles or placings, characters, objects and actions can be selected or emphasized. One scene can become many scenes.

CONCLUSION

The concept of narrative provides a point of access to analysing media texts and producing your own. It identifies the work of formal procedures both shared by and specific to the full range of media texts – written and visual, fiction and non-fiction. Looking carefully at the structure of stories enables us to understand better their effects on us as media consumers. When we see how stories are told and what stories are recurrently told or ignored, we understand more of the relationship between media stories and our social experience. Media texts are narratives and more besides. But understanding what is narrated, how, and who narrates offers powerful analytical tools for understanding not only the media but also our relations to it.

NOTES

This chapter was written in 1986 and updated in 1989.

1 An accessible and polemical account of this argument is in *Literary Theory* (London: Blackwell, 1983) in which Terry Eagleton offers a radical critique of the 'literary heritage' and charts the changes in literary theory over the last fifty years.

2 *The Fantastic – Towards a Structural Approach*, Tzvetan Todorov (Case Western Reserve University Press, 1973) is one of the more accessible examples of structural analysis and useful for writing on the Gothic Horror genre.

3 *Morphology of the Folk Tale*, Vladimir Propp (Texas: University of Texas, 1968).

4 See, for instance, Cary Bazalgette and Richard Paterson, 'Real entertainment: the Iranian embassy siege', *Screen Education* no. 37, Winter,
   1980/1. The essay has given rise to an exhibition of A1-size panels called
   Politics–Media–Entertainment on hire from the BFI Film and Video
   Library.
5 *S/Z*, Roland Barthes (London: Jonathan Cape, 1975).
6 *Film Art, An Introduction*, David Bordwell and Kristin Thompson
   (Berkshire: Addison-Wesley, 1979). The basic conventions of editing
   demand that continuity be maintained. Matching cuts preserve the
   continuities of action, time and space. Eye-lines are 'mirrored' so that,
   for instance, actors in dialogue appear to be looking at each other across
   separate shots. In such a sequence, the camera will not shift more than
   180 degrees from its position in one shot to the next. To do so would
   result in the actors appearing to be talking to an unknown third person.
   Few films intentionally break these rules of continuity unless, like the
   surrealist film *Un Chien Andalou*, in order to oppose them.
7 *Reading Pictures* (BFI) offers an introductory approach, *The Semiology of
   the Image*, Guy Gauthier (London: BFI Education), a more advanced
   exercise. Gauthier's notes are teacherly but the vast range of often
   esoteric images from the 1960s requires critical selection and use.
8 See slide packs available from BFI Education; especially *Some Visual
   Motifs of Film Noir* and *History of Narrative Codes in Film*.

Chapter 4

Institution

Tana Wollen

Imagine a class visit to a television centre. We are led into a studio the size of a football pitch, crane our necks to wonder at galactic electric lights and do our best not to trip over cables coiled like pythons. We are going to watch a TV programme being made and for many of us it happens to be our favourite. On the set the kitchen, living room, bedroom and garden are much smaller than we'd imagined – just painted flats, you couldn't actually live in them. We can see what the viewers will see by noticing which camera has the red light on and by looking at the monitors above us. (Sometimes we can see ourselves, just for a laugh!) It's all worked out in advance by a man in the control room above the studio, behind thick glass. Of course we can't see through that. The actors come on, sometimes they fluff their lines and have to start again. The warm-up man jollies us along and our laughter is recorded, for free. We've had a good look at what really goes on behind the scenes.

Imagine a different visit. The class is taken through the main foyer of the television centre, not through the side door to the studio. They get in and out of lifts, trudge round corridors and poke noses into office after office. Soon a chorus begins to demand why we have come when there is absolutely nothing to see. The most extreme complaints are qualified. There are people on phones, typing, sitting at desks. The offices are well lit and tinged with green plants. There are men in grey suits and younger men in loosely fitting jackets and Italian ties, huddled in meetings. There are some women who answer phones, some who push trolleys and lots who type. And then there is the marvellous view of the whole city seen from the executive canteen on the top floor.

The first kind of visit described above is probably one which many Media Studies classes have experienced but the second would not be allowed. Unlike the concepts 'narrative', 'genre', 'representation' which Media Studies teachers can approach through tangible study materials, 'institution' presents a peculiar pedagogic difficulty: it is invisible. There are signs of institutions – publicity posters or continuity sequences for example – but whereas there are stories to read, slides to show, newspapers or magazines to handle when learning about narrative, genre or representation, it is impossible to grab an institution by the scruff of its neck and drag it up to the teacher's desk for all to quiz and peer at although, ironically, the classroom is itself part of an elaborate institution.

In the most useful article to date about teaching the institutional aspects of television, Gill Branston acknowledges that 'if all concepts are abstract, this one certainly seems far more abstract than others'.[1] Institutions determine the very material of our existence – our housing, our food, our transport, our employment or unemployment, our information and entertainment. Despite this, accurate information about the institutions which involve our lives is often difficult to come by and, especially in the case of the media institutions, it is constantly changing.

Teaching about media institutions involves teaching about processes, about facts and about relations. In negotiating the complex term 'institution', teachers discover daunting vistas and boundaries which change formation no sooner than they are understood. Conceptual confusions and pedagogic unwieldiness provide teachers with reasonable excuses for by-passing it altogether.

This chapter is intended to clear some of the ground and to offer ways of teaching about media institutions which are manageable within the conditions of most secondary school classrooms. Teaching materials which are really appropriate have yet to be produced. We need to find ways of overcoming the difficulties presented by those classroom conditions and by the elusive, protean character of the media institutions themselves.

Like others who have written on the subject, Gill Branston explores Raymond Williams' definitions of 'institution' to elucidate the productive tensions between the meanings it embraces. Williams notes that 'institution' is an example of 'a noun of action or process, which became, at a certain stage, a general and abstract noun describing something apparently objective and systematic'. This is a useful definition because it emphasizes the need to question the origins of what have become familiar edifices, acceptable practices, the habitual way things are run. Williams concludes by saying that 'in the twentieth century, institution has become the normal term for any element of a society'.[2] The normal describing the normal: no wonder the term disguises more than it reveals. In teaching about institutions it is necessary to reanimate our notions of inert, ossified structures, discover the locations of their uneven determinants and reveal the fluidity of processes and agencies which sustain their existence and power.

It is important to show how institutions are structured by historical changes and by contemporary contradictions, overcoming a common tendency to emphasize weighty monoliths and the intractable coherence of arcane conspiracies. The key teaching point is that institutional monoliths and conspiracies exist only because there are human agencies which maintain them. The struggle at Wapping showed that Rupert Murdoch's plant there could only operate with the consent of a workforce. That consent may well be a heavy-hearted one; the prospects of redundancy and flagging support from an enervated trade union movement make hi-tech working conditions and a salaried future more persuasive. Nevertheless, it is important for students to learn about the complexities which determine decisions and to learn that choices other than the 'only available options' need to be made possible. As John Pilger quotes:

> Men such as Murdoch can operate only if they can find pliant men [sic] to assist them. Their power will always be found to rest ultimately, not on their resources, not only on the extensiveness of their organisations but on their gift for searching out men to do their will.[3]

In their search for our students, either as workers or consumers, what should we hope the media institutions might find?

INSTITUTIONS AS INDUSTRIES

On Media Studies courses, the media institutions have been conceived either in terms of a monumental bulk of information which has to be 'got across' (who owns what, for instance) or as co-ordinating sets of social practices (going to the cinema or watching a video fast-forwarding on your own TV). Media institutions, in the first conception, is usually understood to mean media *industries*. Each media form – newspapers and magazines, films, television, radio – has its own processes of industrial production. These can be taught about and imitated, especially on vocational courses. Quite often, studying production processes makes technical constraints the object lesson (particularly when the imitations are done using school or college equipment!). Economic constraints are taught under the heading 'Ownership and Control'. Diagrams representing the tangled webs of shareholdings and directorships, narratives recounting the rise and fall of personnel, diplomacy and barter, are not the lightest of loads to carry into a classroom, however crucial we understand the knowledge of those burdens to be.

Institutions as *industry* is assumed to be 'boring' (even though most students find money completely riveting) mainly because of the pedagogy the transmission of such knowledge seems to demand. Teachers used to discovery-based, child-centred pedagogies fear instructional modes. Teachers' access to who owns and controls what in the media is not easily gained, although trade journals like *Broadcast*, *Variety* and *Screen International* are useful resources in this respect. A more significant anxiety is that in teaching about media institutions in terms of their industrial *constraints*, we are wary lest we overemphasize the powerlessness students may experience along with their increasing knowledge. In Media Studies, the analyses students make of images, of narratives, of representations, often give them confidence in the production of their own meanings. When media institutions are introduced (often in terms of the access students and their media productions would be likely to gain), then either depression sets in as the portals to 'free speech' thud shut or acquiescence takes root and the professionals, the great and the good are allowed to get on with it since 'they know best'. The media institutions are powerful – that is why they need to be taught about – but students should not be taught that media institutions are omnipotent. If, like the many other institutions which determine our social construction, the media change through history then they can *be changed too*.

REGIMENTED VIEWING?

Another approach has investigated how media forms have institutionalized different social practices, different narrative forms and different ways of viewing. These approaches have been largely influenced by John Ellis's work in *Visible Fictions*[4] and by the notion of cinema as a 'regime' elaborated by Christian Metz. Metz worked initially, in *The Imaginary Signifier*,[5] to define a *semiology* of the cinema – to prise open and name the pattern of elements which constitute 'cinema' as a specific discourse (distinct from Literature, for instance). Subsequently, in *Psychoanalysis and the Cinema*,[6] he developed his concept of the spectator as a subject whose cinematic viewing was determined by circumstances in which psychoanalytic processes (narcissistic identification and fetishistic voyeurism in particular) make pleasurable our captivation in fantasy, our raptures before the silver screen. For the purposes of teaching about media institutions, Metz's work on the cinema and the psychoanalytic subject were not so pertinent as his definition of the *cinematic regime* – the spectator sitting anonymously amid a crowd in the darkened auditorium in which vision is projected by a single beam of light onto a screen where images are larger and more luminous than life. The distinction Metz made between 'cinema' as institution and 'film' as a set of textual operations cued approaches to teaching about cinemas as social and economic spaces which audiences use differently according to their cultures and to their histories. Investigating cinema as an institution in this way enables students to take their own viewing habits into account, especially when the 'cinematic regime' could be compared with television or video watching.

This approach has proved to be one of the more successful ways of introducing media institutions. The teacher is able to start with the students' own viewing experience. Each student can keep a viewing diary for a week which lists the programmes, videos or films watched, where and when they were seen, with whom, and enters a short account of any discussion that might have taken place afterwards. Local cinemas and video shops can be mapped out, libraries or the local planning department consulted as to where bygone cinemas could be found. The class can then begin to speculate as to the changes that have been brought about on our high streets and in our cultural pursuits. This kind of work of course requires patient organization and is even easier if carried out with a teacher from the History or Geography department as part of a lower school Humanities course. By locating the historical development of our contemporary viewing practices, students can begin to define their social and economic contexts. Thinking about other ways and conditions of viewing may help to make the habitual historical. Having started with students' own viewing experience and then gaining some historical distance from it, accounts can begin of how the cinema has been determined by a complexity of economic, technological and social factors.

A vast range of determinants could be examined: the *economic* in terms of the star and studio systems, the 'vertical integration' of production, distribution and exhibition, the patterns of ownership in cinema, television and video; the *technological* in terms of lenses, editing, moving cameras, sound, colour, widescreen; the *historical* in terms of how patterns of leisure and cultural consumption have changed this century due to different conditions of employment, week-ends, cars, central heating and home decorating.

Because teaching about media institutions is a way of teaching about relations it is both exciting and problematic. The relations can seem infinite and therefore indigestible in the classroom. The teacher's job is to make the inevitable compromise and select according to the student's interest and the course requirements. There seem to be few alternatives to 'chalk and talk' or to suitably written handouts here. Generally, the teacher will know – or have access to – information which the students will not. Groups could be given specific topics to research in the library and there are a growing number of publications which students can be directed to read in part, depending on their motivation and level of literacy.[7]

A set of notes and slides on 'Early Cinema' has been produced which provide an adequate introduction to how Hollywood cinema evolved. An excellent simulation and information pack, 'Teaching the Film Industry', requires students to negotiate the economic processes of producing and distributing a film and to log accounts at every stage.[8]

CINEMA OR TELEVISION?

As a media institution cinema has been relatively privileged by the number of publications it has spawned, an invaluable resource for those teaching Film Studies where the film industry, especially at GCE 'O' level, was prominent. Nevertheless, many Media Studies teachers are still frustrated by the institutional privileging of what is seen by students as an outmoded media form. A great deal is written about the institutional aspects of television and video in newspapers and trade journals, but these writings have yet to be usefully collated and edited for teachers. The institutional aspects of cinema have been made more easily available to teachers if only because it has been almost relegated to history. The structures of ownership and control, of production and circulation, which constitute television and video as institutions in the 'industry' sense, afford no such distance. The accelerating changes in these institutions are for many the symptoms of contemporary crises. Despite more than sixty years of television, there is still neither government nor industry-sponsored archiving to which anyone can have access: there can be no more careless dismissal of a popular cultural form. Information about institutional structures which are always 'on the brink of change' is the initial frustration for Media Studies teachers, and that is only compounded by the difficulty of deciding how to select and present that information to students in useful and engaging ways.

KEY MOMENTS

Acknowledging the enormity which teaching about just one kind of media institution involves, only to stress the importance of teaching about institutional relations, may seem perverse. The study of media institutions does not simply inform us about those institutions: their history also relates to the development of narrative forms, of genres, of visual and aural styles. The acquisition of the Vitaphone sound process which Western Electric had developed by Warner Bros in 1926 not only plugged financial haemorrhaging but created demands for a new kind of cinema which other film companies would also have to satisfy. The very special special-effects, which films of the late 1970s boasted, marked another phase in the competitive relationship between cinema and television. Movies were temporarily reclaimed for the big screen.[9]

In 'TV as institution' Gill Branston recommends teachers to investigate 'key moments' in the history of media forms and to collect programmes which represent media histories. Key moments in newspaper history might be 1962 with the demise of the *Daily Herald* or March 1986 with the birth of *Today*; in television history, key moments might be in 1954 with the acceptance of commercial television, November 1982 with Channel Four or 1989 with the renewal of ITC franchises. The point of interest in studying media institutions is the heterogeneity of factors which determine moments such as these. Locating 'key moments' avoids identifying the evolution of media forms as the discoveries, appointments or inventions of 'great' men – John Logie Baird to Silvio Berlusconi.

For instance, the arrival of *Today* was preceded by an industrial dispute of novel ferocity. Eddie Shah, given a 'union-bashing' accolade by Mrs Thatcher, undermined the power of the Fleet Street unions by yoking journalists to the latest computerized technology in a new plant at Nine Elms. A number of very different reasons – political, technological and economic – account for this national daily's arrival on the newstands, and for its change in ownership.

The possibilities of a second commercial television channel in Britain were mooted over twenty years ago. The channel's commissioning role and the flavour of its output have been and continue to be the consequences of various group pressures and lobbies and of individual or boardroom dictats.[10] It is this intangible business of political disputes and action which determines the history and development of institutions.

CODES AND CONVENTIONS

How do we teach about these many factors that determine institutions? Since there are few case study teaching materials available, (the teaching pack on *Hammer Horror* providing the most useful example)[11] teachers either have to research a historical moment or keep atuned to all the publicity that surrounds the making of one in the foreseeable future. The teacher can itemize all the various determinants under pertinent headings (political, personal, financial, technological, geographical) in language students will find accessible. These items can be studied by groups and their individual significance assessed. Alternately, the items could be a mixed bag, with students sorting them according to a range of headings provided. The students then debate the significance and the nature of each determinant. This seems an effective way of combining 'learning through doing' with 'gathering facts' which can later be marshalled in argument.

It's a truism that the codes and conventions by which media institutions measure the 'professionalism' of their products change. By watching television clips from the past (more and more programmes seem to plunder their own histories for material) or reading old comics, students can be asked to consider the changes in commentary style, camera movement, editing, lighting, arrangement of studio space or page layout and ascertain, by comparison, which elements constitute contemporary notions of professionalism. Comparing the repeats of *Ready, Steady, Go!* with *The Tube* was a revealing exercise in this respect. Clues from the more self-conscious retrospectives can be gleaned as to how the TV institutions wish their own histories to be represented. The task here is to enable students to distinguish between the programmes' preferred readings and ones which might be made with the advantage of more critical historical or political perspectives.

Teaching about media institutions in this way can introduce students to the codes and conventions of media narratives, genres and representations which are usually the starting-points on Media Studies courses. Rather than 'media institutions' appearing as dreary and disconnected phenomena, learning about the institutional should initiate and then permeate any study of the media.

'Key moments' and 'changing codes and conventions' can be used to raise questions about why changes take place. The received wisdom of institutions as immovable, overbearing edifices (the Church, the State, the BBC) is misleading. In order to maintain themselves institutions have to change: there may be instances of accommodating external pressure or of responding to pressure from within. The risks taken to maximize profits or the uneasy agreements to stabilize them in a limited market seem to necessitate hard-shouldered shoving. Although the basic structures of ownership and control may not have altered greatly under capitalism, the machinations which ensure that some succeed where most fail invigorate a perpetual dynamic. Boardroom shuffles, bankruptcies, litigations and stock flotations in the business pages of the 'quality' press can provide classes with miniature case studies. These need not take up a whole lesson at a time but ought to be discussed as 'Media Studies news items' occasionally so that students will not only become accustomed to taking the institutional seriously but also accustomed to assess the significance of changes as they take place, to predict the likely consequences and to propose their own ideas for changes which ought not to be impossible.

THE MEDIA AND THEIR SOURCES

However students are taught to analyse the ways in which cinema and television represent their own 'key moments', it is not enough to stop teaching at the point of those internal institutional relations.

The subjects of all media discourses lie beyond the media themselves – although that's sometimes hard to believe when the stuff of so many television programmes seems to be other television programmes. A play about surrogate motherhood, the celebration of a 'national' sporting victory, a news item about an imminent epidemic; these are events which originate outside the media institutions. The media

> draw topics, treatments, agendas, events, personnel, images of the audience, 'definitions of the situation' from other sources and discursive formations within the wider socio-cultural and political structure of which they are a differentiated part.[12]

When these 'extra' events are narrativized by the media – in a television documentary or a centrefold special – then the relationship between the media and other institutions (the law, the civil service, the health service) becomes more dialectic. The media institutions frame agendas from topics and events which have originated elsewhere while other institutions have to respond to, pre-empt or refute them. The publicity and press officers of all our major institutions know the dialectics of these institutional relationships well.

News provides the most obvious area to study this institutional to-and-fro and existing teaching materials can be adapted for this purpose. Teaching about news in the media has always had learning about the *construction* of news stories as one of its objectives. The constraints of time (the value of news accentuated by its 'perishability') and space (the impositions on editorial 'freedom'), can be learned about through the experience of doing simulations like the English and Media Centre's *Choosing the News*, *The Front Page* or *Radio Covingham*.[13] But even in these useful packs news stories are 'givens'. A class can assess the different kinds of news deemed appropriate to different kinds of papers by examining their stories not so much for their treatment as for their sources.

Take the local paper as an example. The class could map each story with its likely source and speculate as to how the stories were probably acquired. The dramatically accelerating crime rate can be seen, perhaps, to belong to one reporter's impressions after a couple of days in the magistrates' court; a cheap way of getting 'news'. Some stories will be no more than announcements taken verbatim from press releases. Photos of weddings and of school fêtes ensure that every friend and relative buys a copy. By asking 'how has this got here and why?', a class can begin to estimate how the costings and practices of a local paper produce a certain kind of news. The class should note how often institutions rather than individuals are the sources of 'news' – the police and the courts, the council, schools, hospitals, the football club. By considering what kind of 'news' these institutions are likely to deliver, often as a matter of course, students can begin to learn how the 'newsworthy' is not just a matter of what the public want to buy but what the public has to get.

Investigating overseas news sources in the national press (and why do the tabloids have so few?) can reveal the eurocentric inflections of what's happening 'out there'. A useful simulation to teach about institutional presumptions and news representations of the 'Third World' is *Crisis in Sandagua*.[14]

Comparison between the sources and representations of local and overseas news can be used not so much to prove a teacher's misgivings about what constitutes 'news' but to show how the relationship between the production practices of the media institutions and of other social and political institutions function in their construction of the real. These relationships are not always easy. Newspapers can bash the NHS or schools, the police can voice criticism of the press. How daggers–drawn or hand–in–glove these relationships are at various times is something for teachers and students of the media to work out. Afterwards feature films and 'fictional' television narratives can be considered by a class as to how they articulate with other media products (news items, documentaries) and political campaigns to define an 'issue'. What do *Yes Prime Minister*, *Edge of Darkness* and reports of CND taking the government to court over telephone tapping *together* tell us about the machinations of the state? How do *EastEnders* Angie and Den dovetail with Sara Keays' interview with Anthony Clare in *Good Housekeeping* to construct a changing climate of opinion on adultery? Studying relations between media institutions and others can usefully inform our understanding of the relations between different media texts.

ACCESS AND CENSORSHIP

If plotting the sources of news stories enables an understanding of news as an ideologically-laden commodity, then by studying how information can be channelled or dammed we can gain some knowledge of how institutional processes function and in whose favour. *Access* and *censorship* are the two processes most usually learned about in Media Studies. How can different groups of people represent their news, opinions or dramas on the media? By responding to a carefully structured set of questions, a class can debate the problems that most 'non-professionals' have in gaining access to the organs of free speech. The worthiness of 'visibility' means that you could make your point by staging a stunt (providing of course you furnished it with pre-publicity to make sure the reporters were there); you could spend a lifetime getting the 'proper' education which qualified you to represent the stunts you might otherwise have had to stage; you could train to be a technician, a journalist, a producer, actor or director. Roles and actions can then be assessed in terms of their institutional power or the longevity of their effects.

Questions about who can represent what kind of information in the media can be raised by examining how relationships between the media and the state are structured (or strictured). Processes of external control by the Home or Foreign Office can be learnt about by studying actual case histories. The General Strike in 1926, the Malvinas/Falklands war in 1982, the censoring of 'At the Edge of the Union' in the *Real Lives* series by the BBC in 1985: these are well documented histories.[15] The Official Secrets Act, D-notices, libel laws and contempt of court are legal restrictions on the reporting of news which make timid journalists and broadcasters so that self-censorship begins to replace the time-wasting processes of 'referring up'.[16] Censorship, determined by external and internal political and legal restraints can be taught about by simulating a 'Real Lives' situation. Simulations are signs of an inventive pedagogy but they must be very carefully paced and structured. Students have to be well briefed as to every aspect of their role and in the case of a 'Real Lives' producer, for instance, this may well be very complicated. The most difficult part comes in assessing the learning that has actually taken place. Having 'done' the exercise, how willing are students to assess simulations in terms other than the merits of their performance? How can teachers be confident that the class will be able to apply what they have learnt from the simulation to acquire knowledge about the institutional processes which really operate? These questions highlight the need to prepare thorough follow-up work.

The 'Teaching the Film Industry' simulation referred to earlier is extremely well organized, but it cannot really be used to teach about the relations between media institutions and the state. The Campaign for Press and Broadcasting Freedom have produced an information pack for schools on access and censorship in the media. With appropriate worksheets asking questions and recommending activities, this pack can be divided into parts to be rotated around small groups in a class.[17]

Aspects of access and censorship can be used to teach about decision-making processes in media institutions. Learning about how decisions are made and who can make or overrule them is an important part of learning about institutionalized structures of power. Having assessed, even tested, the opportunities afforded to 'ordinary people' by the media institutions, students might then consider the much greater power of individual and multinational corporations. This has always been an extremely difficult area for Media Studies teachers to deal with. How can the intricacies of large wheelings and dealings be taught without overburdening students with tedious detail? And what would be the purpose of such teaching? Do we aim simply to teach about the processes and principles of capitalism or do we also wish to arm our students with detailed facts and figures? A teacher's decisions will depend on the interest students have in using such statistics, but teaching about the relations between the media, industry and the state is crucial to an understanding of institutions.

We might criticize newspapers or television for personalizing narratives which would be more truthfully told in terms of structural causes and effects. Nevertheless, we cannot deny that the strategy is effective: we might not learn much about oil cartels but J. R. is certainly a popular figure in *Dallas*. By asking students to construct their own case study of a similar, less entertaining real-life figure, a picture emerges of how entrepreneurial, corporate and multinational capital buys, produces and sells our information and entertainment.

MURDOCH ON DISPLAY

Rupert Murdoch provides just the case for such a study. Where possible this might best be done by the class making a wall display, adding new pieces of information, pointing out newly perceived connections, bit by bit. If the display was made gradually, in conjunction with lessons where the class was examining the *Sun*, discussing the possibilities of Direct Broadcast Satellite (DBS) or studying the uses television has for films, then learning about News Corporation could become an integrated part of other lessons.

The key concepts which need to be taught first are 'diversification' and 'vertical integration' (though not necessarily in those terms). One way to start would be with a map of Australia and itemize the businesses other than the eight newspapers, twenty-six periodicals and two television stations in which News Corporation has controlling interests. There are farms, road haulage and air-transport firms, publishing, printing, paper manufacture, computer software, record and tape production and distribution. Why the need to diversify? Little fish get bigger unless big fish gobble them first. Capital is as 'natural' as the 'law of the jungle'. The vertical integration of News Corporation's ownership of all the stages of media production and distribution can be compared, if appropriate, with attempts made by the Motion Pictures Patents company to consolidate a monopoly between 1908 and 1915.

In Britain, Murdoch's 'acquisition' of the *Sun*, *News of the World*, the *Sunday Times*, *The Times*, *Today*, Collins and 20 per cent of the *Financial Times* needs another map and new sets of figures to be added.[18] In 1985 the *Sun* alone made more than half the profits earned by News Corporation worldwide. A study of the dispute at Wapping might educate students as to the lengths that will be taken to secure such rich pickings.

A new map for the classroom and a new citizenship for Murdoch will show how new media technologies depend on old ones. Sky Channel in Europe transmits 116 hours a week to five million homes in fourteen different countries. The expensively-acquired control of Metromedia in the USA means ownership of six independent TV stations and nine radio stations. In 1985 the FCC (Federal Communication Commission) under Mark Fowler, a new Reagan appointment, allowed the number of TV stations a single company could own to rise from seven to thirteen. A fourth American network, owned by Murdoch, virtually exists.

If legislation or state intervention has helped Murdoch (to acquire *The Times* or American citizenship), it also poses problems. Murdoch has had to renounce his Australian citizenship which may mean relinquishing some of his operations there, and repayment of debts and interest require News Corporation to make consistent annual profits of $350 million for the next few years.

Material can be compiled and added to the display by different

THE NEWS CORPORATION WORLDWIDE

AUSTRALIA AND PACIFIC BASIN

Newspapers
NATIONAL
The Australian

QUEENSLAND
The Courier-Mail (1)
The Sunday Mail (1)

Gold Coast Bulletin (1)
The Cairns Post (1)
FNQ Sunday (1)
Tablelands Advertiser (1)

North Queensland Newspaper Group
Townsville Bulletin
(10 various titles – regional)

Quest Community Newspapers (10 various
titles – Brisbane suburbs and regional)

NEW SOUTH WALES
Daily Mirror
The Daily Telegraph
The Sunday Telegraph
Sportsman

Cumberland Newspaper Group
(20 various titles – Sydney suburbs and regional)

VICTORIA
The Herald
The Sunday Herald
The Sun News-Pictorial
The Sunday Sun
The Weekly Times
Sporting Globe
Bendigo Advertiser Group (2 titles – regional)
Geelong Advertiser Group (4 titles – regional)

Leader Newspaper Group (28 various titles –
Melbourne suburbs and regional)
The Wimmera Mail Times (8)

TASMANIA
The Mercury
The Sunday Tasmanian
Tasmanian Country
The Treasure Islander
Derwent Valley Gazette

SOUTH AUSTRALIA
The Advertiser
Sunday Mail
Messenger Press Group
(13 various titles – Adelaide suburbs)

WESTERN AUSTRALIA
Sunday Times

NORTHERN TERRITORY
Northern Territory News
Sunday Territorian
Centralian Advocate

HONG KONG
South China Morning Post
Sunday Morning Post

FIJI
The Fiji Times
The Sunday Times
Nai Lalakai (Fijian language)
Shanti Dut (Hindi language)
Pacific Islands Monthly

PAPUA NEW GUINEA
Post Courier (2)

Magazines
New Idea
T.V. Week (3)
New Woman
Australasian Post
Home Beautiful
Family Circle
Better Homes & Gardens (3)
Your Garden

Books
Angus & Robertson (3)
Bay Books (3)
Gordon & Gotch (3)

Commercial Printing
Progress Press
Norman Keppell
Brownhall Printing
Wilke Directories
Wilke Color
Leader Westernport Printing
West Web Printers
Griffin Press
Multiform Business Systems
Giganticolor
Computer Graphics
Prestige Litho
Willmetts Printers
Mercury Walch
Prestige Colorprint (1)
National Paper Vuepak

Other Operations
Ansett Transport Industries (3)
Australian Newsprint Mills (3)
Computer Power (4)
East West Airlines (3)
Festival Records
F.S. Falkiner & Sons
Independent Newspapers (3)
Lanray Industries
(Sunshine Plantation) (1)

■ 8

Figure 4.1   From the News Corporation International's Annual Report
1989.

UNITED KINGDOM

Newspapers
The Times
The Sunday Times
The Sun
News of the World
Today

Magazines
New Woman
Sky (3)
TV Guide
The Times Educational Supplement
The Times Higher Education Supplement
The Times Literary Supplement
The Times Scottish Education Supplement
Trader (3)

Books
Geographia (3)
John Bartholomew & Son (3)
Robert Nicholson Publications (3)
Times Books (3)
William Collins (3)

Commercial Printing
Eric Bemrose

Television and Filmed Entertainment
Sky Television (6)
  Sky News
  Sky Movies
  Sky One
  Eurosport
Sky Radio (7)

Other Operations
Convoys Group
The Times Network Systems
Townsend Hook
Circle K (UK) (3)
News Data Security Products (5)

UNITED STATES

Newspapers
San Antonio Express-News
The Boston Herald
Daily Racing Form

Magazines
Automobile
European Travel & Life
Mirabella
New Woman
New York
Premiere
Seventeen
Soap Opera Digest
Sportswear International
Star
TV Guide

Books
Harper & Row Publishers (3)

Commercial Printing
World Printing

Television and Filmed Entertainment
Twentieth-Century Fox Film Corporation
  Fox Film Corporation
  Twentieth Television Corporation
  CBS/Fox Inc.
  DeLuxe Laboratories
Fox Broadcasting Company
Fox Television Stations
  KDAF–Dallas, TX
  KRIV–Houston, TX
  KTTV–Los Angeles, CA
  WFLD–Chicago, IL
  WNYW–New York, NY
  WTTG–Washington, DC
  WFXT–Boston, MA (held in trust)

Other Operations
FSI Division
  Product Movers
  Quad Marketing
Etak

Notes

(1) News Group holds **46** per cent interest

(2) News Group holds **63** per cent interest

(3) News Group holds **50** per cent interest

(4) News Group holds **26** per cent interest

(5) News Group holds **60** per cent interest

(6) News Group holds **96** per cent interest

(7) News Group holds **51** per cent interest

(8) News Group holds **67** per cent interest

9 ■

groups in the class – clippings from newspapers, information gleaned from TV news bulletins and the trade journals. From this collective accumulation students will not only have considered some of the facts and processes of a capitalist media industry but they should have a less parochial sense of how media commodities are produced and distributed.

The capacity for distributing broadcast material now far exceeds its production. It is for this reason that Murdoch bought Fox Films in 1985. Hollywood will survive on Satellite TV because 2,500 Twentieth Century Fox features can run and re-run. This is likely to mean an increased demand for independent productions in the near future. Standardized packages of standardized programmes seem inevitable but local preferences exert a much stronger pressure than is often presumed and some innovation and difference will have to be broadcast if global switch-off is to be avoided. Will broadcasting in the 1990s be dominated by monopolistic networks or will there be a competitive ecology of smaller companies? If an independent production is one which has not been produced by a major multinational then of what is it independent: of the state, whether a public broadcasting system or a company in the grant-aided sector? Of capitalist industries which produce the technology?[19]

The relations between states, industries and institutions are in one sense very simple: a few own and control most. We can teach students to discover that simple relationship between 'them and us' and although we cannot necessarily guarantee their desire or will to change it, the multitudinous relations by which the power of the few is maintained and extended over many need, at the very least, to be understood.

For students, an understanding of how power is structured should not be accompanied by a shock-horror realization that everyone is being duped. The best educational moments are often described in terms of scales falling from eyes, of lightening bolts crashing through the barriers of obscurity, but to learn in Media Studies that the media institutions hold us in thrall would be a simplistic assertion revealing less than it disguised. Most of us are perfectly willing to be enthralled, rushing home to the telly, paying for a video or a cinema ticket, buying records, swapping tapes, perusing magazines for tips on lifestyles. There are real delights to savour! Without our consumption the media institutions would not exist, so we have an enormous potential power in our collective ability to reach out and switch over or off. The provisions for our access and the parameters of our choices are limited, but as audiences we do make choices. When studying media institutions we need to consider what and why we choose, as well as how and what is made available to whom.

CIRCULATION

Little that is not abstrusely technical or wide-eyed and marvelling has been written about the new technologies of cable, Direct Broadcast Satellite or interactive video. There is still much to learn about their technological potential and how they will be deployed.[20] We can be certain of one thing: there will be many more media about. The international marketing of films and television programmes, of stars and personalities has yet to be researched. However, there can be no doubt that production is increasingly determined by the possibilities of foreign sales. Many BBC and ITV programmes are now co-produced and Muir Sutherland's promotion in 1982 from chief salesman at Thames Television International to Director of Programmes at Thames demonstrated that selling programmes is as much the business as producing them and that buying is often cheaper than producing.[21]

Since most students will not be receiving cable or satellite TV, the most accessible way of learning about the media circulation of TV is for a class to gauge how much broadcast material is 'home produced' and how much is imported. The class should then measure the preponderance of American imports against the number of programmes from elsewhere – Brazil, Australia, France or Germany, for example. The kind of programmes imported from each country should be noted too. The trans-Atlantic flow is much heavier than any other and apart from Brazil and Japan which export an increasing number of programmes, the traffic from north to south is all one-way. Students should discuss the possible reasons for this.[22].

TV companies produce glossy promotional publicity for the programmes they wish to sell to other companies. These can be obtained free of charge and students enjoy using their own knowledge of a programme to read between the lines of the promotional material. What aspects are being accentuated? What ideas about the production company does the publicity give? What aspects of their favourite programmes would students highlight to sell and which

Come and have a go at television.

If you're in town this week, you could end up being Channel Four's next TV critic.

We've brought the Video Box to Edinburgh. Step inside. Sit down. Face the camera. Press the 'record' button.

Say what you like about television. (Or, of course, say what you don't like). Talk sense and your tape could wind up on our 'Right to Reply' Show. Then you'll be speaking to hundreds of thousands of Channel Four viewers. Beats mumbling away to yourself.

The Video Box. St Cuthbert's Churchyard, between Prince's Street and Lothian Road. August 26th-31st. 10am-6pm. (Then back in London from September 1st).

66THE VIDEO BOX99 4

countries would be likely or unlikely to buy them? What representations of Britain are most saleable? What representations of the USA seem to be most frequently bought?

If there are to be more media competing for more of our time, money and attention then the loud appeals for our consumption that media institutions make are themselves worth studying. How

SPEND A QUIET NIGHT IN WITH LILLIAN GISH.

This Autumn, Channel 4 is showing a short season of silent film classics. Tonight at 9.00 see Lillian Gish in 'The Wind', the film that made her famous, and in two weeks' time she appears in 'Broken Blossoms', a striking melodrama directed in 1919 by D.W. Griffiths. Meanwhile on October 3rd, there's 'Show People', King Vidor's malicious 1928 satire on Hollywood, and on October 17th, 'A Woman of Affairs', a 1928 Garbo film never seen on television before. All have new scores composed or conducted by Carl Davis.

Figure 4.2   What corporate identity is being promoted here? Why do we need reminding?

are we 'sold' programmes, films, magazines, videos or records? Listings magazines, *Radio Times*, *TV Times*, advertisements and continuity sequences offer an abundance of study material.[23] What aspects of the product are emphasized? Who is the advertisement's target audience? Why this particular audience? These questions are familiar to textual analysis: here they can make the textual reveal the context, they can be used to show how we are constructed as audiences by the media's address.

From potential viewers or purchasers we become ratings. As consumers of products we ourselves become commodities to be delivered to advertisers in the case of the commercial media and as ratings to public service broadcasting which has to compete with 'independent' broadcasting companies. How are we sold media products so that we can in turn be sold to other producers as potential consumers?

Through questions such as these, students can begin to understand how variously audiences are perceived by media institutions. The notions which programme producers might have of their audience's tastes and tolerances are not the same notions of audience that an advertising director might have. Both these notions are likely to be very different from the ones we might have of ourselves – watching, reading, listening, buying. New work is beginning to appear about the meanings people bring to media products and the meanings their active readings produce.[24] This chapter suggests the relative power we have in the roles offered us by media institutions and by our study of them. To take the cue from Raymond Williams, if we cannot say we are determined not to be determined, at least we can be determined to determine whatever positions we occupy.

CODA

Since this chapter was completed in the autumn of 1986 the broadcasting ecology in Western Europe has changed dramatically. Although the basic teaching strategies suggested here may still hold good, recent changes make different approaches necessary.

In Britain, the Broadcasting Act 1990 has accelerated what is referred to as de-regulation. Independent television companies will be awarded franchises only if they can outbid other applicants; their advertising revenue will be destabilized by new competition from cable and satellite channels and so, they argue, production of quality programming and for regional and minority audiences will suffer. Financing of the BBC will be reviewed in 1996 but in the meantime the intense competition for audiences will mean, some fear, taking the cost-saving option and importing ready-made productions from the United States.

Proponents of the Act argued that by breaking the BBC/IBA

duopoly, and by allowing fiercer competition, quality television would be enhanced rather than diminished because only the best would survive. If nothing else, the Act has stimulated debates about broadcasting: about its function and provision, about quality, about audiences and about control. While the Act proposes a de-regulation of the markets, concern about questions of 'taste and decency', of state security and of political bias has meant that the de-regulated market has to be *re*-regulated in other ways. It is these new regulatory bodies which should be the objects of study and discussion in lessons about media institutions.

What are the functions and remit of the Broadcasting Standards Council? Could a class measure these against a few of their own 'test' cases? How will the ITC (Independent Television Commission) apply a 'lighter touch' than the IBA? How will relations between the BBC Board of Governors and Cabinet Ministers develop over the next few years? What is the brief of the Press Council and why is it a comparatively toothless body? By closely studying the histories and activities of bodies such as these, students should begin to learn how the media are being both de-, and then re-, regulated in British society. By doing so they may become attuned to the contradictions within a political system which in apparently extending choices can also centralize control.

NOTES

This chapter was written in 1986 and updated early in 1990.

1 Gill Branston, 'TV as institution', *Screen*, vol. 25, no. 2, 1984.
2 Raymond Williams, *Keywords* (London: Fontana, 1983). See also 'Institutions' chapter in Manuel Alvarado, Robin Gutch and Tana Wollen, *Learning the Media* (London: Macmillan, 1987).
3 John Pilger quotes Henry Fairlie in *Heroes*, p. 533 (London: Jonathan Cape, 1986).
4 John Ellis, *Visible Fictions* (London: Routledge & Kegan Paul, 1982).
5 Christian Metz, 'The imaginary signifier', *Screen*, vol. 16, no. 2, Summer 1975.
6 Christian Metz, *Psychoanalysis and the Cinema* (London: Macmillan, 1971).
7 See David Pirie, *Anatomy of the Movies* (New York: Macmillan, 1977); Michael Chanan, *The Dream that Kicks* (London: Routledge & Kegan Paul, 1980); Martyn Auty and Nick Roddick, *British Cinema Now* (London: BFI, 1985); Steve Neale, *Cinema and Technology: Image, Sound, Colour* (London: BFI/Macmillan, 1985); Douglas Gomery, *The Hollywood Studio System* (London: BFI/Macmillan, 1986). A more succinct and very useful account of early Hollywood and its determinants

is to be found in Nancy Wood's 'The film industry', June 1985, a BFI Education Advisory Document.

8 *Early Cinema* is available from the Clwyd Centre for Educational Technology, Mold, Clwyd. *Teaching the Film Industry* is available from The Media Centre, South Hill Park, Bracknell, Berkshire.

9 The development of Hollywood narratives and their technological and economic determinants have been most thoroughly charted by David Bordwell, Janet Staiger and Kristin Thompson in *The Classical Hollywood Cinema: Film Style and Mode of Production to 1960* (London: Routledge & Kegan Paul, 1985). For teaching narrative see Adrian Tilley's chapter in this book.

10 Stephen Lambert, *Channel Four: Telev sion with a Difference* (London: BFI, 1982).

11 *Hammer Horror* (London: BFI Education, 1980).

12 Stuart Hall, 'Encoding/decoding' in Stuart Hall *et al.*, *Culture, Media, Language* (London: Hutchinson, 1980).

13 Available from the English and Media Centre, Sutherland Street, London SW1.

14 Available from Development Education Project, Manchester Polytechnic, Didsbury, M20 8RG. See Ivor Gaber, 'The media and the Third World', *Multiracial Education*, vol. 9, no. 2, Spring 1981.

15 The *Guardian*, 29.7.85, 3.8.85, 9.8.85, 12.8.85; *New Statesman*, 2.8.85.

16 These inter-institutional relationships are lucidly explained by David Barrat in *Media Sociology* (London: Tavistock, 1986).

17 *Right of Reply* is available from the Campaign for Press and Broadcasting Freedom, 9 Poland Street, London W1.

18 A very useful diagram of media ownership and control in the form of a poster is updated and published by the National Union of Journalists (NUJ), 314 Grays Inn Road, London WC1X 8DP. Posters currently cost 50p each.

19 Most of the information here has been taken from two articles: Douglas Gomery, 'Vertical integration, horizontal regulation – the growth of Rupert Murdoch's US media empire' in *Screen*, vol. 27, nos 3–4, 1986, and Manuel Alvarado, 'Rupert Murdoch' in Richard Paterson and Manuel Alvarado (eds), *1987 International TV and Video Guide* (London: Tantivy Press, 1987).

20 John Howkins, *New Technologies, New Policies?* (London: BRU/BFI, 1982); Timothy Hollins, *Beyond Broadcasting: Into the Cable Age* (London: BRU/BFI, 1984).

21 See Appendix 4, William Phillips, 'Another view of Thames Television' in *Made for Television, Euston Films Limited* by Manuel Alvarado and John Stewart (London: Thames/Methuen, 1985).

22 Armand Mattelart, Xavier Delcourt and Michèle Mattelart, *International Image Markets* (London: Comedia, 1984).

23 See Ed Buscombe, 'Disembodied voices and familiar faces: television continuity' in *Television Mythologies*, edited by Len Masterman (London: Comedia, 1984) and John Morey, 'The space between programmes: television continuity' Media Analysis Paper 1 (London: Comedia 1986).

24 Ien Ang, *Watching 'Dallas'* (London: Methuen, 1985); Bob Hodge and David Tripp, *Children and Television* (London: Polity Press, 1986); David Morley, *Family Television* (London: Comedia, 1986); Philip Simpson (ed.), *Parents Talking Television* (London; Comedia, 1987).

Chapter 5

Audience

Gill Branston

> The family is sitting in front of the TV, staring blankly at a fuzzy, low-quality image. Their eyes are glazed, their limbs hanging laxly from unhealthy bodies. Junk food is pushed mechanically into slackly open mouths. There's no conversation; just the occasional grunt as programme becomes advert and then becomes programme again.
>
> Jane Root, Open the Box,
(Comedia 1986: 7)

This glum shot of 'an audience' (like the version which begins 'Children spend more time in front of the TV than they do in front of a teacher ...') is regularly used against TV viewers and, by extension, media users generally. Let's first think about what it means for us to be called 'an audience' for leisure activities as diverse as watching TV, listening and dancing to pop music, and reading magazines and comics.

The term 'audience' invites us to imagine media users in certain ways and not others. It suggests meeting together in social gatherings, often in silence, to witness (and especially to *hear*) special events such as a concert or a play. It evokes a serious, public occasion and emphasizes an attentiveness on the part of those gathered together. Yet it also seems to ignore social differences within the audience, paying scant attention, for instance, to who can afford the best seats or who laughs and when during a performance. One TV pundit said about this way of imagining TV users: 'It's fatal to start thinking: how smart are they? No one's ever *seen* 10 million people together – that's twice as many people as there were at Gandhi's funeral'.[1] Other terms for large groups of people gathered together in public don't suggest the strange mix of passivity and attentiveness that 'audience' does. We don't use 'audience' for 'crowds' at sporting or political occasions, for 'congregations' at religious ones, nor for 'assemblies' or 'classes' of school students.

But there's a twist in the way 'audience' describes media users. Because they are clearly *not* gathered together in public, media audiences are imagined as a huge but privatized, amorphous *mass*, consuming small-scale diversions at home rather than larger events, more seriously, in the separate public world outside. And, of course, they're imagined as people isolated from each other (unlike the *apparently* unified theatre audience) with no chance to talk about the event together. The term 'audience' here works to exclude a sense of critical and public activity as well as any kind of meaning being made by viewers. This 'audience' just sits and listens, a familiar replica of the 'empty vessel' student in some educational philosophies. Finally, such thinking generally excludes the critic or campaigner who writes about proposed effects on 'an audience' while remaining untouched him/herself. This implication is particularly useful for self-styled moral majorities, otherwise we might wonder how *they* have escaped the evil effects of all those nasty videos, suggestive pop songs and wicked comics.

Interestingly, audiences for areas like literature, painting or art cinema, though often large, aren't usually considered a mass. The appeal in much literary criticism, for instance, is to an imaginary community, which our individual reponse to this poem/novel/film may let us join. We're invited to feel a *reader* rather than part of an *audience* and both critical and creative activity are usually assumed, or at least hoped for, in the written or spoken response. If there is a worry here about an audience, it is usually the audiences for popular forms such as music hall, cheap books, comics and videos.

So, to describe as an audience the many types of groupings in which people use TV, radio, pop music, etc. is already to sustain certain attitudes and values – both to people and to the media themselves. Developments in current understandings of 'the audience' for contemporary media can be described as existing between two extreme attitudes: the idea of the *all-powerful message* and the idea of the *all-powerful viewer/receiver*.

ALL-POWERFUL MESSAGE

The most familiar instance of the first is the so-called 'effects' or 'hypodermic' model.[2] This seizes on the idea that the mass media 'do things to' a mass audience. This emphasis on the 'massness' of 'mass' culture is helpful. It recognizes that the audience for 'high' cultural products is a highly selective – maybe even a minority – one and it makes it possible to consider how numbers of people joined in particular cultural activities relate to technologies and to patterns of ownership and control in the cultural industries. All these concerns seemed especially urgent in the 1930s when reasons were sought for the mass appeal of Fascist movements and work theorizing the media and their audiences began.

But generally in such an approach the potential gains from emphasizing a large audience are lost when 'mass' is used to describe an aggregate of isolated persons bombarded with messages they are helpless to resist. This theoretical model is straight out of stimulus/response experiments in the behavioural sciences. The effects which are supposed to be produced can be caricatured as inactivity (the zomboid slump in front of the box) or, at the other extreme, a manic activity (ad-watchers obeying the ad-message, or do-badders who've just watched a 'video nasty').[3] Significantly, it is groups who are deemed 'weak' and vulnerable who are most worried over: women (the nineteenth-century novel, soap operas), children (comics, TV, toy ads, video nasties) and the 'lower orders' generally (working-class readers of cheap print forms in the nineteenth century; unemployed and working-class viewers of video nasties; 'Third World' audiences for *Dallas* and, by extension, all American cultural products).

As these examples suggest, the approach is alive and well today, still able to command money for research projects commissioned to produce 'hard and fast' (i.e. statistical) evidence and results;[4] still able, too, to command space in newspapers and on TV to report such results. 'Hypodermic' assumptions are even embedded in some apparently more radical and critical approaches: for instance, in the way some progressive media workers speak of 'injecting' new meanings into the media and, by implication, their audiences. Or take the argument that commercial TV works by selling audiences to advertisers.[5] This is a useful challenge to the idea that the audience is a bunch of rational, free, empowered consumers just waiting to pick n' choose their way through the programmes on offer. Of course, it is in the interests of advertisers and commercial TV time-renters to argue that the money paid in order to reach, say, the 10 million social class AB Thames viewers from 9.00 p.m. to 9.01 p.m. is well spent. Such 'effects' arguments, however, ignore research into the work audiences do with texts – and that includes ads.

Nevertheless, concern about the possible effects of the media is an important motive in trying to understand and teach about their workings. Worry, outrage and even panic are often voiced in school staffrooms and in homes and can seem dramatically confirmed by the apparently unanswerable power of the toy ads – especially at Christmas time. And it is in this over-heated context that attempts to introduce Media Studies are often welcomed insofar as they might 'inoculate' students against effects or protect 'the family' against the intrusive power of TV. Tales of pupil hours spent in front of the telly or hooked into the Walkman, of non-stop video and chips in working-class front rooms, are often told in support of Worries – and even Censorship.

Of course, it *is* staggering to see the demands for electricity placed on the Central Electricity Generating Board at the end of *The Thorn Birds* (Figure 5.1) as millions of viewers turned on lights, made tea, and used electrically pumped water to flush the toilets. But many people want to jump straight to the conclusion that this is indisputable evidence that viewers form a regimented, stupefied mass. Such jumps in interpretation actually condense all kinds of anxieties about, for instance, the nature of and opportunities within

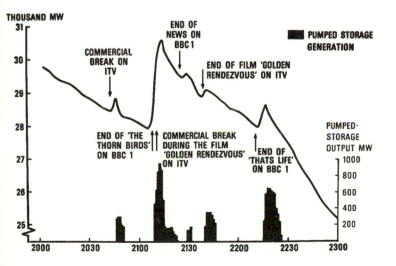

Figure 5.1

leisure in our society. They need to be contested by understanding how media forms might be working with audiences. This would have to include both a more detailed exploration of what happens in the *process* of watching TV (which is not at all the same thing as being in a room with it switched on). And it also requires some attention to the fuller social context so often ignored in those panics where the power of the media looms so terrifyingly large. This context for the fascination of the media includes inadequate child-care provision, solitary domestic labour and ill-funded cultural and leisure activities. Unless these more adequate understandings of 'audience' enter the classroom, the power of the effects lobby can turn teaching into a struggle either to give popular forms the status of high culture or to endlessly deconstruct the forms that are popular with the poor deluded students ... and, perhaps, with poor deluded old you and me?

However, because the effects lobby has serious and often politically dangerous limitations doesn't mean there are no grounds for concern and even anger at the operations and power of the media. Fortunately, other accounts have been developed which try to come to terms with these – in fact more urgent – concerns about the ways the media might shape our imaginings, prop up certain identities at the expense of others, and help form the success or failure of all kinds of large and small struggles for a better world. In such contexts terms like 'effects' and 'offensiveness' take on quite new meanings and possibilities.[6]

Agendas and address

For the moment let's consider other approaches to audience which can help teaching. Running alongside the 'hypodermic' conception of audience is a crude form of content analysis which suggests that counting, say, 'acts of violence' in texts (and here *Thundercats* might be treated as though it were the same as *The Professionals*) is enough to identify a Very Violent Programme *and* to predict its effect on its audience. Part of the challenge to such naive models of how the media work is the development of concepts such as *agenda setting*.[7] This refers to the idea that through a whole range of different kinds of programmes, images and forms the media are able to set an agenda of what is to count as newsworthy, as 'good' music, as funny, as an acceptable image of a particular activity, etc.

When we think of the media in terms of 'setting an agenda' it becomes easier to see that some subjects are routinely deemed acceptable, 'top of the agenda' and are therefore quite common ways of organizing debate, while others are unacceptable, and therefore 'off the agenda'. Significantly, too, some subjects suddenly become important or get linked together while others seem to vanish overnight. So yesterday's panic over video nasties gives way 'quite naturally' to an obsession with 'hard' drugs. Or, conversely, the Ethiopian food crisis does *not* get regular coverage nor does it get insistently linked to questions of the repayment of 'Third World' interest on loans to the big banks. Such an approach has usually been applied in the field of news and TV documentaries but it can be extended to entertainment forms and the implications of the kinds of pleasures and fantasies they routinely invite us to join and the ones they exclude. This would clearly relate to the way the process of stereotyping can set 'frames' for expectations about certain groups.[8]

A related idea is that all acts of communication have assumptions built into them about their audience. This is termed *mode of address*. As labelling theory and our experience of teaching and learning tells us, if we are repeatedly addressed as stupid or bright or nervous, we are likely in time to respond accordingly, thereby reinforcing the label in a process that becomes self-fulfilling.

If TV repeatedly addresses us as though our central identities are as consumers or members of traditional families or people with a short span of attention, we may in time take up the proffered identity, especially if few others are being offered. More noticeably, perhaps, if we are repeatedly addressed as though we are white or male or middle class, we may come to feel inadequate or deviant if we can't make that enjoyable, friendly-feeling identification with the rest of the audience whom we imagine to be 'out there', nor with those characters on the screen. Noelle-Neuman[9] has even suggested that a 'spiral of silence' may get set up in audiences, whereby those who perceive themselves, on the evidence of media agendas, to be in the minority fall increasingly silent, while those who are confident of majority support become more vociferous. Such *discourses* (interpretations backed by power) can keep offering identities in which we are to recognize ourselves, which may contradict but more often reinforce and overlap each other.

The problem with some versions of such useful emphasis on agendas, mode of address, textual positionings is that, paradoxically, they end up with a model of audiences as irretrievably positioned and as helpless as those in the 'effects' scenario. This is perhaps most visible in the way I suppose many of us have taught advertising at one time or another. For the sake of a lively analysis of attractive texts, it's easy to risk implying that we can take for granted the effects ads have on their audiences, effects which we and our enlightened students of course can only too easily resist. It's a problem risked by many 'deconstructive' approaches too, insofar as they imply that 'cracking the code' of the text is all that needs to be done.

ALL–POWERFUL RECEIVER

The most familiar example of the 'all-powerful viewer/receiver' side of debates about audience has been the 'uses and gratifications' model.[10] This suggests that audience behaviour is explicable by the various needs and interests its members have as free individuals, as consumers gratified through the market place by certain kinds of films, magazines or videos. Such approaches have been criticized (a) for the excessive stress on what they conceive as the individual rather than social identities of audiences, (b) for a rather crude sense of 'basic needs' like 'the need for esteem' which could mean a thousand and one things or 'sexual satisfaction', which is usually described in terms which reveal that the 'individual' being assumed as 'the audience' is white, male and middle class. In addition, (c) for the conceptualizing of the notion of basic needs and the ways programmes are thought to satisfy them, which share the weaknesses of many similar market models. The needs can only be conceived and registered via the market research of the interested industries themselves. They tend to rest ultimately on the status quo and on what the existing industries can readily provide, rather than on encouraging the expression of needs which it would take more than the provision of a different product to satisfy and which are therefore 'off the agenda'.

As these models are applied to the media, the helpful emphasis on the audience's role in the production of meaning can obliterate the fact that texts are *not* open to any meaning at all and cannot be used in any way they please by their individual 'consumers'.[11] And, of course, the 'market place' itself can only be reached by those with a certain amount of money (and with control of the channel button!).

Consumers and pleasure

Some of these problems apply to current uses of the term 'pleasure'[12] which, in some emphases, becomes a hold-all term to celebrate anything that escapes a rigid emphasis on the rational, ideological meaning of a text. But first, let's see how the concept can inform discussion of many media products in valuable ways. With a game show like *Blind Date*, for instance, it may reveal not only enjoyment of the wit and aplomb of some of the contestants, and the use of a soap opera 'cliffhanger' link from one show to the next, but also a fascination with the programme's play around areas of social embarrassment. This kind of reading deserves space to be heard in a climate that denies the intelligence of audiences for such game shows. However, the very *different* experiences described by 'pleasure' need to be *socially* characterized and differentiated. Male/ female, black/white, old/young people will enjoy very different parts of *Blind Date* – and sometimes very little of it. The 'pleasure' of housewives carving out a little space of leisure in the working day in the home to watch a film or soap needs to be distinguished from the 'pleasure' of feeling oneself part of a large audience (perhaps even for a media event you're not particularly interested in) and the anticipation of being able to talk about it to friends and workmates the next day. And these pleasures need differentiating from the 'pleasure' of answering back when TV or the *Sun* makes us angry.

None of these are exactly the 'textual' pleasures concentrated on in media teaching. There is a need to find ways of teaching, for instance, how large audiences – the presumed proof of 'the popular'[13] – are prepared for and produced. How do distribution and exhibition practices determine what we get to see at the cinema, on TV – or in the local supermarket, as follow-up to advertising for that matter? Whenever huge audience figures are produced for media events, it's worth asking what else was there to do and who had access to it? How are we made to feel if we resist an almost inescapable event like a Royal Wedding? – a weirdo, a killjoy or a smartass? What enjoyments are there to 'serious' television or to independent practices? And why aren't they advertised as pleasures?

Space needs to be created for students and teachers to discuss the *spectrum* of different pleasures produced by audiences in their interaction with the media – from enjoying the sound of television as the background to other activities through to cheerful scorn, glee and even joy. For instance, we may agree that Prince Charles seems OK, but why are we talking about *him*? How has that agreeable feeling of community been produced? At the other extreme, voice needs to be given to those social recognitions which can suddenly make us jubilantly feel part of larger, but usually invisible, groups and affiliations. Such recognitions may arise when an interview suddenly slips out of control or when a few lines in a pop song stop us in our tracks. An idea that deserves classroom space is that certain popular forms (musicals and quiz shows are only the most obvious) offer audiences pleasures that can be called 'utopian' in their celebration of abundance, spontaneity and transparency[14] in a social world that routinely effaces them. The emphasis on audience pleasure has been important in complicating simple models of the ideological poison assumed to be injected into audiences by popular entertainment forms. But a teaching space is surely also justified for exploring audience *anger* and *frustration* with parts of the media, for imagining what other forms might be like – and celebrating them when they do get on air.

Viewing contexts

Still on the side of the active viewer, some work of the 1970s (much less well-funded and publicized than the Broadcasters' Audience Research Board (BARB) surveys (Figure 5.2, p. 118)) has pointed out that we come to texts with certain social identities which lead us to make different readings of the same programmes.[15] A bank manager, for instance is likely to perceive and respond differently to a programme on a long-running strike than a shop steward. Some working-class students reject the kind of critical teaching of TV news coverage of strikes which emphasizes, for instance, the privileged access to respectable settings of management figures or top union brass over the image we're offered regularly of bedraggled strikers outside the factory gates. For such students, the arrangement of these sequences may be completely subverted by their identification with the strikers, who look more like their parents,[16] and by the immense popularity of programmes like *Spitting Image* with their debunked authority figures.

This opens up the possibility of thinking and talking about the everyday ways in which we are all able to resist – or maybe just take a sarcastic or distanced view of – media messages, as part of a body of work which enables us to see *ourselves* among the audiences; no longer just outside, dispassionately observing and judging, but also inside. At the centre of this model is a figure rather different from the individual, 'pickin' n' choosin' consumer of the uses and gratifications school. But it's worth asking whether the figure isn't still assumed to be male, researched mostly in his relation to factual and documentary programmes, away from the domestic context in which most of us watch TV most of the time. This early work may also have tended to privilege class as *the* main determinant on how programmes are understood.

The most exciting recent work on audiences[17] has followed the figure home, away from work or media research centre. Paying attention to how that domestic context affects the process of TV viewing, such work has revealed:

(a) differences between 'homes' (dependent on such factors as class, race and whether or not the household is a 'traditional family');

(b) that the home is by no means isolated from social power (especially according to gender and age and how these relate to who gets to control TV viewing);

(c) the place of home in relation to work and to leisure. Video recorders are one more commodity which reduces the need for people to experience their leisure outside the home – the place where they now expect a lot of their entertainment to take place. For men, often coming home after work outside it, viewing can be a very different experience than for women who, whether or not they also work outside the home, see it as the place of their work. Children, of course, occupy yet another position, one not yet explored in much detail but which work on these aspects of audience might open up;

(d) how all this leads to different kinds of viewing. It's far more common for the man to watch in a sustained, uninterrupted way than it is for the woman, who is anyway less likely to be watching the programme of her choice, and who is often expected to 'manage' the continuous little interruptions, demands and disputes that often break out among children who are also perhaps not watching a programme of their choice;

(e) how, within all these complex social relations, TV is used for many purposes other than simple viewing. It may be used to 'mind' a child or an old person, as something that provides a welcome reason not to talk for the moment, to take time off housework or as a way of ensuring you can take part in conversations about a programme the next day at work or in school. (Indeed, one of the fears around deregulated fragmentation of the airwaves is that many opportunities for conversations and exchanges which can easily begin around programmes may be lost.)

This work is important in several ways. It surely pulls the last props away from simple models of either hypodermic effects or the free, self-gratifying consumer. Instead we have to see the home, the sacred ground of the private, as being not at all insulated from social differences but structured by them in similar but different ways to other social areas. Age, gender and class operate both *across* different kinds of families and *within* particular ones. Just as a completely passive viewing rarely takes place, so the image of completely free active viewers is also an exaggeration. Media users make meanings, yes, but not in conditions of their own choosing. Viewing habits, competences, reasons for an interest in or enjoyment of a programme are bound up with all kinds of power relations and competences. Women's enjoyment of soap operas, for instance, has derived partly from soaps' concentration on areas in which women have had to become extremely skilled and experienced – the management of personal relationships, 'caring', interpreting the behaviour of those we're closely involved with, witholding punitive judgement. Such work means we can begin to think about the effects of the media in a much more sophisticated way. To take an often controversial example, instead of seizing on the notion that toy ads should be banned because they brainwash kids we might explore how the provision of childcare, leisure facilities and money for toys relate to the power of toy manufacturers within and outside TV. It also becomes important to ask how *different* viewing groups handle such consuming demands (as well as how the children actually handle the toys, which may be in quite *un*stereotypical ways). We can then rethink the effects of toys and ads insofar as they relate more broadly to gender identity and socially-sanctioned violent behaviour.

TEACHING AUDIENCES

The organizing potential of this concept 'audience' in the classroom is great. The main point becomes not study of the text as site of meaning and effect, the puzzle to be solved, but the active production of meaning on *both* sides of the text. Students, too, become the subject of study, recognized as active media users with all the advantages for teaching this brings in student confidence and knowledge. Teaching 'audience' also enables classrooms to be related to the 'outside' world of home and public–political areas. Just as we teach literacy as reading *and* writing (albeit only handwriting, not print), so we can teach media literacy by first emphasizing the activity involved in audiences reading texts so students may then be encouraged to 'write' their own, this time in the more publicly available media of print, radio, photography, video and perhaps even with a 'real' audience at the end of the process.[18]

Of course there are problems in teaching 'audience', a relatively new teaching concept with few materials yet developed. There is the danger of falling into a confusion of differences with endlessly relative readings and points of view. Or, in trying to avoid that, there is the danger of seeming to want to reduce the complex differences between students' viewing experiences to an overarching economic or gender explanation, where you are telling them what they *really* enjoyed – or that they shouldn't 'really' have enjoyed it! How can these dangers be avoided? How is it best to teach 'audience'? The most obvious approach is the use of simple questionnaires, interviews, participant observation work – especially, but not only, at home – on how the media are used and how they get discussed.

A possible questionnaire
Who usually has command of the channel control? Is there a pecking order in your home? If so, have you ever managed to subvert it? How? When and where have you heard programmes/ records/ads being discussed this week? How do you watch TV? In a group? In your own room? Do you talk about the programmes at all during/before/after them? How is the video used in your home? Who mostly controls it? What do you record on it? Do you avoid the ads or positively watch out for some of them?

Following this, discuss the ways people admit to a liking for certain programmes which we often say we're 'hooked' on. Why are images of addiction, junk foods and drugs used to describe this attraction? What kinds of discussion does it prevent? Why do we say we 'just happened to have the TV on' when a certain programme came on or were 'too busy' to watch another that friends are discussing? Are there any programmes we say we never watch, but find we can join in conversations about? Play 'Confessions', asking people to admit to the programmes they least like to admit to watching, exploring why such resistance is felt, maybe ranking the programmes and looking at why they have such low status.[19] Do simple research into whether such preferences and dislikes are shared in the classroom. It's often striking how boys will at first say they don't watch soap operas but later betray quite detailed knowledge of various characters. Keep simple diaries, collate and display the results or even send them to your local radio or TV station.

Play a TV or radio scheduling game. Ask what the schedulers seem to be taking for granted about audience preferences, lifestyles and even bedtimes. Why that magazine format from 6 p.m. to 7 p.m.? Why this insomniac ghetto for minority video or Open University programmes? How does the continuity voice between programmes encourage us to estimate those programmes and ourselves? Students might be asked to dub their own commentary onto a continuity sequence. Or they might report back on how a night's TV 'schedules the family', timing particular programmes against a presumed family's bedtimes; so soaps on at 6.30 p.m. or 7.00 p.m. cannot handle the 'adult' language or situations of those coming on later. Compare this to the actual schedules of the domestic groups watching TV, whether in TV's presumed traditional family units or not. Take two programmes – one seeking to gain a large audience, the other a more specialized one – and devise advertising for them. This is especially effective in relation to studying articles in the *Radio Times* or *TV Times*, in Sunday colour supplements, press handouts, continuity trailers both long term ('the autumn season') and short term ('later tonight'). Assemble ome publicity material for a film – storyline, pictures, graphics, slogans, critics' comments – and ask students to arrange them into posters intended to attract different audiences – 18, 15, PG, U, art house, men, women – and compare the results. Or take extracts from early morning radio, covering the switch-over from an address to, among others, male commuters on the way to work to one which assumes a housebound, largely female audience.[20] How is the change-over done? How do we know who's being addressed and when? Does the advertising change? Throughout these exercises, students can devise and produce their own schedules, commentaries, advertisements and posters.

Scheduling work can spark other connections with advertising, that staple of media-related courses. The BARB ratings figures and, if possible, one of their detailed, minute-by-minute charts of an evening's viewing figures can be discussed along with charts of the rates charged by the ITV companies for advertising space at particular times.[21] Students can then be given an existing TV ad and a fixed budget, playing out the role of advertising agency. They have to decide both the mode of address of the ad (who it is seeking to construct as its audience) and where to place it most suitably in the schedule within the constraints of their budget. Students can then discuss how they actually and differently enjoy and *use* ads (for jokes, allusions, conversations, keeping up-to-date with fashions, etc.). This may avoid the risk of simply assuming the guaranteed brainwashing effects of ads and can expose the limitations of the number-crunching style of BARB's results (Figure 5.2).[22]

To explore the relation between social identity and the media's pleasures, try to discover how far your students feel that (once they think about it) even when deeply involved in a text, they're not completely 'swallowed up by it' but *allow* themselves to go along with it. This is particularly helpful in enabling younger children to talk about their engagement with comics or cartoons[23] rather than reacting to complaints that *Thundercats* is a Very Violent programme with terrible effects on its young audience. Do your students feel that they take on a kind of temporary identity in watching TV programmes? How do they choose the ones they want to go along with as they flash by during channel-hopping? Which media forms have they encountered the least, or feel they are least likely to enjoy? The range will go all the way from opera to soap opera, and neither end should be dismissed out of hand. Nor should it be assumed we are divided into watertight compartments, in one the audience for *The Singing Detective* and in another the audience for *Dallas*. Once established, a cultural form, whether 'popular' or 'high', can go on building up pleasurable reference and play for its audiences. It can rely on that comfortable familiarity for the sake of which our recognitions of how social groups are being routinely represented may be disavowed or willingly suspended. This may

RATINGS

NATIONAL TOP 10s

BBC1

		millions
1	EastEnders (Th/Su)	23.75
2	EastEnders (Tu/Su)	23.40
3	Bergerac	15.15
4	The Paul Daniels Magic Show	14.25
5	Bob's Full House	13.10
6	Miss Marple: Nemesis	12.95
7	That's Life	12.85
8	Antiques Roadshow	12.75
9	Last Of The Summer Wine	12.10
10	A Question Of Sport	11.95

BBC2

		millions
1	Moonlighting	5.55
2	Crufts '87	5.50
3	Indelible Evidence	5.45
4	Food And Drink	4.55
5	Gardeners' World	4.40
6	Nozzers	4.30
6	Northanger Abbey	4.30
8	International Bowls (Su 15:20)	4.00
9	M*A*S*H	3.95
10	Charlie Chan In Castle In The Desert	3.75
10	Mission Impossible	3.75
10	The Mistress	3.75

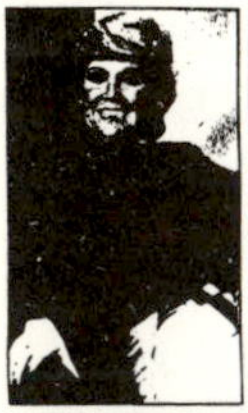

ITV

		millions
1	Coronation Street (W)	18.40
2	Coronation Street (M)	16.25
3	Wish You Were Here (M/Various)	15.95
4	This Is Your Life	14.00
5	Surprise, Surprise	13.00
6	The Equalizer	12.80
7	Crossroads (W)	12.20
8	Crossroads (Th)	12.15
8	The A-Team	12.15
10	Crossroads (Tu)	11.85

CHANNEL 4

		millions
1	Treasure Hunt	6.30
2	Brookside (Tu/Sa)	6.25
3	Brookside (M/Sa)	6.15
4	The Chain	5.25
5	Cheers	3.50
6	The Waltons	3.05
6	A Severed Head	3.05
8	Countdown (Th)	2.95
9	The Blue Dahlia	2.80
10	Countdown (W)	2.75

BREAKFAST TV

	Reach millions M-F	Sa/Su	M/Su
BBC1	6.3	N/A	N/A
TV-am	11.3	7.3	14.4
Individual millions Peak Qtr Hr Audience Average			
BBC1	1.2	N/A	N/A
TV-am	2.6	3.1	2.4

S4C Welsh Speaking

		000s
1	Pobol Y Cwm	63
2	Ffermio	46
3	Hel Straeon	45
3	Cadwyn Cerdd	45
5	Bwrlwm Bro	43

S4C All Viewers

		000s
1	The Chain	147
2	Golden Girls	129
3	Valentine	114
4	Brookside (W)	112
5	Snwcer (Th)	107

THE WEEK'S VIEWING IN SUMMARY

HOURS OF VIEWING SHARE OF AUDIENCE

	Average Per Head (Hrs:Mins)	Share of Total (%)
All Any TV	27:44	100.0
BBC1 (inc Breakfast Time)	10:25	37.6
BBC2	3:02	10.9
Total Any BBC	13:27	48.5
ITV (inc TV-am)	12:04	43.5
Channel 4/S4C	2:13	8.0
Total Any ITV	14:17	51.5
S4C (Welsh Speakers)	2:46	9.3

AUDIENCE REACH

	Average Daily (%)	Average Weekly (%)
All Any TV	81.0	94.6
BBC1 (inc Breakfast Time)	69.1	93.1
BBC2	39.1	82.0
Total Any BBC	72.9	93.6
ITV (inc TV-am)	67.1	92.2
Channel 4/S4C	32.7	77.1
Total Any ITV	70.9	93.2
S4C (Welsh Speakers)	36.4	74.7

ITV DAY/NIGHT

	ITV	C4	Total ITV
All Hours	43.5	8.0	51.5
Before 18.00	44.5	7.3	51.8
After 18.00	42.9	8.4	51.3

BBC DAY/NIGHT

	BBC1	BBC2	Total BBC
All Hours	37.6	10.9	48.5
Before 18.00	37.9	10.3	48.2
After 18.00	37.4	11.3	48.7

AREA TOP 10s

Week ending February 15, 1987

LONDON

		Shown	TVR
1	EastEnders (Tu/Su)	BBC1	41
2	EastEnders (Th/Su)	BBC1	39
3	Bergerac	BBC1	31
4	Coronation Street (W)	Thames	29
4	Miss Marple: Nemesis	BBC1	29
6	Wish You Were Here (M/W)	Thames	27
6	Paul Daniels Magic Show	BBC1	27
8	Holiday '87	BBC1	26
8	News, Sport & Weather (Sa 21:24)	BBC1	26
10	Coronation Street (M)	Thames	25
10	Rumpole Of The Bailey	Thames	25
10	Bob's Full House	BBC1	25
10	Antiques Roadshow	BBC1	25

SOUTH & SOUTH EAST

		Shown	TVR
1	EastEnders (Th/Su)	BBC1	40
2	EastEnders (Tu/Su)	BBC1	37
3	Bergerac	BBC1	30
4	Wish You Were Here (M/F)	TVS	29
5	Paul Daniels Magic Show	BBC1	28
6	Coronation Street (W)	TVS	27
7	Antiques Roadshow	BBC1	26
8	That's Life	BBC1	24
9	Coast To Coast (M)	TVS	23
9	Coast To Coast (Tu)	TVS	23
9	News At 5:45 (W)	TVS	23
9	Coast To Coast (W)	TVS	23
9	A Question Of Sport	BBC1	23
9	Bob's Full House	BBC1	23

NORTH WEST

		Shown	TVR
1	EastEnders (Th/Su)	BBC1	47
2	EastEnders (Tu/Su)	BBC1	45
3	Coronation Street (W)	Granada	44
4	Coronation Street (M)	Granada	38
5	Wish You Were Here (M/Su)	Granada	36
6	Paul Daniels Magic Show	BBC1	32
6	Surprise Surprise	Granada	32
8	The Equalizer	Granada	30
8	Bergerac	BBC1	30
10	Emmerdale Farm (Tu)	Granada	29
10	This Is Your Life	Granada	29
10	Cannon And Ball	Granada	29

SOUTH WEST

		Shown	TVR
1	EastEnders (Tu/Su)	BBC1	48
2	EastEnders (Th/Su)	BBC1	43
3	Coronation Street (W)	TSW	39
4	Wish You Were Here (M/F)	TSW	37
5	Miss Marple: Nemesis	BBC1	36
6	That's Life	BBC1	35
7	Coronation Street (M)	TSW	34
7	Antiques Roadshow	BBC1	34
9	Holiday '87	BBC1	33
9	Mastermind	BBC1	33

EAST OF ENGLAND

		Shown	TVR
1	EastEnders (Tu/Su)	BBC1	46
2	EastEnders (Th/Su)	BBC1	45
3	Coronation Street (W)	Anglia	37
4	Coronation Street (M)	Anglia	33
4	Paul Daniels Magic Show	BBC1	33
4	Bergerac	BBC1	33
7	Wish You Were Here (M/F)	Anglia	31
8	Bob's Full House	BBC1	30
9	Holiday '87	BBC1	29
9	This Is Your Life	Anglia	29

MIDLANDS EAST & WEST

		Shown	TVR
1	EastEnders (Tu/Su)	BBC1	42
1	EastEnders (Th/Su)	BBC1	42
3	Coronation Street (W)	Central	33
4	Bergerac	BBC1	30
5	Coronation Street (M)	Central	29
6	Wish You Were Here (M/W)	Central	27
7	Paul Daniels Magic Show	BBC1	26
7	Last Of The Summer Wine	BBC1	26
9	This Is Your Life	Central	25
9	Bob's Full House	BBC1	25
9	That's Life	BBC1	25

NORTH EAST

		Shown	TVR
1	EastEnders (Th/Su)	BBC1	40
2	EastEnders (Tu/Su)	BBC1	38
3	Coronation Street (M)	TTT	32
4	Coronation Street (W)	TTT	31
5	Wish You Were Here (M/F)	TTT	29
5	Antiques Roadshow	BBC1	29
7	Paul Daniels Magic Show	BBC1	27
8	The Equalizer	TTT	26
8	The A-Team	TTT	26
8	Bergerac	BBC1	26

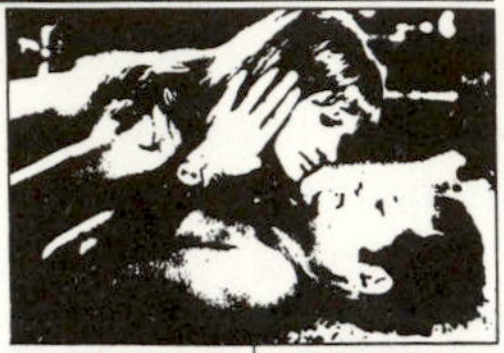

YORKSHIRE

		Shown	TVR
1	EastEnders (Th/Su)	BBC1	47
2	EastEnders (Tu/Su)	BBC1	46
3	Coronation Street (W)	Yorkshire	38
4	Coronation Street (M)	Yorkshire	37
5	Wish You Were Here (M/F)	Yorkshire	36
6	This Is Your Life	Yorkshire	30
7	Emmerdale Farm (Tu)	Yorkshire	28
7	Paul Daniels Magic Show	BBC1	28
7	Bergerac	BBC1	28
7	Bullseye	Yorkshire	28
7	Surprise Surprise	Yorkshire	28

WALES & THE WEST

		Shown	TVR
1	EastEnders (Th/Su)	BBC1	39
2	EastEnders (Tu/Su)	BBC1	36
3	Coronation Street (W)	HTV	35
4	Coronation Street (M)	HTV	33
5	Wish You Were Here (M/F)	HTV	29
6	This Is Your Life	HTV	27
7	Crossroads (Tu)	HTV	25
7	Emmerdale Farm (Tu)	HTV	25
7	Crossroads (W)	HTV	25
7	Crossroads (Th)	HTV	25
7	Emmerdale Farm (Th)	HTV	25

BORDER

		Shown	TVR
1	EastEnders (Th/Su)	BBC1	51
2	EastEnders (Tu/Su)	BBC1	47
3	Wish You Were Here (M/F)	Border	42
4	Coronation Street (W)	Border	40
5	Coronation Street (M)	Border	36
5	This Is Your Life	Border	36
5	Antiques Roadshow	BBC1	36
8	The Equalizer	Border	34
9	Surprise Surprise	Border	33
10	Bugs Bunny	BBC1	32

CENTRAL SCOTLAND

		Shown	TVR
1	EastEnders (Tu/Su)	BBC1	46
1	EastEnders (Th/Su)	BBC1	46
3	Coronation Street (W)	STV	34
4	Bob's Full House	BBC1	33
5	Dempsey And Makepeace	STV	31
5	Murder She Wrote	STV	31
7	Surprise Surprise	STV	30
8	Wish You Were Here (M/W)	STV	29
8	L.A. Law (Tu)	STV	29
8	The Newlyweds Game	STV	29
8	The A-Team	STV	29
8	Catchphrase	STV	29

NORTH SCOTLAND

		Shown	TVR
1	EastEnders (Tu/Su)	BBC1	45
2	EastEnders (Th/Su)	BBC1	38
3	Coronation Street (W)	Grampian	37
4	Surprise Surprise	Grampian	35
5	Catchphrase	Grampian	34
6	Highway	Grampian	31
7	This Is Your Life	Grampian	30
8	Dempsey And Makepeace	Grampian	29
9	Coronation Street (M)	Grampian	28
9	Crossroads (Tu)	Grampian	28

ULSTER

		Shown	TVR
1	EastEnders (Th/Su)	BBC1	51
2	EastEnders (Tu/Su)	BBC1	48
3	Coronation Street (W)	Ulster	41
4	Coronation Street (M)	Ulster	35
5	Surprise Surprise	Ulster	34
6	This Is Your Life	Ulster	33
7	Crossroads (W)	Ulster	30
7	Dempsey And Makepeace	Ulster	30
7	Bullseye	Ulster	30
10	Wish You Were Here (M/W)	Ulster	29

MONTHLY RATINGS

BARB MONTHLY AUDIENCES – JANUARY
Share of Total Viewing by ITV Region

	ITV		CHANNEL 4/S4C		BBC1		BBC2	
	JAN %	(DEC) %	JAN %	(DEC) %	JAN %	(DEC) %	JAN %	(DEC) %
London	41.4	(42.9)	7.1	(7.3)	40.8	(41.0)	10.7	(8.7)
Midlands (E & W)	45.2	(45.9)	7.7	(7.4)	36.4	(37.8)	10.7	(9.0)
North West	43.3	(44.6)	7.7	(7.4)	38.2	(38.9)	10.9	(9.1)
Yorkshire	44.3	(46.8)	7.8	(7.3)	37.8	(37.9)	10.1	(8.0)
C. Scotland	40.8	(43.8)	9.9	(9.3)	38.2	(37.9)	11.1	(8.9)
Wales & The West	46.3	(46.5)	6.7	(6.4)	35.7	(38.0)	11.3	(9.1)
South & South East	41.9	(42.5)	6.5	(6.3)	40.4	(41.6)	11.2	(9.6)
North East	43.0	(44.6)	8.5	(8.0)	38.1	(38.4)	10.4	(9.0)
East of England	43.2	(44.2)	6.7	(6.6)	40.0	(41.1)	10.1	(8.0)
South West	41.4	(42.9)	6.9	(6.4)	41.2	(42.3)	10.5	(8.4)
Ulster	42.1	(44.7)	8.0	(6.9)	38.6	(40.1)	11.3	(8.4)
Border	46.5	(48.7)	7.4	(6.9)	36.8	(37.1)	9.3	(7.3)
N. Scotland	45.2	(47.8)	8.3	(8.0)	37.2	(37.2)	9.3	(7.0)
Network	43.3	(44.6)	7.9	(7.4)	38.0	(38.9)	10.8	(9.0)

HOURS OF DAILY VIEWING AND SHARE OF TOTAL VIEWING OF INDIVIDUALS IN JANUARY

Channel	Average Daily Viewing per Head JAN Hrs:Mins	(DEC) (Hrs:Mins)	Share of Total Viewing JAN %	(DEC) (%)
All TV	4:23	(4:10)	100.0	(100.0)
BBC1 (inc. Breakfast Time)	1:40	(1:37)	38.9	(38.9)
BBC2	0:28	(0:23)	10.8	(9.0)
Total BBC	2:08	(2:00)	48.8	(47.9)
ITV (inc. TV-am)	1:54	(1:52)	43.4	(44.6)
Channel 4/S4C	0:21	(0:19)	7.9	(7.4)
Total ITV	2:15	(2:10)	51.2	(52.1)

Broadcast 27 February 1987

25

Figure 5.2 BARB chart.

be especially so for audiences seeking relaxation after or during work who are therefore very ready to 'join in the game' of the text.

How do phrases like 'it took me out of myself' relate to where we repeatedly get taken to? Do we sometimes want to 'escape' to a quite different place, at other times to one where we can rehearse in imagination problems we are encountering in the rest of our lives? Where do we *not* get routinely taken to? And, on the other side of the 'game', are there places where we refuse to go, well-crafted jokes we refuse to laugh with, because the stubborn resistance of other social identities refuses even the pleasures on offer? Such an approach can also counter a common tendency to treat a story as though all it was about was its ending, 'the moral', whether that be defeat or an enforced sacrifice, etc. Ask a classroom audience what they remembered or responded to most vividly as a story took its course and which few moments they talked about afterwards. Rarely is the ending mentioned.

Work on the routine, institutionalized address of the media to its assumed audience has another advantage. Having explored how powerfully assumptions about us are embedded in conventional practices, students may be able to approach unconventional, usually marginalized programmes, sounds and images far more encouragingly, without the intimidating heading of 'artistic creations' or 'serious work'. Here you might invite along members of your nearest video and film workshop or any other 'alternative' production group. The text itself will get more sympathetic and lively attention than if it's presented in a mystifying way as a 'work of art'. Some students, especially if encountering young, local independent cultural workers for the first time, may feel empowered to begin work on their own representations.

With appropriate pedagogies and classroom work, the concept of audience has the potential to develop understandings of the cultural power of media institutions in ways that won't reduce down to 'brainwashing' or 'ideology' the variety of relations we enter into with texts. Teachers have to engage with those very pressing concerns of parents and others about the effects of the media. But we may better be able to resist calls to inoculate or protect if the effects can be understood as varied, as complex, as often beneficial, and as overlapping with other social forces which are damagingly ignored if we simply assume media are doing the harm.[24] It may also be able to produce not only critical and complex understandings of media products and processes but also students who feel empowered as active, socially-positioned users making their own representations and finding their own voices. Few concepts seem better able to begin this than 'audience' which is concerned to explore groups and experiences about which students, once they begin that thinking, have a wealth of knowledge. Such work can suggest and build on a fuller meaning for 'popular' than the statistics of the quantifying industries. It might also change classroom work, for some of the time, into something livelier and more like

LWT RATE CARD NO 33
STANDARD RATES

FRIDAY

Time Segment		10 sec	20 sec	30 sec	40 sec	50 sec	60 sec
1.	1715–1800	5,000	8,000	10,000	13,300	16,600	18,000
2.	1800–2240	12,500	20,000	25,000	33,250	41,500	45,000
3.	2240–Close	5,000	8,000	10,000	13,300	16,600	18,000

SATURDAY

Time Segment		10 sec	20 sec	30 sec	40 sec	50 sec	60 sec
1.	Up to 1730	5,000	8,000	10,000	13,300	16,600	18,000
2.	1730–2230	12,500	20,000	25,000	33,250	41,500	45,000
3.	2230–Close	5,000	8,000	10,000	13,300	16,600	18,000

SUNDAY

Time Segment		10 sec	20 sec	30 sec	40 sec	50 sec	60 sec
1.	Up to 1930	5,000	8,000	10,000	13,300	16,600	18,000
2.	1930–2230	12,500	20,000	25,000	33,250	41,500	45,000
3.	2230–Close	5,000	8,000	10,000	13,300	16,600	18,000

Spots of longer duration are pro rata to the 60 second rate and are only available in multiples of 10 seconds.

Figure 5.3 London Weekend Television's advertising Rate Card no. 33 (1989); figures represent charges in £s.

work with an active and engaged audience than classes often seem to be.

NOTES

This chapter was written in 1986 and updated in 1990.

1 Clive James, the *Independent*, 22 May 1987.
2 See David Morley, *The 'Nationwide' Audience* (London: BFI, 1980), especially Chapters 1–4 for a succinct account of this and other dominant ways of thinking about 'the audience' for the media.
3 See Jane Root, *Open the Box* (London: Comedia/Channel Four, 1985) and the first programme of the series it was written to accompany (available through the BFI Film and Video Library) for a lively account of the imagery and extremes of the 'effects' case. For a helpful discussion of the 'video nasties' panic, see Julian Petley, 'A nasty story', *Screen*, vol. 25, no. 2 and Annette Kuhn's reply, *Screen*, vol. 25, no. 3.
4 *Video, Violence and Children* (London: Hodder & Stoughton, 1985) by the so-called Parliamentary Group is a recent example of such work. See also David Lusted, 'Feeding the panic and breaking the cycle', *Screen*, vol. 24, no. 6, for a critique of the area.
5 Len Masterman gives an account of one such theorist, Dallas Smythe, in his chapter on 'Audience' in *Teaching the Media* (London: Comedia/M K Media Press, 1985).
6 See John Caughie, 'On the offensive: TV and values', in David Lusted and Phillip Drummond (eds), *TV and Schooling* (London: BFI, 1985).
7 For a clear account of the earliest, news-centred work around 'agenda setting', see Dennis McQuail and Sven Windhal, *Communication Models for the Study of Mass Communications*, pp. 62–4 (London: Longman, 1981).
8 See *Selling Pictures* teaching pack, Listings, p. 211.
9 E. Noelle-Neumann (1974) 'The spiral of silence: a theory of public opinion', *Journal of Communication*, vol. 24, no. 2.
10 See McQuail and Windhal, op. cit., pp. 75–83.
11 The word 'consumer' in conceptions of audiences has shifted interestingly. It was once used as a way of dismissing the complicated processes of 'reading' texts, serving to link these with the 'consumption' of alcohol, nicotine, junk food, as in much 'effects' rhetoric. Recently, though, it has been used in ways which converge with other celebrations of 'consumer power' and the importance of 'market mechanisms'.
12 See especially Dorothy Hobson, *Crossroads: The Drama of a Soap Opera* (London: Methuen, 1982); Charlotte Brunsdon, '*Crossroads*: notes on soap opera' in *Screen*, vol. 22, no. 4; Ien Ang, *Watching 'Dallas'* (London: Methuen, 1985).
13 See Raymond Williams, *Keywords* (London: Fontana, 1984, revised edn) for the complex history of the term 'popular'. In 'Melodrama' (*New Statesman*, 24 April 1980) he outlines two major conflicting but

related meanings: 'popular' as 'active majority interests and issues' and 'popular' as 'highly organized and increasingly monopolistic capitalist cultural markets'. These two meanings seem to converge with the similarly opposed meanings of 'freedom' in recent market models and rhetoric.

14 See especially Richard Dyer in Rick Altman (ed.), *Genre: The Musical* (London: BFI, 1981).

15 Stuart Hall, 'Encoding/decoding' in S. Hall *et al.* (eds), *Culture, Media, Language* (London: Hutchinson, 1981); David Morley, *The 'Nationwide' Audience*, op. cit.

16 This example is taken from Cary Bazalgette, 'Making sense for whom?' in *Screen*, vol. 27, no. 5.

17 See David Morley, *Family Television, Cultural Power and Domestic Leisure* (London: Comedia, 1985); Ann Gray, 'Women and video' in Helen Baehr and Gillian Dyer (eds), *Boxed In: Women On and In Television* (London: Routledge & Kegan Paul, 1987); Philip Simpson (ed.), *Parents Talking Television* (London: Comedia, 1987).

18 See the experience of co-ordination between school and college students and the Rio Cinema, Hackney, described in papers by Trish Jenkins and Nicole Stephenson for the 1987 conference Teaching Alternative Media, produced by SEFT.

19 See Ien Ang, *Watching 'Dallas'*, op. cit, for a detailed account of how audience members have to struggle to justify their liking for a low-status cultural form like *Dallas*.

20 See Helen Baehr and Michele Ryan, *Shut Up and Listen!* (London: Comedia/Campaign for Press and Broadcasting Freedom, 1984) for an interesting account and discussion of the address of local radio to women listeners, especially in chapters 1, 2, 5 and 6.

21 Commercial TV companies will supply their current rates for advertising space on request (Figure 5.3). Comment on and extracts from the ratings are published in the *Media Guardian* (Mondays). Back copies of the BARB weekly ratings figures and charts are sometimes available from BARB, 56 Mortimer Street, London W1N 8AN.

22 See John O. Thompson's stimulating piece 'Advertising's rationality' in M. Alvarado and J. O. Thompson (eds), *The Media Reader* (London: BFI, 1990).

23 See Bob Hodge and David Tripp, *Children and Television* (London: Polity Press, 1985) especially chapters 2, 3 and 4.

24 For a refreshingly positive yet discriminating approach to children's TV contact British Action for Children's TV, c/o 21 Stephen Street, London W1P 1PL.

Chapter 6

Representation

Gillian Swanson

At its most basic, the term 'representation' refers to the way images and language actively construct meanings according to sets of conventions shared by and familiar to makers and audiences.

Conventions form part of our cultural knowledge – we know 'what to do' with the media products we come across even if we don't do it – and the conventions used are as familiar to the participants of a particular culture as the meanings they make. Assumptions, 'common knowledge', common sense, 'general' knowledge, widespread beliefs and popular attitudes are all part of the *context of meanings* within which representations are produced and circulate. They also form the basis of our own cultural knowledge, varied though it may be. This context and our individual ranges of knowledge, values and attitudes is governed in turn by a system of power that offers varied legitimacy to these meanings, ideas and responses. In this system, there is a hierarchy in which some meanings come to be dominant and others marginalized. Approaches to representation incorporate the way the media use conventions, how audiences make meanings from them and how representations work and are used within a cultural context.

There can be no absolute version of 'how things are' but only many competing versions, some of which are more highly regarded than others in society and hence are circulated more widely. In looking at the media as 'representation' we may examine the versions that have currency, the elements that are repeated across them and the relation to common-sense definitions we acquire as participants within a culture. We study narrative, visual structures, character or whatever, to get at something else – the *way* in which meanings are offered to us and *our part* in actively making sense of them for ourselves.

Our sense of self is organized according to various *categories*, those of gender, race, class, age, sexuality and so on, as well as those encompassing different 'interest groups' which include, say, political affiliation. And the *characteristics* associated with these categories include the way we look, how we behave, the lifestyle we adopt, even the car we buy. We come to recognize how certain characteristics are considered more or less socially appropriate or acceptable. For example, drunkenness in a sexually assertive woman might be considered licentious and unrestrained, a threat to established roles and forms of behaviour, especially if she's an older woman. Drunkenness in a young, apparently virginal woman might alternatively be seen as a sign of her lack of experience of alcohol, emphasizing her vulnerability, innocence and naivety, and invoking the need for protection.

Ideas about what people are like and how they are meant to be understood already prevail in our culture. They give meaning to our sense of self and allow us to position ourselves in relation to others. Such meanings and attitudes are reproduced in representation but the *way* representations are constructed is as important as the ideas and meaning they project, since they offer *positions* for us, through which we recognize images as similar, or different from, ourselves and those around us. We continually define ourselves in changing relations to these meanings; images change over time and the meanings which are legitimated by the social or cultural context change as well.

UNDERSTANDING REPRESENTATION

The different questions one might ask of representation have been usefully set out by Richard Dyer in *TV and Schooling*.[1] Put simply:

1 What sense do representations make of the world? What are they representing to us and how?
2 What are typical representations of groups in society?
3 *Who* is speaking, *for whom*?
4 What does this example represent *to me*. What does it mean to others who see it?

Dyer links what representations are saying to how they work as entertainment by asking 'what the enjoyment is about',[2] suggesting that we investigate the pleasures offered and who they are for. From whose *point of view* is a text pleasurable and why? What are the elements which constitute pleasure in a certain representation? These questions not only enable us to look at how pleasure is constructed, at who within society is offered pleasure and on what basis, but also at the position others have to take up in order to get pleasure.

The investigative procedure prompted by Dyer raises the issue of who we are in a more personal way, dealing with our responses – our likes, dislikes, identifications and fantasies. It involves our *sense of self*, inviting teacher and student alike to investigate what a particular representation says we are and what we think of it. The way we understand ourselves and define our identities depends very much on attitudes derived from cultural experience. We see ourselves or who we want to be in others: friends, parents, popular figures, etc. This constitutes the process we call *identification*. In representation, this sense or image we have of a 'self' is constructed through the feeling we have of becoming absorbed into a character's role or position in a narrative, understanding their thoughts, feelings, reactions and taking on their point of view. Alternatively, we may *recognize* the characteristics attributed to a particular kind of person (male/female, black/white, working class/middle class, old/young or whatever) in our own social make-up.

In order to engage our interest, to involve us, media representations must show some aspect we recognize or want to adopt as part of ourselves and give us something we will find pleasurable. But the question of from whose point of view a narrative, scene, line of dialogue or image can be found enjoyable or pleasurable causes much discussion. For example, protests against sexist or racist jokes are often met by the response 'Haven't you got a sense of humour?' that assumes we can all equally share in the enjoyment of the joke. But jokes position us differently and mean different things to different people. This works in film or television narratives, too. In a thriller which has shown us the rape or murder of a woman through the 'eyes' of the male perpetrator, suspense may be caused by our desire to find out if and how he gets caught. Girls and boys may not identify with him in quite the same way, however. If the only way to participate in the suspense of the narrative is to adopt the male point of view, female spectators may be able to do so through their familiarity with the *conventions* of this kind of story. But the clash between the social formation of our identity (here, female) and the position we are asked to occupy to get pleasure (here, male) may produce anxiety in our viewing and response.

This issue of *point of view* means we must consider in our study both the power of the text – in the way meaning is structured and produced – and the way spectators can climb in and out of the various pleasurable positions offered. Who likes what is offered? Why? What may it mean to refuse the offer? Such questions can reveal power relations in who has the right to speak and to whom. They can help identify the elements in our social make-up which are necessary in order to take up the positions offered. They can make sense of displeasure as an indication of tension between our own sense of self and the identification offered.

Questions like these examine how the kind of cultural know-ledge we possess helps us to take up the *address*, the way of 'speaking to' us, that media representations offer. They go beyond looking at images and narratives and at their forms since address is hidden behind the apparent 'naturalness' of such conventions. We need to analyse modes of address as part of our concern with how meaning is formed and how pleasures are constructed.

The ways in which we make sense of representation is governed by a set of norms. Our own cultural positions become defined according to the degree of coincidence with or deviation from any norm. But if we were merely to describe the way norms are constructed, we would not allow space for expressing the *resistances* and *negotiations* which certain members of an audience make during their viewing experience. Incorporating these 'other' readings into the exploration of meaning acknowledges differences rather than deviations from norms. Teaching about representation, then, requires a pedagogy that pursues this enquiry, one that can dismantle the conventional ways experience and identity are cate-gorized and defined, one that allows us to ask how to make sense of the cultural framework we operate within, one that contains the possibility of *changing* models of thinking and redescribing experience and identity.

For this reason, there is a need to draw on more than the material most widely circulated in the media. While it is true that this material makes up the bulk of most people's viewing experience, other forms need to be seen in order to transform the ways we can understand and describe those elements of our experience mar-ginalized by the mainstream media. Other kinds of representations can allow us to make different meanings and help us to construct the ways we make sense of ourselves in alternative, challenging ways. It may mean using independent film and video, experimental photography or painting, graffiti, alternative magazines or journals and using them to pose questions about mainstream representations and forms of knowing. Hopefully, this may also lead to using these media forms to develop alternative processes of representation.

TEACHING ABOUT REPRESENTATION

I will attempt an *approach* to teaching about notions of sexuality and gendered identity as a way of understanding the conceptual framework of representation. I am using this as a specific example but the method can be related to teaching about other categories of social differentiation and cultural identity. In order to get at these categories, I suggest a link between materials and activities that is thematic rather than generic (e.g. news, soap opera, the single play). This is because it is an approach which works with *knowledge* as its basis. Our knowledge of generic *codes* (how, say, news is divided up, presented, uses still images, location footage, interviews, etc.) is part of a wider investigation into how meaning and pleasure are constructed.

Questions about cultural identity could be introduced through a study of, say, TV sitcom[3] once skills in visual analysis of images and an understanding of genre conventions have been acquired, perhaps through study of a set of slides on genre recognition.[4] Work on other elements such as narrative[5] or stars[6] also provides a familiarity with discussing and analysing images and the forms they take. Then one can move on to study a category like gender, to question the ways representations are constructed and meaning is made.

Any culture attaches a range of characteristics, expectations and assumptions to the biological sexes of male and female. 'Gender' refers to the particular ranges that define 'masculine' and 'feminine' qualities. 'Sexuality' – individual sexual identity – expresses any particular composition of characteristics, expectations and assumptions. Masculinity and femininity may seem biologically distinct categories but a focus on gender enables us to see how sexuality is a cultural construction rather than an identity determined by one's sex.

To teach about gender/sexuality at secondary level it may be necessary, first of all, to 'translate' these terms. It may be possible to start by discussing common-sense definitions of 'what girls/women are like' and 'what boys/men are like', how they are meant to look, sound, behave, etc. Alternatively, we can start with the terms 'male/female' and gradually draw out the difference between these biological categories and the cultural definitions or expectations of what they are (or ought to be) like. Using the terms 'sex' and 'gender' can help draw out this distinction between biology and culture. As Gill Branston points out: 'Sex says "It's a boy!",', gender says "Oh good!" and gets the baby clothes and little train sets ready.'[7]

Next, we can ask what the labels 'male' and 'female' can be applied to or what could be referred to as 'he' or 'she', and what this says about these categories. A *car* may be referred to as 'she', for instance, but what characteristics tie in with this categorization? We might note that it is an object of possession conventionally attributed to men whose ownership signals status and sometimes virility. There is an emphasis on shape and bodywork, 'performance', temperament; it is ritually 'worked on' and looked after; money is spent on it. The symbolic meanings attributed to this object and the activities it stimulates obviously exceed its function as transport and tell us more about conventional notions of masculinity and femininity than they do about cars. It is hard to imagine a car taking on similar meanings when owned by a girl or a woman. An *iron*, on the other hand, may be seen as more feminine precisely because it is an object more often used by women and connects with various assumptions about femininity and domestic labour. 'Male' objects – such as *motorbikes* and *guns* connoting power, speed, control, perhaps destructiveness, or *shovels*, demanding strength, associated with the 'outside' and activity – equally suggest a range of characteristics associated with masculinity.

Abstract concepts can be used as well as objects. The *nation* and the *country* have personal associations of home, belonging and the domestic which are associated with the family (hence *mother*land) and made physical (the '*body* of the nation'). The *state*, however, is a more 'masculine' construction, associated with intellectual rather than emotional functions, part of the public world of legal, parliamentary and financial institutions, governing individuals and determining the future. Through comparisons like these we can show how such categories are not natural but constructed, building up associations by the way they are conventionally used.

From here we can move to characteristics in people, to think through what 'masculine' and 'feminine' can be applied to in behaviour, looks, possessions, decor, emotional responses, ambitions. This may be done verbally or could form part of an exercise involving images or text from magazines, newspapers, promotional leaflets, mail order catalogues and extracts from novels, fictional stories, autobiographical articles or news reports. This forms the groundwork to study how representations are constructed – even though at this stage it is the 'what' that is being dealt with – in the way meanings are divided into two opposing (if not always opposite) categories and definitions of male and female.

As an exercise, consider the following extracts from *Fever* by Charlotte Lamb (London: Mills & Boon, 1979; new edition 1985):

> She looked at him properly then, her catlike green eyes wide and sharp, absorbing the tall, powerful body and black hair, the harsh strong lines of his face, realising that he had a face she would like to paint; drivingly individual with features which were at war with each other, a sensuality in the mould of his mouth which did not match the hard cold blue eyes. Sara gave him a cool little smile.
>
> (p. 6)

> Her eyes lifted again to his face and found him staring down at her, the black bar of his brows meeting over his eyes. Sara tilted her head, her red–gold hair glittering in the light as she moved and his blue eyes took on an open insolence, slowly wandering down her body in a fashion little short of insult.
>
> (p. 8)

> She had fine-boned sensitive features; a delicate little nose, slanting green eyes with gold-tipped lashes, high cheekbones and smooth creamy skin, but Sara was too well aware that her mouth was far too wide for her face, far too generously cut, the fullness of the lower lip promising a passion which her cool green eyes denied.
>
> (p. 20)

What different characteristics are emphasized in the descriptions of the male and female characters in these extracts? And what are the descriptive and metaphorical *terms* which are used to define these characteristics? This tells us something about the power relation between characters and how it permits them to act towards each other and express their desire. It is also useful to consider how point of view works in the text to position *us* in this relation and to suggest a potential readership.

We are moving towards observing the versions of femininity and masculinity we find and the expectations we have of relations between the sexes. What *combination* of characteristics do these rely upon? Could they be made into different combinations? What would this mean?

At this point, we can connect the cultural knowledge we bring to representations with an analysis of how sexuality[8] and gender are signified. How do we recognize the *signs* that help us to understand the images we are offered? How do they form part of the system of social forms of knowledge that categorize our experiences and identities? This is also a way of thinking through how we construct or represent *ourselves* in relation to such categories.

The male/female categories of gender represent themselves through a system of characteristic signs. Visual signs of height, build, length of hair, dress, etc. contribute to defining a 'position' within such categories. This offers a *version* of femininity or masculinity, a definition of sexuality or how sexual identity can be expressed. A study of the way these signs work to define sexuality can show how precarious are norms and 'standard' versions. Re-organizing the signs, according to a different pattern, can provide a *re*-definition, perhaps confusing our expectations about gender and sexuality.

Moving from talking through general ideas about gender and sexuality and how they form certain patterns, definitions and boundaries, to studying specific images prevents wild and un-revealing generalizations being made. We can unravel how images call on certain forms of knowledge and how the signs operate to make specific statements about any particular version of masculinity or femininity.

Stereotyping

Using stereotypes is a conventional way into teaching about representation, since meanings are more highly circumscribed within apparently very fixed categories. The value of this approach lies in the instant recognizability of a stereotype, its apparently widespread yet culturally specific manifestation, and the extreme and caricatured way in which it draws on commonly-held impressions and assumptions.

As a particular gender representation, the dumb blonde stereotype[9] is useful for its incorporation of character traits and visual characteristics. Examples would be Marilyn Monroe, Judy

Holliday, Jayne Mansfield and Barbara Windsor but the image is not, of course, necessarily attached to a star persona. One of the features of the stereotype is that it makes anonymous actors/ characters recognizable.

1   Composing a list of characteristics of the dumb blonde type

In order to go beyond just discussing 'what' a dumb blonde is in general terms, we can begin by analysing the *constituent elements* and how they are organized in one particular example. (Different versions might stress different aspects, providing a formulation far from other versions.) One might arrive at a list such as this:

strange logic
innocence and naivety
manipulativeness
humour
blondeness and other characteristics which emphasize the body
childlike nature
adult 'knowingness' and seductiveness.

2   Which characteristics change and which remain the same?

One can then point out how a particular representation appears to contain *contradictory* elements: both child and adult, innocent and manipulative. How can they appear to co-exist so naturally? Such a line of enquiry leads us into searching out elements which are *repeated* in order for the stereotype to be instantly recognizable and how the combination and selection of elements *differ* in different representations. These enquiries concern the way images work as a series of conventions. There is always a pattern of *similarity* (characteristics such as heavy make-up and curvaceous figure, signifying, through their conventional use, glamour and sexuality) and *difference* (in some cases, a spectacular display of sexuality may be seen as enjoyable exhibitionism and sensuality while in others it may be seen as crude, grotesque, socially inappropriate or unpleasantly 'voracious').

3   Which characteristics describe and which make judgements?

What else is signified by the combination of characteristics? What tells us that any particular character is 'dumb'? Aspects of behaviour, visual appearance, physical presentation and dialogue are combined in ways that comment on the character's femininity. While 'blonde' serves to describe the stereotype, 'dumb' makes a judgement. This serves to regulate the ways in which women can be seen to 'succeed' or attract approval. Characteristics such as movements over-emphasizing the body are considered negative according to one criterion (low expectations of intellectual ability) but positive according to another (increased sexual allure) and so set the agenda for feminine identity. The ways in which 'dumbness' is suggested in some versions of the type extends beyond an assessment of intelligence to *define* femininity.

The following categories serve as examples, along with judgements that can be ascribed to them:

Childlike	*Inappropriate*	*Unconventional*
High or breathy voice, rounded face, wide eyes; deliberate, self-conscious or awkward movements; naive responses, lack of concentration, an emphasis on 'fun' and 'play'; irresponsibility and emotional indulgence.	Behaviour or appearance showing 'inability' to grasp (or refusal to obey?) rules of conventional (particularly middle-class) social contact. Includes over-dressing, unrestrained voice (volume/pitch) or especially 'excessive' laughter.	Unusual forms of logic, exaggerated gestures, unexpected responses; characteristics, behaviour and desires which do not concur with feminine roles; emphasizing a unique individuality.

Childlike qualities may signify 'acceptable innocence' in the dumb blonde but the suggestion that this is natural helps the dumb blonde to represent sexuality and an uninhibited expression of it at that. They may suggest a passive dependence which fits in with notions of acceptable female sexuality. The dumb blonde remains childlike, it is implied, because the type *has not yet learnt* certain rules of behaviour. The type is incomplete, open to being formed by one who can impose norms and 'fill up' this empty vessel, a role conventionally played by a male character who is mature, learned, streetwise or just plain determined.

Inappropriate behaviour, often associated with class difference, implies an unfamiliarity with conventions of femininity, exclusion from situations where conventions have to be obeyed or inclusion in cultures where other rules are learned. While childlike qualities can be seen as endearing, inappropriate qualities alternatively invoke disapproval, ridicule or simply embarrassment.

The type, then, is a site for replaying *differences* in social groups, but from a certain perspective, one which does not admit that legitimacy is socially organized and conventions variable, one that includes and excludes according to the authority of social norms. It is a perspective which therefore denies credibility to alternative characteristics, identities or forms of behaviour. This version of the type is judged and found wanting according to modes of acceptable femininity.

The line between inappropriate and the third category, *unconventional*, is blurred but it can be drawn according to the degree to which 'knowingness' and 'idiosyncrasy' are emphasized. How far are the unconventional elements seen as accidentally out of step or knowingly and wantonly different? While 'inappropriate' suggests acceptance of the conventions but a lack of agility in adapting to them, 'unconventional' indicates a challenge to those conventions. Does this version of the type refuse to conform to the system that defines what *is* conventional, thus redefining how it is to be understood? Finally on this point, we might ask why qualities considered unconventional overlap with those considered inappropriate?

4   Which characteristics are ambiguous?

Unearthing ambiguity in the dumb blonde stereotype is, as with all types, a key area for discussion. Not only does it allow us to ask if she is *really* dumb but also to discuss what we make of her at all. Stereotypes may be instantly recognizable, but they contain ambiguous and contradictory signs. The way in which ambiguity works in an individual star image or character persona allows us to investigate the range of different readings available.

Some signs refer not only to conventional notions of intelligence/dumbness but also to what is judged appropriate and acceptable feminine behaviour according to sexual, class and ethnic expectation. Mask-like make-up, for instance, can simultaneously suggest vacancy and cluelessness, glamour and attractiveness, as well as a certain class position through connotations of brashness and overt sexuality. It may equally well suggest a deliberate refusal to be accessible, as in more recent stars such as Annie Lennox and

Madonna, their resistance to definition implying an inscrutable impenetrability. The same questions could be asked about how we recognize the signs of glamour, how blondeness is used (not least in helping to define acceptable sexuality as white) and how relationships to men are characterized. 'Masculinity' serves to 'complement' the passive and unassertive function assigned to female characters whose acceptance of conventional standards may be ambivalent and in need of clarification by this sexualized relation.

5   Investigating variations of the type

Many representations do not fall neatly into the dumb blonde category. Actresses like Cybil Shepherd, Jamie Lee Curtis and Jessina Lange accentuate blondeness without dumbness. While these stars incorporate some elements of the stereotype, still other stars and characters upset the meanings associated with the dumb blonde. Doris Day's wisecracking and emotional excesses of anger or frustration and the maternal characteristics of *Dynasty*'s Krystle Carrington tip the balance away from seeing them as solely objects of sexual desire. Some types may be given an active role in a narrative or be set within forms such as the 'realist' soap opera that do not offer space for spectacular objects of desire, e.g. Bet Lynch in *Coronation Street*. Diana Dors, Dolly Parton and other parodies of the type exploit visual enjoyment and control narratives through their use of comedy.

When intelligence is added as a characteristic that *opposes* the terms of 'dumbness', the remaining elements function differently. So Jessica Lange's wide open smile, blondeness and nervy wriggle suggest a kind of frank and childlike (unrestrained) enjoyment of her sexuality which do not undermine her intellect. Such qualities refer less to her body as object of display than to a sense of energy and physicality which connects to an abstract and less passive image of sexual promise. With actors such as Cybil Shepherd and Jamie Lee Curtis, the tension between the glamour of blondeness and the determination and resourcefulness that are part of their personae lead to their narrative activity as well as their visual fascination. Christine Cagney in *Cagney and Lacey* provides another example of this tension but with a different emphasis. Her blondeness tends to 'soften' her capable, streetwise cop character and signifies an aspect of femininity different from the 'glamorous' image.

Detailed textual analysis of a particular representation will discover how it is both similar to and different from the *repeated* model.[10] This allows us to get at the relation of elements in the categories outlined in 3 above: how our judgements and responses are influenced by what happens to the character; how the character relates to the structure of conflict in the narrative; how it differs from other characters; how it is looked at by them and the camera; how it may offer the realization of other characters' desires or act on its own.

6   Explore how the type has changed over time

Are there elements or assumptions found in the stereotype which could help to describe more contemporary, even more (apparently) 'liberated' images of women? Can studying the dumb blonde stereotype give us knowledge about the way femininity is constructed that could help us analyse the power of feminine images? For instance, are there elements of visual appearance, character traits, narrative function, etc. in Figures 6.1 and 6.2 which correspond to notions of femininity raised by the dumb blonde stereotype? In what ways do they rework dominant images of spectacular sexuality? To what extent do they call up different expectations and understandings of female self-definition?

It is not simply that different images of women 'escape' the stereotype but that, in their combination of typical with untypical elements, they change the terms according to which they can be understood. How, for instance, do these images also call up our knowledge of other female types and other social categories? The article these two images accompanied labelled them 'The Stylist and the Girl Next Door', drawing on contrasting feminine representations that imply different class contexts and different expectations of their accessibility. The girl next door, it is implied, fits into one's everyday experience – always available, but ordinary – while the stylist is an exotic fantasy image to be desired from a distance. The different styles of publicity photo draw this out. Diahann Carroll is starkly lit, hard-edged and brilliant-surfaced, set against an anonymous studio background, whereas Susan Tully is softly lit and focused, blended in to an unobtrusive but recognizable background.

Contrasts between the genres in which each of their images more usually appear also illustrate the differences. Carroll's high-gloss

Figure 6.1 Diahann Carroll.

exoticism emanates from *Dynasty*, a soap opera based on melodramatically-charged narratives of conflict and power among the 'flaunt-it' super-rich, with confrontation expressed in moments of visual spectacle linking the sexual to other forms of power. Tully's image is coded according to the demands of social realism which inform *EastEnders*, the attempt to represent the 'ordinary' through

Figure 6.2   Susan Tully.

subject matter, dialogue, character and visual appearances. As such, Tully's image is given a more 'natural' look – a less ornate hairstyle, no visible make-up, little jewellery and everyday clothes made from inexpensive materials; street fashions rather than couture style. Her pose and expression are also less studied, giving an impression of being 'caught' by the camera rather than arranged before it.

These are very different representations of femininity, both breaking with conventions of the stereotype of glamorous sexuality. Neither is blonde: Figure 6.1 in order to become the 'first black bitch on TV', Figure 6.2 in order to maintain an opposition to 'the exceptional'. The generic contexts in which they are set give us a different relation to them: we *use* them in different ways, connect them to different parts of our social experience and personal identities.

7   Other representations of femininity

How are other images of women different from those of sexual desirability? If some images of women do not stress sexuality, what do they stress? How wide is the range of images by which women are understood? How do expectations concerning femininity change according to age, race and class? (Figure 6.3)

Notice that there are similarities in the characteristics of roles played by women even where visual display is not so accentuated (e.g. the characteristics of motherhood common to Sue Ellen

Figure 6.3   Coronation Street women.

in *Dallas*, Bet Lynch in *Coronation Street* and Sheila Grant in *Brookside*). How are those characteristics shown differently in images of Princess Di or mother-types used in advertisements? The way in which other categories such as class or race might alter the way women are represented in particular roles needs to be brought in here.

Having looked at types like the dumb blonde and other popular images, we can analyse images of women that seem more ambiguous in their meaning (Figure 6.4).

Figure 6.4   Still from *Images and Blacks*.

How do we make sense of an image such as this? With the limited information we are given visually, we struggle to 'place' the figure securely in a gender category. We can talk about the colour of skin and hair, length and style of hair, lack of make-up, expression, and also background, lighting, the look at the camera, close-up framing. Other factors stressed by the image might raise different expectations of the kind of person this may be and why the photograph was taken. Potential narratives build up around the event of the photo, the making of the image, partly because of the lack of clarity over its codes and conventions and partly because it is an isolated image, separated from the context in which it might be found. The combination of these factors may make us less certain of the figure's gender than its race. For some audiences, the signs of gender differentiation might be organized in unfamiliar ways or signalled less strongly through photographic codes stressing meanings which are not so common in the conventional representation of women. If members of a group have more knowledge of the cultural signs deployed, it would be useful to tease them out. How does this image 'speak' to different people in different ways?

8   The audience

It is useful to assemble a variety of images than enable work to be done on different cultural identities. How do we know what those identities are? Do we recognize ourselves in any of them? Do they offer pleasure to us? Why?

To avoid repetition, use a range of activities deploying different skills and knowledges, drawing out contrasts in genres (news, soap opera, game shows), media (television, film, magazines, advertising) and audience/address (taking magazines for women or men and looking at the different female/male audience implied). Even products for a specific age range (e.g. comics for girls or boys) demonstrate different subject matter, treatment and presumed interest while assuming similarities in the identities of the audience they address. *Selling Pictures*[11] includes a number of exercises and materials of this kind, raising 'questions about audiences for images' using women's magazine covers, showing 'the *narrow range* of ways in which these magazines appeal to women's images, concerns and self-images, *how* the magazine covers construct the particular and limited appeals they make', looking at the similarities of their appeals and the differences of detail between images.

It is a cliché that men are found furtively reading women's magazines. To explore the ways in which one group might enjoy a representation intended for another unearths processes of identification and positioning that initially appear so difficult to talk about. What do different members of the class 'tune into' with one particular magazine? Perhaps the range of answers will show that pleasure is not dictated by the text but is a contract between what the text offers and what we want. This tells us at least something about the difficulties of maintaining a coherent 'image' in the face of the numerous ways we are invited to enjoy varying forms. It also suggests that representations imply a use, or a series of uses, rather than a concrete audience.

Alternatives

Alternative forms of representation might be brought into the classroom to present different images and provide different forms of engagement, pleasure and meaning. Studying alternative and less widely circulated media texts helps to re-pose questions concerning how identities are understood. Alternative media products show up just how 'learned' are our familiarities and expectations. They encourage us to look at what is included and excluded in dominant representations, and at what representations are marginalized. Exercises which show up the restricted range of possibilities imply that *others* are possible.

The choice of study objects could be made from those alternative media which address issues particularly relevant to the teaching and groups involved. Those films or videos made *by* groups of young people *for* young people which speak of their own experiences provide an address and engagement not found in television programming or feature film production. They pose questions about how they are different from other forms of representation even while perhaps adopting some elements from mainstream forms.

Taking on the category 'youth' can bring in a number of associated questions and break down the assumptions that 'youth' is a fixed and heterogeneous category. Videos[12] like *Us Girls*, *1 in 44* and *Girl Zone* deal specifically with issues of gender and youth. The first two consider how the options open to girls also depend on class and education and influence work, home, leisure and relationships. *Girl Zone* deals not only with assumptions about girls but 'what girls want'. *Framed Youth* explores gay identity and experience, countering the stereotyped assumptions often made about gays with images that defy heterogeneous descriptions and their categorization as a 'social problem', instead asserting diversity and exploring the pleasures and passions of gay relationships. *Giro – Is this the Modern World?* raises questions about how unemployment affects young people and how they deal with its effects, countering the assumptions behind the conventional image of 'unemployed youth'. *MsTaken Identity* shows how adult attitudes to young women influence the way their identities can be expressed and explored. It attempts to counter the limited representations of young black women ('You hardly ever see black people enjoying themselves on television . . . if you see them they're shown rioting . . . as problems . . . or in other countries') by constructing their own representations through sketches, song and dance, filming themselves doing the things they like to do and talking about them together.

The variations in the way young people represent themselves in this small selection cross other social categories and form new images with different signs and meanings. These representations show how far definitions remain open to change even while they maintain dominance. They may provide a space to allow students to think about ways they want themselves represented and defined.

Practical media work, including students' own production, is *part* of this kind of study rather than a separate activity. Together, this range of activities is designed to stimulate students to define meanings and express their own engagements, to re-order their experiences according to a new framework for thinking: active, critical and *transforming*.

PEDAGOGY

A certain pedagogy ties in with the understanding of representation I have outlined, one that allows us to consider the *range* of meanings any representation offers, the limitations to this range and what this indicates about commonly-held ideas and attitudes, how these are offered and how we come to make sense of what is being said. At each point connections should be made with 'common sense' or dominant ideas and definitions about 'how things are' and the way social relations are organized.

This pedagogy asks pupils and students to examine what 'common sense' is, how ideas about who we are and what the world is like are composed and ordered into a certain view of reality. And it asks how *we* are placed within this view, how our different positions might influence the ideas and assumptions we make. This ties in with how we might react to media representations, how different audiences make different kinds of sense of them, take up a different set of meanings from the range on offer, bringing different knowledges and experiences to them. It also proposes that our reactions to certain representations contain various elements, some of which we may want to work against, and others which we may wish to hold on to and use in defining our own demands, needs or pleasures. Discussion of these responses should be directed as an *approach* to cultural knowledge and the media. Responses become *material* for learning rather than the outcome of discussion. It is important that students and pupils are aware of this as we are asking them to take risks in offering responses in this way. It is one of the pleasures and problems of Media Studies that discussion can be lively and engaged because people are used to discussing media such as television, music, films and perhaps also magazines and adverts. But how to deal with views and responses once they are out in the open is a tricky area.

Once we recognize that representations have no final meaning, no 'answer' to the questions of what they mean, then no one response is 'better' than another. All have to be understood. This means we do not ask students to guess at what we want them to say – the 'right' answer. It is up to us to respond to each observation they make, grouping responses together and making connections between them. Considering the delicacy of this activity, it is important not to set up students to be criticized, not to lure them into saying something we can hold up as a pernicious, illogical or offensive belief. They are hardly likely to change their minds if this happens. To avoid hardening attitudes of students on the defensive, it is important to jettison evaluative notions such as good or bad. I would also avoid confronting students with accusations of sexism and racism, preferring to ask them to examine how they come to hold such ideas, what social groups hold them and why it might be in their interest that such ideas are held or devised and, very importantly, what other points of view may provide different readings to their own. A class made up of a range of social groups might offer alternative opinions, requiring the teacher to ask (or point out) what the significance of each of the contributions is to understanding how meaning is organized.

The important point is not to force students into positions they feel compelled to defend and not to crash down on them from the height of superior knowledge because they got it 'wrong'. It is a different matter when they crash down on each other, however. My solution is to let those whose racist or sexist comments have incurred opposition feel the weight for a bit and then defuse it so they have a chance to examine it less personally in the light of such resistance. If those wielding sexist or racist comments have the upper hand, then obviously the weight needs to be lifted by focusing upon the inflammatory comments.

Using specific representations allows us to examine the way knowledge and ideas are produced rather than what they are and if they are right or wrong. Looking at how we are *encouraged* to think leads us to examine ideas we may or may not hold, analysing how they are constructed, what they include and leave out and how they intervene in forming our beliefs. Through this procedure, it can be shown how it is possible to adopt commonly held beliefs while also showing that this is not the whole story (and how the rights of certain groups to express their points of view and be understood may be damaged). Instead of assuming those who do not hold them are simply foolish, it suggests we think around them and 'place' them in a wider context, showing them as incomplete, with vested interests, denying the places of others and countering them with other ideas that may, in effect, break them apart. The teacher's role is to begin such a process of scrutiny.

NOTES

This chapter was written in 1986 and updated in 1989.

1 Richard Dyer, 'Taking popular television seriously' in David Lusted and Phillip Drummond (eds) *TV and Schooling* (London: BFI, 1985), pp. 44–5.
2 ibid., p. 41.
3 Cary Bazalgette, Jim Cook and Andy Medhurst, *Teaching TV Sitcom* (London: BFI, 1985) is a teaching pack containing notes and slides. An accompanying video tape of a compilation of extracts is available for hire from the BFI Film and Video Library.
4 *Genre Recognition* is a component of *The Western Project*, one of many slide sets available from BFI Publications. Other BFI slide sets include *Narrative*, *Film Noir*, and *Genre*: teaching packs such as *Teaching Coronation Street* and *Hammer Horror* could also be used. I suggest using these slide sets selectively. They can be repetitious if used 'en bloc' and some are more useful than others. It is also interesting to compose a set from a number of different packs, perhaps also from those dealing with other questions apart from genre.
5 Using the description of the continuity system in David Bordwell and Kristin Thompson, *Film Art: An Introduction* (Berkshire: Addison-Wesley, 1979) or David Bordwell, Janet Staiger and Kristin Thompson, *The Classical Hollywood Cinema* (London: Routledge & Kegan Paul, 1985), one could select a number of slides from various film title sets or use the *Narrative* teaching pack (all BFI).

6 See Richard Dyer, *Stars* (London: BFI, 1979) or the teaching booklet *Star Signs* (London: BFI, 1982).

7 Gill Branston, *Film and Gender* (London: Film Education, 1986).

8 From the perspective offered in our culture, sexuality is seen as a collection of inherent urges and desires culminating in the playing out of physical and therefore 'natural' acts. By this sleight of hand the social organization of these relations are endorsed as absolute and unchanging rather than specific to certain cultures in certain places at certain times.

9 For this section I have drawn on the material available in Richard Dyer, *The Dumb Blonde Stereotype* (London: BFI, 1979) and the student notes for the Stars Module of *Popular Culture*, Open University (second level) course U203 Notes (Milton Keynes: Open University Press, 1981). Also relevant is *Star Dossier One: Marilyn Monroe* (London: BFI, 1983) and Richard Dyer, *Heavenly Bodies* (London: Macmillan, 1986) contains a recent update of Dyer's position on Monroe.

10 See Steve Neale, 'The same old story', *Screen Education* 32/33, Autumn/Winter 1979/80, for a discussion of the problems of over-emphasizing similarities in stereotypes at the expense of differences between them.

11 *Selling Pictures*, a teaching pack about representation and stereotyping (London: BFI, 1983).

12 *Us Girls* (Albany Video, 1979); *1 in 44* (Nottingham Youth Theatre, 1983); *Girl Zone* (Birmingham Film and Video Workshop, 1986); *Framed Youth* (Lesbian and Gay Youth Video Project, 1983); *Giro – Is this the Modern World?* (Birmingham Film and Video Workshop/Dead Honest Soul Searchers, 1985); *Ms Taken Identity* (Albany Video, 1985), all available from Albany Video, Douglas Way, London SE8 4AG.

Chapter 7

The production process

Jenny Grahame

The fourth-year English group cluster expectantly around the TV monitor awaiting playback of a soap opera episode they scripted and performed over the last six lessons. To their horror, they discover that in audio-dubbing their sound-track, someone has managed to erase the final cliff-hanging sequence; or that poor lighting conditions have plunged their carefully-dressed set into a pea-souper fog; or that the running battle for director's role has resulted in barely twenty seconds of completed video. And the results of this scenario – all too familiar to teachers working with students in video production – meet an inevitable response from colleagues: 'You mean it took them four double periods to produce *that*?' or 'I'm sure they *learned* a lot, but I'm not quite sure what . . .'or 'It's not like real telly, is it?', culminating in the real killer, 'Wouldn't it be a lot easier just to *write* about *EastEnders* instead?'

Well, frankly, as most Media Studies teachers would agree, it would. But would writing be enough? Despite the daunting array of logistical, institutional and technical obstacles to worthwhile classroom production work, many teachers now believe that a media education curriculum based on analytical study alone is *not* enough. They argue that hands-on experience of the production process is essential if students are to understand and question the forms through which the media produce meaning and the ways in which those meanings are understood. A re-evaluation of the status and methodology of practical production work is long overdue.

No neat solutions will be provided here. What will be attempted is a brief outline of some of the pedagogical debates which have underpinned (and sometimes undermined) production work in schools, together with a tentative rationale for a structured production curriculum. Three key issues are addressed: methodology, organization and evaluation. In other words, what such a curriculum might look like; how it might function within the everyday constraints of the real classroom; some possible survival strategies; what 'works', who learns what, and what the wider implications of that learning are. Finally, it is also useful to raise questions about the place of production work within and across the formal and informal curriculum, in relation to similar work in other educational sectors, to other institutions and to the wider community.

What is meant by 'the production process'? It implies a single integrated procedure focusing on and resulting in a finished product. But in a classroom end results are rarely 'finished' tidily or purposefully. Any practical activity involves a great many learning objectives, skills and outcomes, and frequently what is learned through the process of production is far more important than the end–product itself. So it describes here any exercise which actively engages students in the process of producing meaning through sound and image. It will refer mainly to video activities, since developments in video technology have increased the accessibility and use of video in schools, extending its flexibility as a medium to incorporate many of the formal properties of film and photography. The term 'production' will cover a diverse range of activities: from image analysis using closed–circuit TV to teacher-directed deconstruction exercises or to the manipulation of extracts from broadcast TV through the structured production of short narrative or documentary extracts using a single video camera. It will also extend to increasingly complex and sophisticated pupil-directed projects employing a variety of technical processes and skills and resulting in fully-fledged programmes within specific genres and for specific audiences. While not denying the function of the end product (of which more later on), the emphasis here is on producing *meanings* rather than products. The *process* of media production must be seen as a discipline in itself, integral to, and shaped by, its theoretical context.

What should students be producing? Why? And how? Where might such work be located on the timetable, and how might it relate to other institutionalized production activities such as the recording of the school play, the production of teaching tapes or the promotional video for the Parents Association? By what criteria should this work be evaluated? What conceptual, analytic or technical skills can be realistically developed? And how, and by whom, should these skills be prioritized and assessed? These questions are worth raising because they tend in practice to be answered arbitrarily according to the needs and limitations of particular situations, the resources available and the expertise and confidence of particular teachers. Sadly, such questions are all too often a luxury when set against the very real logistical difficulties in devising a range of activities to engage constructively twenty-four fourth years (or even sixteen extra-mural students) with a single video camera and a fifty-minute lesson.

Production work suffers from a general lack of status, shared experience and critical writing.[1] Since it is relatively new in schools, little attention has been given to the construction and establishment of a practical curriculum. The result is a lack of consensus about the objectives, functions and purposes of practical production work. My suggestions are tentative, therefore, raising issues rather than offering solutions.

'I'm sure they learned a lot, but I'm not quite sure what'

The increasing accessibility of domestic film and video equipment has significantly advanced the technical quality of work produced by young people in schools and colleges, but the pedagogic basis of that work has not always been clearly defined. Bob Ferguson[2] describes how video has been variously exploited to motivate alienated under-achievers, to extend self-expression and to develop individual creativity as ends in themselves. Such work tends to mystify, to reinforce rather than challenge dominant media forms and confirm for students their technical and aesthetic inadequacies. Ironically enough, the emphasis on personal experience that characterizes so much pastoral and pre-vocational education actually reifies the experience at the expense of the learning that comes from experience. Far from developing skills in making meaning and understanding how one has done it, these approaches have, perhaps unintentionally, contributed to the undervaluing of both the work and its producers.

Film and video production in schools is also widely used (in Humanities or English teaching, or in youth work, for example) to open up social or political themes: gender, racism, images of youth, environmental issues, etc. These content-based approaches to production are almost invariably confounded by students' reliance on conventional media forms and techniques which are difficult to reproduce given their limited skills, experience and technology.

Stuart Hall, from a specifically anti–racist perspective, argues for the radical implications of the production process for students:

> it is important to get people into producing their own images because ... they can then contrast the images they produce of themselves against the dominant images which they are offered, and so they know that social communication is a matter of conflict between alternative readings of society.[3]

But without a full understanding of the forms, the institutions which produce them and the meanings they generate, the political or subversive potential of production cannot be fully exploited.

Another tendency in practical media teaching has been to concentrate on the technical skills of production. This 'How To Do It' approach argues that only through emulating, and failing to achieve, professional practice can students fully understand the complexity of media production. Recently this view has developed a more vocational bias, paralleling the growth of the new 16+ B. Tec and City and Guilds courses and capitalizing on the generous resourcing offered by local authorities for TVEI (Technical and Vocational Educational Initiative) schemes. The acquisition of sophisticated equipment and the opportunity to challenge and explore its uses in professional broadcasting offers enormous potential for media educationalists. But this potential may not always be fully tapped by pre-vocational courses and tasters more concerned with technical and skills–orientated instruction than a wider definition of production.

From a more radical pedagogical perspective, Bob Ferguson argues persuasively for deconstruction exercises in manipulating, reconstructing and ultimately challenging familiar media conventions and techniques, in consciously breaking the conventional rules to question the meanings they produce and to develop the ability to produce other meanings. Clearly these exercises can have little value unless they are integrally related to study of the professional practices and institutions which they subvert. Alone, they offer no rationale for production. Since classroom production is in any case undertaken under very different institutional conditions from professional practice, a concentration on rule-breaking and deconstruction may prove sterile and over-theoretical. Indeed, over-emphasis on such exercises can inhibit and demotivate students from developing and constructing their own meanings and conventions. Nevertheless, the approach does suggest a more clearly defined function for production work as a vehicle for analysis and interrogation, and a firm commitment to a structure and methodology closely linked to the theory it embodies.

'Wouldn't it be a lot easier just to write about "EastEnders" instead?'

Practice and theory are complementary and interrelated. All production activity must be informed by specific theoretical concepts and theory can only be fully understood in relation to specific media practices and through practical application. Students can be taught theoretically about, say, the nature of mediation in TV news film. They can explore the concept through close viewing and analysis of voice-overs, edits, juxtaposition of images, and so on. But so prevalent and deep-rooted is the myth of the news as transparent, as immediate reality, that for many students it will continue to be experienced as 'the truth', the way things really are, *until* they participate in their own news selection, shooting and commentary-production. But here lies the first major caution. If media education is ultimately about how meanings are constructed and understood, then production work must actively extend students' understanding of the ways those meanings are generated as well as their ability to construct alternatives. But what sort of production activities will enable analysis of forms, conventions and institutions without merely replicating, reinforcing and internalizing the very meanings they should be questioning? Won't their own news bulletins merely join the 'endless wilderness of third-rate imitative "pop"-shows, embarrassing video dramas and derivative documentaries' pessimistically predicted by Len Masterman?[5]

I would say no: not if production is fully integrated at every level of a media course and structured developmentally with the same rigorous objectives as the theoretical concepts it explores. The study of news values and mediation need not involve producing a full-scale news bulletin. It may be far more effective and manageable to employ a range of short exercises such as audio-dubbing alternative commentaries over pre-recorded newsreel, or attempting to extract thirty seconds of newsworthy material from a longer interview, or filming a news interview from unconventional angles. These are very specific and limited processes which are an integral part of the lesson rather than a specialized, separate activity. Obviously such exercises require particular technical skills, but if these too are developed over a period of time and gradually increase familiarity with equipment, the technology will become more accessible, less controlling and an accepted tool of learning. If, as it can and should be, practice is implicit, valued and integrated throughout an entire curriculum, it will acquire the status of a formal discipline with its own methodology, skills, and organizing principles – a discipline it has long lacked and desperately needs.

'It's not like real telly, is it?'

The first obstacle to useful practical work is the technology: unfamiliar, shrouded in a mystique of professionalism, marketed by the media industry as a leisure/pleasure facility and unlikely to be initially perceived by students (nor, alas, colleagues) as material for a serious and structured discipline. Add the teachers' apparent lack of expertise, the potential unreliability (not to mention health and safety hazards!) of their equipment, as well, of course, as the inevitable comparisons between the embarrassingly amateur product of the classroom and the glossy production values of professional broadcasting, and the problems can seem insurmountable.

However much we may resist the mystifications of the 'high-tech' media industries, we do react to an end–product which doesn't look like 'real telly'. By its very nature, the technical quality of classroom production work is very different from professional production. This must be accepted as the first principle of a production methodology. Paradoxically, this apparent limitation can be put to use to define manageable tasks appropriate to the medium, specific learning objectives and the needs and abilities of the students. It's neither feasible nor desirable for the fourth-year English group to reproduce a look-alike *Dynasty* for its case study on soap opera; neither the resources nor the skills are available. But a structured exercise around the single scene which examines formal properties, camera conventions or significant objects is both achievable and appropriate for analysis, particularly when students are introduced to the technology through a series of controlled activities which explore its limitations as fully as its potential. This may not at first placate those students who resent and resist the tight structure imposed on activities they normally associate with entertainment and freedom of choice. But if working conditions are discussed and negotiated, and the future development of the work made clear, most pupils will accept, and eventually value, a disciplined framework for their learning.

A second principle related to classroom technology concerns expertise and the status of those who have it. Many pupils will bring to the classroom considerable out-of-school experience of video equipment and will handle it with considerably more confidence and skill than their teacher. This offers the potential for democratic collaboration, allowing pupils' own expertise to be shared, valued and given status, and the teacher's role to be reinterpreted as facilitator, negotiator or student rather than omniscient authority. Thus, while it's a teacher's responsibility to become as familiar and fluent with the technology as the pupils (perfectly possible given a weekend at home playing with 'the gear' and discovering its pitfalls), lack of expertise should never be concealed and in fact be exploited positively in co-operative, non-hierarchical learning activities.

Co-operation must be a central feature of production methodology, not only for its pedagogic value,[6] but also for the very obvious reason that all media products are defined and constructed by groups rather than individuals. Collaboration and teamwork require a commitment and discipline which may not come naturally to students whose learning experience has been primarily individualized and teacher-led. Group decision-making, negotiation, and role-allocation all need to be learned and developed as rigorously as analytic and technical skills. Collaboration then becomes an organizing focus for a production methodology. Students can start in pairs working on simple visual image exercises, moving into larger groups with more clearly differentiated roles and relationships for more complex activities and simulations, before attempting open-ended and self-determined projects. The experience of failure can in itself be a productive learning process. For example, a narrative sequence abandoned in chaos because individuals have been unable to negotiate an ending, or an incomplete interview rendered unintelligible because of disagreement between director and camera operator can raise valuable questions about industrial organization and professional codes. But for any exercise to be effective, the group dynamic must allow for constructive criticism and evaluation. An appropriate classroom ethos must be developed.

A further priority for a production methodology is for pupils to evaluate and make explicit what they learn, how they learn it, and how that learning relates both to classroom theory and their own media use. Again, a series of skills must be learned. Pupils may rely heavily on teacher assessment initially. They may find it hard to be objective about processes in which they have engaged so actively and which compare so apparently unfavourably with professional practices. There will almost certainly be resistance to writing up experiences and processes which they consider self-explanatory. The discipline of pre-planning, story-boarding (outlining in visual shorthand exactly what each shot will involve) and scripting for each assignment needs to be explained from the start. Verbal and written analysis must be established as routine elements of production work. The filing of rough notes, story-boards and detailed records will allow pupils to build up a dossier which will become increasingly valued as a record of their learning and progress. Written work which documents decision-making processes, accounts for failed or non-existent end-products and relates their own experiences to more general media concepts will also reinforce the status of production work as serious, valued and as valid as more conventional classroom study as well as being 'fun'. Written work will also form the basis of examinable folder work for those courses which require it.

So far, this outline methodology has been about limitations – of technology, expertise, ability, the pupils' capacity for classroom interaction – and strategies for using them productively within a structured discipline. But what might this discipline actually look like?

MAKING PRODUCTION INTO A DISCIPLINE

The suggestions that follow are skeletal and non-specific, to be developed or amended to meet differing contexts and curriculum requirements. They might be the organizing focus of a two-year Media Studies course or equally the concentrated core of a half-term's work in the English Department or a TVEI module. The outline assumes minimal resources and no expertise. Most activities are designed for use with a single video camera, no editing facilities, classroom support or studio area and no special timetabling requirements. They rely mainly on in-camera editing (shooting in sequence to avoid post-production editing), partly to minimize the constraints described above but also because the technique requires rigorous planning and thus imposes a control on pupils' work. Similarly, the early exercises deliberately avoid dramatic action or performance skills which can distract from, and sabotage the process of, constructing meaning. Drama techniques may be exploited later or in more open-ended projects.

Schools fortunate enough to own TV studio set-ups or editing facilities possess potentially invaluable resources. I emphasize 'potentially' because the mystique, sophistication and status of such technology can pose as many problems as it solves. Access to a two- or three-camera studio, vision mixer and sound deck offers students an experience of programme-making which engages them fully in every aspect of industrial production. It can also result in productions of an extremely high standard which may reproduce and exploit techniques of professional broadcasting most effectively – a real asset where audiences are concerned. But it can equally divert attention away from the concepts it illuminates; it can intimidate and deter potential producers who perceive themselves as 'un-technical'; it can lead to an emphasis on 'how it's done' rather than 'what it means and why it's done that way'. For these reasons, I strongly recommend very cautious induction and a developmental approach to studio work through a series of controlled exercises, until pupils have experienced the discipline and methodology imposed by single-camera exercises, no matter how tempting it may be to launch straight in.

Image-reading exercises – whole-group work on selection and visual ambiguity

Exercises in decoding, selecting and reconstructing visual images form the base-line of every media course. A closed-circuit video set-up is ideal for a series of brief, discrete camera exercises which are non-threatening for students, require minimal resources – a range of magazine adverts, news images, contact sheets, everyday objects – and help reduce teacher wear-and-tear. This set-up also allows individuals to take turns with the equipment, enabling them to acquire basic camera skills and to experiment with the effects of angle, framing, focus and cropping, which are simultaneously observed and discussed by the rest of the group.

Anchoring and encoding meaning

Pairs of pupils might then juxtapose, sequence and record a series of pre-selected images to anchor them to a particular context, theme or issue. Meanwhile, others might be logging the effects of their choices before going on to select a sound-track or scripting a voice-over to reinterpret the meaning of their sequence. Others might go on to a worksheet constructed to enable them to articulate and evaluate what they have learned. Each exercise might last as little as ten minutes, result in less than two minutes of recorded images and alternate with more conventional writing tasks. Evaluation and discussion are emphasized at every stage; brevity, diversity and controlled objectives will help to demystify the technology and break down pupils' assumptions that production work is in itself specialist and separable from other aspects of their learning. The emphasis will be on their own selection processes and the range of meanings they have constructed.

Image, text and context

As a follow-up, simple small-group exercises involving the manipulation and anchorage of still images with sound can be used to introduce and explore central concepts. Issues of representation, for example, might be raised through the construction of a commercial from a limited range of magazine images and recorded sound-tracks for a particular product and target market specified by the teacher; perfume and soft drink adverts are particularly useful subjects for examinations of gender and youth respectively. News photographs anchored by alternative voice-over commentaries can be used in a similar way to represent differing views of a particular news issue, or images sequenced and captioned to reinterpret key events of a particular year. Similar work around narrative structure might involve the amended use of available teaching materials,[7] recording the images onto video with synchronized sound-tracks. Alternatively, other exercises based on the same materials might examine the significance of visual codes, concentrating particularly on the conventions of chronology or suspense through camera techniques such as the fade to black, the dissolve, or the time allocated to particular images. Such activities are not in themselves new or original, relying as they do on tried and tested materials which require little amendment. It could be argued that the concepts involved could be learned just as effectively and with much less hassle using cut–and–stick techniques or worksheets. Yet video offers greater possibilities: of additional facilities such as movement and sound, of actively rather than notionally producing in and for a particular medium, and of end results which can be viewed and evaluated by a group audience.

Visual conventions and the functions of editing

A next step might be towards problem-solving exercises, where groups of pupils are given clearly defined tasks which question the apparently 'natural' visual conventions of TV and film. For example, pupils can be set simple continuity or animation exercises using jump-cuts and single frames to magic people and objects on and off the screen. They might then tackle the deliberately unachievable task of shooting a dramatic dialogue (a soap opera confrontation, perhaps) with a single camera. Or an action sequence (a chase, or an exchange of glances, or the passing of a message) can be filmed unedited with a single camera rather than several to reveal by omission the normally invisible intervention of the editing process. Access to an editing suite allows groups of pupils to experiment on a single series of shots with the effects of resequencing, altered timing or cutaway shots. Such exercises will develop technical skills, and begin to establish a pattern for group collaboration. More importantly, they will develop pupils' understanding and interrogation of the constructed and industrial nature of narrative, however naturalistic. Such activities can then be extended to cover 'actuality'; news footage may be shot and then crash-edited[8] from one recorder to another; interviews can be filmed, reassembled and intercut with 'noddy' shots,[9] to raise questions about the media's tendency to make stories across a range of different factual and fictional forms.

Genres, audiences and industry

Brief and accessible exercises like these lay foundations for the practical application of theoretical concepts. They set an important precedent, developing a greater respect for the processes of production and a less reverent attitude to the end-product. But more sophisticated technical skills, a greater degree of group collaboration and planning, and an increasing sense of audience will be required for areas such as the manufacture of TV news, or the marketing and distribution of film, or the scheduling of advertising which foreground the relationship between industrial practice, big business, and forms of representation. These areas, too, can be examined with minimal resources if coupled with a tightly structured assignment organized through a series of related tasks, clearly defined production roles and realistic expectations. The development of story-boarding skills is particularly useful here in organizing pupils' ideas, objectives and technical skills. The production of a TV or film trailer, for example, might be a vehicle for the analysis of audience expectations of a particular style or genre, for investigation of marketing or scheduling strategies, or for a simulation around the constraints of industrial production. Producing a trailer also offers possibilities for a number of other related practical assignments – poster design, reviews, press releases and publicity interviews, and so on – as long as the production activity itself is controlled by its specific brief, limited by the constraints of the form, and can be achieved with available technology and skills.

Opening scenes, title sequences, advance publicity, continuity segments, single news items – these are structured activities with specific objectives, yet all offer sufficient flexibility for pupils to make informed decisions, negotiate roles, and develop original ideas. The basic premise of this structured approach emphasizes analytic and technical skill rather than the need to produce the perfect product. Production is not seen as an end in itself, but a tool through which students can eventually work in a more open-ended way both to construct their own meaning and become 'active readers' of media texts.

Products, institutions and simulations

This doesn't mean that every exercise should not be completed to the highest possible standards, nor that an end-product isn't desirable. Inevitably, pupils will demand the opportunity to extend their developing technical skills through longer and more complete projects. Equally, work related to concepts of institution and audience can have little validity unless they actually do result in productions shaped by institutional processes for specific audiences. Here, the limitations of equipment and expertise can to some extent be avoided by schematically-organized simulations. While these present certain problems (expecting students to 'be' programme controllers or commissioning editors is unrealistic, not to say absurd), there are benefits to be gained from processes which reflect industrial practices, as well-used print simulations such as *The Front*

Page[10] testify. The pressures and constraints of industrial practices can be effectively explored by producing a three-minute news bulletin with items selected by an editorial team from an incoming flow of pre-determined news stories which are written up, captioned and presented to a strict deadline, or the creation of a thirty-second advert within a tightly controlled budget to a client's brief. It will also result in a complete and satisfying piece of television.

Studio production and industrial practice

With a well-established working group and the additional technological sophistication of a studio facility, the simulation can be taken considerably further. Research, preparation, selection and editing of their *own* news material, with a specific school or community audience in mind, requires little time. Given a longer period of preparation and transmission time, students can also shoot their own TV news footage with appropriate commentary, prepare their own captions and photographs, and explore both the mediating effects of sound and vision mixing as well as the specific roles and interaction of editorial and production teams. On a theoretical level, they will be employing a growing range of analytic skills and concepts to uncover insights into the priorities and values of news selection, and the relationship between information, entertainment, industry and institutions. These are highly complex questions about the nature and function of news and newsworthiness.

On a practical level, work can be structured to employ all the technical skills painstakingly developed through earlier exercises and deconstructions. Most importantly, students will have produced, under industrial conditions, a fully developed product which may be seen and evaluated by an audience for which it was intended. Through this multi-layered learning, they will be confronting in practice the theoretical questions which lie at the heart of media education: Who is producing what and for whom? How is it produced, and whose interests does it serve?

Setting up production work ... and how to survive it

However disciplined its objectives, the methodology outlined above makes light of the daunting array of organizational obstacles to be negotiated in the classroom and it is pointless to underestimate them. However well-resourced and supported, most teachers are likely to be faced with at least one, and probably several, of the following problems: large teaching groups unused to collaborative work; individual pupils with little English or little motivation or large behavioural problems; one working camcorder (if you're lucky); no editing facilities; little or non-existent technical expertise, lack of support or maintenance from a Media Resources Officer or Audio-visual technician; no separate working space, requiring different groups to work at different stages in different corners of the classroom; inflexible time-tabling and lessons which end as soon as the equipment is set up; the constraints of a departmental policy or an exam syllabus which pay lip-service to media work but prefer folders to practical work; unsupportive colleagues who may not be actively hostile but simply don't see the point of production work. And that's just for starters . . .

A conscious methodology should minimize some of these handicaps but it cannot eradicate them. As each school will present its own particular organizational nightmares, I can offer only general, basic strategies which have been found useful in anticipating and avoiding pitfalls.

The function of the following questions is to help design and structure an activity which not only meets desired learning aims but is also achievable. Failed practical work can be productive but, if expectations are too high or the task impossibly demanding, teacher-stress and pupil-disaffection can be extremely unproductive.

Some classroom survival strategies

The survival strategies below represent a pragmatic attempt to work within limitations in a disciplined way, hopefully without undermining pupils' autonomy or skills.

What are the objectives of the exercise?

- Exactly what do you expect/want pupils to learn from the exercise?
- Which concepts/processes/skills do you hope particularly to emphasize?
- Exactly what is its context?

How can the learning best be organized?

- Which production processes are most appropriate/manageable and what skills will students need to employ – e.g. story-boarding/camera skills/performance/direction, etc?
- What working groups will be most effective?
- How can you best exploit and organize available equipment and space?

What will pupils produce?

- Will this be an exercise with an expendable product unlikely to be completed; an ongoing exercise; a simulation; or an open-ended, pupil-directed product, complete in itself?
- Will there be a finished product and what is its status?

For whom are the pupils producing?

- For themselves, in order to compare and record their learning? For a notional target audience (as for a title sequence, advert, trailer, etc.)? For assessment or examination purposes? For a real audience?
- How will the concept of audience shape the task they are set?

By what criteria should the work be assessed?

- How will pupils evaluate their work – written production logs, taped discussion, report-back, presentation on video?
- What steps will you take to ensure that the activity is contextualized, followed up and related to previous analysis?
- What will *you* be looking for when you assess it – and how will you evaluate individual learning and contributions to group products?

Some classroom tips

Know your equipment

- Familiarize yourself and gain confidence with it, if possible over a weekend at home.
- Get to know its limitations (poor light sensitivity, slow telephoto lens or whatever) so you can advise students to work around them.

- Get support from your MRO or technician, mug up on the handbook and experiment.
- Make a checklist of component parts and any necessary accessories (extension lead, charged batteries, double adaptor, etc.).

Construct assignments which bypass problems

For example, avoid dialogue if the microphone is poor, set tasks involving long slow shots if in-camera edits are messy.

Negotiate optimum working conditions

Wherever possible, bargain for:

- double-periods, (always allow for time lost in setting-up and putting away)
- time to organize a classroom in advance, if possible
- secure and accessible storage for equipment
- a light room large enough for different areas of activity (preferably not on the main corridor) with display areas for story-board, photographs and mounted stills
- access to alternative spaces for small-group planning.

Prepare the class

- Ensure pupils have worked through initial excitement/ embarrassment via use of closed-circuit TV beforehand.
- Define their assignment, clarify and explain objectives and working methods, and outline realistic expectations.
- Throughout every activity, encourage pupils to relate experiences to what they've watched and studied, and to articulate what they've learned.

Organize the classroom

- However you may define your own role (advisor? facilitator? crew member? director?), once work has started minimize chaos and maximize participation through rigorous forward planning.
- If appropriate, select groups to accommodate class dynamic or allocate specific production roles to engage pupils at appropriate levels.

- Set each group time limits for the use of equipment and deadlines for different stages of production; stick to them, issuing written timetables if necessary.
- Don't dismiss constructive observation, but always provide a range of ready-prepared follow-up activities, log-keeping or writing tasks to contextualize work and relate it back to theory/analysis. None the less, accede to a limited degree of chaos and warn colleagues accordingly!

Work collaboratively

- Despite strict classroom management, be prepared to admit your own lack of expertise and to validate pupils' own skills and experience by learning with and from them. In redefining your own status, you'll also have the chance of re-evaluating them in the light of unrecognized or previously undervalued skills.

Enlist support

- The more technical, practical and moral support, the better.
- Use people shamelessly, including Head of Department, MRO, technician, support teachers, community resources, local workshops, sixth-formers or other students, etc.
- Wherever possible, get classroom back-up – an MRO who will team-teach/facilitate rather than simply act as technician is invaluable.
- Investigate and exploit local sources of support/expertise, alternative working spaces, existing projects, potential audiences for finished work, etc.

Look outwards

- Consider ways in which pupils' practical skills could be developed through hands-on experience lower down the school – as far down as possible.
- In the light of the National Curriculum, investigate other curriculum spaces for media practice, from First Years upwards – the Lower School English syllabus, CDT, the Art Department.
- Investigate cross-curricular liaison on practical projects in the Lower School, to develop pupils' confidence and collaborative

skills, and to pave the way for more specialized working practices later on.

Be prepared to justify the work

- Rehearse arguments in favour of your work in order to persuade unsympathetic colleagues, HoD, hierarchy, etc.
- Outline curriculum context and objectives of work; where appropriate, build into the project conventional elements such as writing tasks, folder assignments, formal accounts or other visible record of skills pupils have employed, and relate them to National Curriculum Programmes of Study and Statements of Attainment if possible.
- Warn colleagues in advance of possible problems; play strictly by the book until production work is firmly established on the curriculum.
- Familiarize yourself with the institutional channels through which its place might be secured.

EVALUATION – 'YOU MEAN IT TOOK THEM FOUR PERIODS TO PRODUCE THIS?'

At some point every media teacher will be expected to justify production work – to argue for its validity with colleagues who question its objectives or pedagogy, or who compare it unfavourably with the unattainable standards of professional practice or syllabuses which assess only in terms of written output. There may be reluctance to resource active learning which is not seen as examinable, vocationally useful or prestigious. So, first, how do you evaluate the product itself? This is a question which has never been satisfactorily answered. How do you assess a polished piece of video which illustrates technical and observational skills but merely emulates existing conventions and cultural forms? How does it compare with an unfinished or technically-unwatchable product which reflects a genuine attempt to explore the construction of meaning or analyse the production process at the expense of the end-product?

Much of the learning, and a great deal of the input of individual students, will be invisible – the exchange of ideas, acts of negotiation, planning and collaboration at various levels of production, the roles and developing skills of individuals within a group, and so on.

Yet this is essential evidence which must be recognized and evaluated in some way. Additional problems arise where the work itself is to be externally examined, especially where it is undertaken through non media-specialist subject areas like English or Art (where it may not even be submittable) and where appropriate criteria have not yet been agreed.

In promoting self-evaluation and documentation, students should be encouraged to keep a production log. The nature of production work often requires intense commitment and personal investment; it is often difficult for students to distance themselves from what they have produced sufficiently to articulate what they have learned. The production log therefore offers a structured framework for objective analysis. It should include a detailed blow-by-blow account of the production process from the initial assignment through to a critical evaluation of the end-product, full records of the decision-making processes of the group and individual contributions to it, and attempts to articulate what has been learned. Its form might vary to include visual or photographic evidence, annotated story-boards, draft scripts of synopses, notes or tape-recorded discussion, depending on the context and the needs of individual students. Whatever its form, it should represent for students a measure of their own achievement, identify and value productive failure and provide tangible evidence of strengths, weaknesses, skills and differing levels of conceptual understanding.

Log-keeping is an invaluable resource for the teacher in pupil assessment, particularly given the increasing spaces for practical media projects in TVEI, GCSE or CPVE modules. It is also a fertile area for the investigation of issues related to gender, culture and language. Pupils' perceptions of their own experiences, together with teachers' observations and monitoring, will raise important questions which have not yet been adequately researched.[11] Are boys really more technically competent than girls? How far does an understanding of media technology depend on linguistic competence? Are there gender differences in the way pupils learn from practical activities? How might production work be harnessed for the implementation of equal opportunities policies? These issues cannot be fully addressed without a range of different forms of evaluation. These might include teacher documentation of each practical session, classroom observation and video-recording of pupil discussion and interaction before, during and after production, or the structuring of practical activities which require pupils to discuss specific concepts or materials they have produced. Such strategies, and the development of appropriate monitoring techniques, will provide some evidence, at least, of the complexity of the learning processes involved in production work and set an agenda for the diverse range of issues it might generate.

The question of evaluation has further implications for the status of production work and its position within the curriculum. As a relatively recent and potentially radical discipline, it has yet to be legitimated and its methodology has yet to be proven. It will have to be fought for in many schools and this struggle will involve consciousness-raising, challenging the expectations of colleagues and lobbying for an audience, support and resources. If media education is to involve production, properly recognized and validated, it must first be made visible, and that means active promotion. Screen and display work wherever possible, no matter how 'unprofessional': use logs, story-boards, rough drafts of scripts, photographs of students at work and stills or artwork illustrating particular projects. Even more crucial, construct work for a 'real' audience, so that students are producing for a specific purpose and will have the chance of seeing their work received and evaluated. Arrange public screenings where pupils will participate, explain their work and reply to criticism. Invite the responses of staff, other students, parents. Whatever the technical merits of the work, create as high a profile for it as possible and be prepared to justify that profile. It may be a long, slow process of consciousness-raising, but media production work must be put on the agenda if it is to acquire the credibility and status it deserves.

GETTING PRODUCTION ON TO THE AGENDA

In an already overcrowded curriculum, where might production work appear? Specialized Media Studies courses, where they have already been fought for and established, are ideal sites for the extensive development of production skills but, as Ben Moore suggests,[12] other subjects also offer opportunities. And given the recurrent, and often conflicting, references to media education across the range of subjects in the National Curriculum, and the recommendations of the Programmes of Study for English we cannot afford to waste these opportunities.

Lower school English or Humanities work, for example, will be free from the constraints of examinations, and more likely already to employ many of the teaching strategies (group work, active learning in a range of different media, emphasis on explicit analysis of how knowledge is produced and understood) which underpin effective production work. Modules within GCSE English courses might be organized around controlled multi-layered simulation or production activities which could be appropriately examined either as part of the oral communication requirement or through detailed written logs. CPVE courses provide an ideal opportunity for the development of production work in a ready-made modular structure. Not only is there a framework for group media work at the Exploratory/Project stage of any CPVE category but certain categories lend themselves particularly to specific Media Studies content. The unit on Mass Communication Industries offers a site for the integration of production practice and theory, as usefully documented by Tim Blanchard.[13] TVEI courses offer similar potential for structured modules, with the additional motivation of (for once) adequate resourcing. Although the historical development of such courses has too often been to resource first and justify later, they too make possible theoretical learning through the production process.

Production work has traditionally been an acceptable if problematic element in other curriculum areas such as Art, Drama and the Performing Arts generally. This area too could be productively exploited through interdisciplinary collaboration. So, the record of the drama group's Christmas panto might be the focus for a documentary project by fourth-year Media Studies pupils, or the Art Department's display of examination work represented with appropriate music, voice-over analysis and commentary.

A further step might be the production of materials specifically for teaching purposes, either related to specific media concepts (a brief sound-image sequence, for example, that comments on the significance of selection or different types of narrative construction) or as assignments examining the work of other departments. Real assignments with real audiences are an essential way of validating the production process for both pupils and teachers, yet they are few and far between in most institutions. Cross-curriculum liaison and course-planning can actually create and exploit such opportunities, extending the arena for media study across subject barriers.

Taken a stage further, production work has an even more crucial function in schools with a policy of 'media education across the curriculum'. Schools such as North Westminster Community

School[14] are attempting to integrate specific aspects of media study into subjects which are co-ordinated by a whole-school policy. As with many such cross-curricular innovations, the practice of such a policy has enormous, radical implications for individual subject curricula, and its implementation requires coherent organization. One approach might be to structure integrated media work around the focus of cross-curricular practical production projects. Work on advertising, for example, spans commerce skills, graphics, visual arts, language study and Humanities work. Through the focus of a production project, the inevitable diversities of perspective can be co-ordinated and controlled within the context of media theory and practice. Although in its infancy, and fraught with difficulties, this approach offers an important function for production work and a role open to further investigation. The production process, then, far from being a marginalized specialism, has potentially far-reaching implications as the organizing focus for a whole-school approach to media education.

Production work has radical implications beyond the school too. Until recently, there has been a tacitly-acknowledged no-mans-land between those who teach formally about the media, and professional and community practitioners. Interaction has been sporadic and inconclusive, expertise and resources have been under-exploited; restricted distribution and access have separated products from the audiences they were produced for. Yet the educational potential for liaison and collaboration is increasingly recognized by independent producers, broadcasters and teachers. From a community base, youth workers, arts workshops and adult education projects seek increasingly to underpin production work with a theoretical framework, just as teachers in schools are increasingly motivated to justify and extend theoretical concepts through active learning. That interaction must be exploited; it is exemplified in the work of groups such as the Cockpit Cultural Studies team, and their long-standing and well-documented photographic projects in schools.[15] Their model of classroom involvement within existing curricula is used increasingly by regional film and video workshops, for whom schools are potentially both audiences and producers.

Such interaction is an invaluable resource for classroom teachers. Not only does it offer life-saving moral support, technical expertise and resource-sharing, it also opens up possibilities for real links with the community and access to many different audiences. There are real benefits for students in working with non-teachers with specific media skills. Interest may be generated in alternative forms of media activity or in more autonomous community-based projects. Technical expertise and vocational possibilities will be extended. Projects which are jointly developed and which look *outside* the school to produce specific products for specific purposes through applying in practice the theoretical concepts explored in the classroom are the tangible objective evidence of pupils' learning. In purely pragmatic terms of internal school politics, they offer forceful arguments for production work and, in the longer term, they may play a vital role in shaping the relationship of the school with its local community.

This sort of interaction has recently proved a particularly useful way of delivering the practical course work elements of GCSE and 'A' Level Media syllabuses. It has been shared and developed through exam board consortium meetings and other local groupings set up by LEA curriculum working parties and informal media education interest groups which are equally useful information networks and sites for local activity. Further support has been offered by the regional groups of teachers, broadcasters and parents set up in response to the DES report *Popular TV and Schoolchildren*,[16] and by regional Arts Associations.

It may be that there are even more important connections to be made through these groups. Len Masterman suggests the development of local Media Centres[17] to encourage productive interchange between all those involved in media education. In a similar way it may be that localized ongoing production work might function as a link between different schools, sectors and agencies so that institutions within a particular area, from further education down to primary or even nursery, might collaborate with parents, youth workers, community workshops or independent production groups in sharing resources, expertise, skills and ideas. Such co-operations could challenge and redefine the conventional hierarchies of learning and, through the genuinely democratic process of constructing meanings from and for the community, establish the development of a life-long commitment to media practice and media education.

Postscript

In the six years since this paper was originally written, there have been significant changes both in the organization and assessment of the secondary and tertiary curriculum and in funding arrangements both on an LEA basis and within individual institutions which have had profound implications for the status, management and resourcing of practical production work, particularly in the 16+ sector. While these developments are not fully explored in the body of this paper, its underlying argument and the pedagogic issues it raises remain fundamentally unchanged.

NOTES

1 Notable exceptions which summarize and challenge a range of different approaches to practical work in media education include: Bob Ferguson's cogently argued essay 'Practical work and pedagogy', *Screen Education*, no. 38, Spring 1981; Jim Hornsby's paper on 'The case for practical work in media education', *BFI Education*, January 1984; David Buckingham, 'Theory and practice in media education', *Open University Course E207: Communication and Education*.
2 Ferguson, op. cit.
3 Interview with Stuart Hall, *The English Magazine*, no. 5, Autumn 1980.
4 Hornsby, op. cit.
5 Len Masterman, *Teaching About Television* (London: Macmillan, 1980) p. 140.
6 See Carol Lorac and Michael Weiss, *Communication and Social Skills*, (Wheaton/Schools Council, 1981) for an investigation into media use in general subject teaching.
7 Pre-packaged photoplay materials offer a range of possibilities for introductory exercises. Packs such as *The Station, The Fairground* or *The Visit* produced by the English and Media Centre (distributed by SEFT) are particularly useful for investigating narrative structure, mood or point of view. There are a variety of similar photoplay exercises in Andrew Bethell, *Eyeopeners One and Two* (Cambridge: Cambridge University Press, 1981), many of which are framed reassuringly around familiar environments or situations (a school, urban streets, family albums) which may suggest ideas for student-made photography projects. All these exercises are flexible and may be amended to serve specific objectives.

Similar activities can be constructed from commercial photoplays from magazines such as *Jackie* or *My Guy*; blanked-out speech balloons allow for the construction of alternative narratives; different meanings can be encoded through the re-sequencing of frames. Alternatively, students can choose from a teacher-compiled selection of diverse press images of an identifiable group, according to class, subculture, age or occupation as appropriate, to construct a particular perspective of that group – the homeless, the elderly or the police, for example. This exercise is extremely effective with a combination of documentary images and recognizable fictional or advertising characters.

Again, sequences can be constructed from a dossier of newspaper photographs of an ongoing news issue (unemployment, football violence, industrial action), or a major news event (industrial action, a natural disaster, a Royal Wedding). Montages representing students' perceptions of a specific period of time can also be produced using a range of teacher-selected news photographs intercut with images of contemporary music, fashion and lifestyle of the students' choice. These exercises are slightly more labour-intensive for the teacher, since picture research is time-consuming and the images may need mounting and numbering. However teacher input is useful to avoid the distractions of potential magazine-swapping sessions and to ensure an appropriate range of images. The development of a mini picture library which can be regularly updated makes this infinitely less arduous.

8   Crash-editing involves the transfer of recorded material onto a second tape using two connected video recorders (VCRs), thus allowing scenes to be re-sequenced, shortened or omitted altogether. The use of this technique allows students to lose unwanted material, to re-construct pre-recorded or original footage, to insert new footage or to repeat sequences (as in 'scratch' video). It is a relatively crude process which requires careful logging and timing of selected material, and can never guarantee split-second accuracy. It is also time-consuming and frequently frustrating, particularly since with each transfer of material the quality of the image deteriorates. However it allows considerable flexibility, not least in the elimination of mistakes and re-takes.

9   Noddy shots are a standard technique of interview editing where the responses of the interviewer are filmed separately and then cut in to an interview to disguise the loss of continuity caused by editing. Cutaway and reaction shots are similarly used extensively in fictional narrative. Such techniques can be used very productively with pre-recorded material and also to salvage errors or heighten atmosphere in students' own productions. The most recent range of VCRs feature an insert-edit facility which allows cutaways or insert shots to be dropped in over existing material with no loss to picture quality before or after, thus making the technique immediately accessible to students.

10 'The Front Page', in Ken Jones, *Nine Graded Simulations* (vol. 1) (Oxford: Blackwell, 1974).

11 Some of these issues have more recently been explored in David Buckingham (ed.) *Watching Media Learning* (Basingstoke: Falmer Press, 1990).

12 Ben Moore, in the next chapter.

13 Tim Blanchard, *Media Studies and the CPVE*, Media Analysis Paper 7 (London: University of London Institute of Education, 1985).

14 'North Westminster Community School Whole-school Curriculum Policy for Communications and Media', September 1982. The policy offers a draft media education curriculum for eleven- to sixteen-year-olds; key extracts, including specific recommendations for the role of practical production work, are reproduced in *The English Magazine*, no. 15, Autumn 1985.

15 The Cockpit Cultural Studies team published extensive accounts of their work. A useful example of a specific project and its relationship to classroom practice appears in *The English Magazine*, no. 16, Spring 1986. The issue also contains several other articles on media education, including a particularly useful piece on classroom video practice by Peter Male.

16 *Popular TV and Schoolchildren: The Report of a Group of Teachers* (London: DES, 1983), reproduced and discussed fully in David Lusted and Phillip Drummond (eds) *TV and Schooling* (London: BFI, 1985).

17 Len Masterman, *Teaching the Media* (London: Comedia, 1985).

Chapter 8

Media education

Ben Moore

'If education is to have any credibility at all, then media
education must move from te periphery of the curriculum
towards its centre. This movement will, moreover, be paralleled
within each subject. For, as more and more information is
transmitted via electronic media in every discipline, problems of
interpreting this material will attain the kind of significance that
reading now has at all curriculum levels.'

> Len Masterman, 'Why teach television', in *Understanding
> Television* (The English Programme, Thames TV, 1983)

THE CURRICULUM

There are so many pressures for change in education at this time,
especially in post–14 provision. Since 1983 and the advent of TVEI,
especially, this phase of schooling has been in almost continuous
change. In matters relating to the curriculum, these pressures are
deeply conflicting. From one direction come plans to *narrow* the
curriculum into a national core, differentiating between forms of
general and pre-vocational education and assessment procedures.
From another direction entirely come anti-racist, anti-sexist and
other *expanding* curriculum initiatives. These and other plans for
change are inevitably serious challenges for teachers, not least
because of the power of the groups enacting them.

Claims for media education are part of these expanding initiatives,
yet they are less crucial and mostly expressed by educational rather
than political groups. If media education is to become a term within
the new curriculum initiatives, then the extension of ideas and
strategies from Media Studies 'across the curriculum' into all
subjects and disciplines, is a priority.

Among the many government and DES reports on curriculum matters,[1] cross-curricular issues tend to be identified in three areas: competencies (or skills), dimensions and complementary studies (or themes). *Competencies*, defined as 'skills which are developed right across the curriculum', are the responsibility of all teachers regardless of subjects being taught. The DES document *The Curriculum from 5–16*[2] describes skills as creative and imaginative skills, numeracy, oracy and, of course, literacy.

The concept of literacy is central to media education which extends and develops the familiar sense of the term within English teaching. As Cary Bazalgette writes:

> Most people agree that fully literate readers bring many under-standings to a text: they can recognize what kind of text it is, predict how it will work, relate it to other texts in appropriate ways. They can thus understand it critically, enjoying its pleasures, engaging with its argument, reading 'between and beyond the lines' .... . Every medium can be thought of as a language. Every medium has its own way of organizing meaning, and we all learn to 'read' it, bringing our own understandings to it, and extending our own experience through it.[3]

This account is accepted by the first of the Cox Reports[4] though it is not spelled out so clearly.

The School Curriculum Development Council (SCDC) identifies three cross-curricular *dimensions* which 'should permeate all aspects of school life'. These are multicultural education, equal opportunities and the integration of pupils with special educational needs. Media Studies can have an important role to play in fulfilling these aims.

Complementary Studies are identified as those subjects which complete the national curriculum. The list is long: economic awareness, preparation for the world of work, careers education, health education, education for parenthood and family life, information technology, media education, moral education, law-related education, political literacy, environmental education, aesthetic awareness/design education, European/Commonwealth/International understanding.

Teachers may initially feel understandably perplexed about the possibility of accommodating such a list in a curriculum which is already crowded. Certainly most of the above list will not appear as named subjects on the timetable but learning in these areas cannot be left to chance.

Media education, like English, does not specify its content. So much of it will be going on naturally and spontaneously during classroom work where the focus is ostensibly on other subjects. 'Media education', therefore, describes not so much what is to go on in all forms of teaching about and with the media, but the *process* of disseminating and developing these new curriculum arrangements.

The promise of media education is twofold. First, to provide teachers of existing subjects with strategies for dealing anew with aspects of the media in their own teaching. At the simplest level, this means ways of dealing with films, TV programmes, photographs, etc. There is nothing new about the use of media in subjects like History, Geography and Science: the media have been used as evidence and stimulus for many years in education. What is different about media education is ideas for treating study texts as dynamic *producers of meaning* about history, geography, science or whatever.

Second, media education recasts assumptions about the ways learning about those subjects through the media takes place, at the same time extending understanding of how teaching can develop more effective learning. This pedagogy is particularly important for mandatory sectors of schooling where forms of resistance to learning and the institution of schooling are frequently met. Conventional knowledge-based and even skills-based curricula pose more problems for learning than are often acknowledged, since they inherently assume the *transmission* of knowledge and skills from teacher to pupil. Media education, however, offers the possibility of a more *transactional* pedagogy through a conceptual framework and a classroom practice that seeks to engage student understandings and sense of self quite directly.

Media education encourages teachers to draw on what students already know about the operation of media languages and encourages young people to become self-conscious of *how* they know what they know. This can be done by drawing upon their expectations of any particular media text, considering how those expectations are based upon familiarity with like media texts, how texts 'call up' their recognitions and identifications, and their knowledge of institutional issues like who produces texts, for whom, and why. This knowledge can be informed by the production of their own videos, magazines and exercises in all media.

Many teachers commonly use news or documentary forms in the

classroom. Rather than use these forms as if their meaning is self-evident and unequivocal, teachers could give greater weight to how learners render the meanings of such forms in a multiplicity of ways, defined in some part by their age, gender, race and class position. Rather than seek to register a 'correct' reading, teachers could be sensitive to readings asserted from these positions, and recognize that their own, although maybe preferred, are as governed by context and experience as those of the pupils they teach. The consequent strategy is to first establish the reasons that account for the differences: to ask '*How* do we know?'

Anti-racist and anti-sexist initiatives in education have alerted teachers to many of these issues, making more public the discriminatory practices that lead to educational failure for black pupils and rejection of science and technology subjects among girls.

Much of the argument about how we learn and how we make meaning differently turns as much on our familiarity with the languages of the media as it does on our familiarity with the written, printed and spoken word. All this is an argument for media *literacy*.

The process of accommodating cross-curricular themes in the national curriculum is a complex one and will need to be undertaken in a detailed way. Curriculum mapping is needed to determine when and where they will be covered and to ensure that features of progression and continuity are taken into account. The management of cross-curricular matters will require new institutional agreements. Drawing upon co-ordinators from non-specialist backgrounds is a strategy favoured by SCDC. All specialist subject teachers will have a contribution to make.

What follows is some thoughts on the general contours of a curriculum map which arise from this concern with the place of media education in the plans for a national curriculum, in particular with its place across the curriculum.

History

The objectives of the Schools Councils History project might be related without much disturbance to a Media Studies GCSE syllabus:

(a) to comprehend evidence and place it in its context
(b) to analyse, detect bias and point to gaps and inconsistencies in evidence

(c) to distinguish between fact, opinion and judgement

(d) to compare sources and reach conclusions based on evidence.

The concept of 'evidence' is being problematized here and it only needs the introduction of fictional texts to extend the range of primary evidence available for historical study. There is a recognition that meaning is produced by a 'reader' of History as she attempts to make sense of historical evidence. Modes of textual analysis that seek out the point of view of historical objects are consistent with those of Media Studies.

Teaching about the news is a staple ingredient of many Media Studies courses. Newspapers and TV programmes provide a wealth of historical material for study and there are many resources and simulations available for this purpose.[5] This material encourages an active pedagogy in its use of small-group exercises, and skills of textual and institutional analysis.

The late Professor Lawrence Stenhouse has said of History:

> An understanding of historical context does not yield productive generalisations but it improves our estimate of situations and hence our judgement of possibilities thereby helping us to escape being surprised – in the sense of being ambushed – by the future.[6]

An historical perspective is often lacking from Media Studies courses and resources where teaching can be very much caught up in contemporary media. To place media texts and institutions in an historical perspective allows the meaning of many rituals and practices to be interrogated productively. For example, the controversy arising from Michael Foot's overcoat worn at the Remembrance Day service before the 1979 election could be regarded as part of an historical struggle over the meaning of such services. Here was a self-proclaimed pacifist remembering the dead of the First and Second World Wars. Was the coat, described by the press as 'a duffle coat', really a mark of disrespect or did it provoke hostility because it threatened the conventional meaning of the ceremony?[7] Was the controversy a symptom of the same beliefs and fears that exclude participation of USSR leaders in European Remembrance ceremonies? Similarly, many of the cultural rituals which appear timeless or steeped in centuries of repetition are more recent in origin. Discovering the origins and attempting to account for their emergence casts an important light on their contemporary functions. The Open University course on 'Popular Culture'[8] offers an excellent case study on Christmas, examining representations of children, Christmas traditions like cards and crackers, and the ways in which the media articulate a variety of representations of the family as an ideal institution (symbolized most notably of course by the Windsors). The unit and its TV programmes unpicks the seams from one of the most 'national' of our festivals. It examines how widespread resistance to the celebration of Christmas from both employers and employees as late as the mid-nineteenth century finally gave way in the twentieth century when Christmas became a national holiday. Topics and analyses like these usefully connect approaches from History and Media Studies and deserve to be more widely known.

Geography

The relationship between Geography and Media Studies provides more examples of the value of cross-curricular approaches to media education. An aim of virtually all geography teaching is: 'to encourage an understanding of different cultures' (NEA Geography GCSE).

The central way in which students understand different cultures is through the way we see them in the media. In his excellent section on Geography and Media Literacy in *Teaching the Media*,[9] Len Masterman draws on the work of Jenkins and Young at Oxford Polytechnic to demonstrate the connection between what he describes as visual literacy and 'the natural environment'.

Problematizing what seems to be 'natural' is the first step, as Masterman points out, to perceiving the term as an ideological construction; that is, recognizing that 'natural' has a range of possible meanings allows us to see in whose interest or on whose behalf it is being defined at any specific moment.

M. J. Young suggests that Geography teachers could investigate 'image regions' which are 'often popular and non-rationalized images of, for example, climate, social systems, terrain, social attitudes and more. They are the naive images that we rely on to explain things rapidly to ourselves.'[10]

Third World countries are judged, often on the basis of news coverage, either Safe or Unsafe. Fictions about or referring to terrorism often use idealized versions of English landscapes against which to contrast the 'foreignness' of the villains.[11] These same idealized images of Britain are used by multinational corporations like Shell in promotional films freely distributed to schools. Masterman points to links between images of the countryside appropriated by Shell and those used in advertisements for brown bread, cheese, pickle and other 'traditional' factory foods, describing this as a 'mythic, arcadian, and entirely mystificatory' process. What is consistently missing from such imagery, he suggests, are problems of rural poverty, exploitation, unemployment and poor communications. To investigate these concerns in the classroom, students can be asked to produce accounts of particular regions from a range of viewpoints, including their own.

Students can also investigate images of their own locality or region. As an example, take the region I am most familiar with, the North-East of England. *Get Carter* is one of an extremely small number of mainstream feature films set in this region. How does this media text relate to other media images of the North-East? Early in the film the gangster hero, played by Michael Caine, travels to Newcastle where the action takes place largely in pubs or on cobbled streets of terraced houses and culminates with a gunfight on Blackhall Beach near Hartlepool. The beach is the site of a coal mine, the industrial setting made even more bleak by being shot on a grey winter's day. This image of industrial decay and regional drabness is sustained throughout the film, rendering the North-East in a way that corresponds only fitfully to the experience of those who live in or travel through the region. Passengers on trains to Newcastle from the South are greeted by the spectacular vista of the River Tyne flowing past grand architecture and the Tyne Bridge, upon which the Sydney Harbour Bridge was modelled. The film avoids this impressive sight and any other suggestions of the North-East as modern or picturesque by its significant absences (even at one stage having the hero arrive at night?). *Get Carter* can be seen as part of a cultural process caught up in dominantly producing depressed images of the region.

As a case study of how media institutions tend to ignore events which do not conform to available stereotypes, recent events in the North-East offer rich pickings. A recent Tall Ships Race turned the riverside into a festival site with fairgrounds, a magnificent firework display and maritime events. The local television station, Tyne Tees, produced a lyrical evocation of the event with scenes of the ships sailing up the river with their crews standing on the masts

Figure 8.1   Invisible ships! Picture taken by a pupil at Montague Primary School in Newcastle.

and tearful young girls exchanging messages with young Russian sailors before they were due to set sail.

Over a million people visited the city during the five days the ships were moored there, yet the national networks neglected to tell the rest of the country about it. This typifies the way 'national' news tends to focus on events in London and the South-East.

As well as noting absences, any case study should look at other images which counter the dominant ones. Returning, as example, to the case of the North-East, Amber Films produce work rooted in the conditions of the region. *Sea Coal* deals with the lives of the sea-coalers of Lynemouth. It is a fiction film and contrasts visually the huge seaside mine at Lynemouth with the caravans and horses of the gypsy sea-coalers whose land is just half a mile from the National Trust-owned Druridge Bay (a region, the guide books tell us, 'of unspoilt beauty').

Figure 8.2   Does this image confirm or overturn stereotypical images of the North-East? (*Sea Coal.*)

Trade Films – like Amber, a film workshop based in the region – have completed *North* which also deals with some of these contradictions. Using time-lapse photography, the film deals more directly with North versus South issues. Both these films and others offering alternative views of this and other regions are available for hire to schools.[12]

Working on the range of meanings of an area you are familiar with, and on the reasons for the prevalence of some meanings over others, can subsequently help clarify what is at stake in studying the range of images of countries and cultures removed from our direct experience. With such images we have little or, more likely, no experience to add to the range of representations available to us. The temptation is to find the measure of any image of an event or place unfamiliar to us by reference to other images we *are* familiar with.

The degree of our familiarity with textbooks, wall charts, TV documentaries, *National Geographic* magazines, etc. offer the framework within which we tend to make sense of any representation of unfamiliar countries and cultures. Much of this imagery tends to be exotic, as in travelogues and holiday brochures, or distressing, as in charity posters and Band Aid coverage. The Third World, especially, is represented as 'a holiday for us and a hell for them'.

Much work has been done by media academics on the role of dominant images in producing ethnocentric and eurocentric attitudes. *Teaching the Media* cites Hicks' list of categories of dominant representations and their attenuated explanations in this area:

1 Poverty is due to inbuilt obstacles and/or chance.
2 If you do the right things, 'take-off' to development occurs.
3 There are too many hungry people in the Third World.
4 Peasant farmers need education and everyone needs help.
5 Colonialism didn't happen, except for the benefits.
6 Minorities don't exist or need our help.

Coming to understand the meanings of dominant images of other nations and peoples also helps to sort out how groups who are 'not like us' are constructed as *other*, not just abroad but in Britain, too. Defining what is different from ourselves helps us to define what *we* are and this is a particularly pertinent perspective for teachers committed to multicultural geography.

Anti-racist strategies

These ideas also offer something to anti-racist strategies in education, helping to understand not only *what* part images play in constructing 'ourselves' as different from, even superior to, 'others' but also *how* they do this.

Anti-racist teaching, in whatever subject, has many problems arising from its engagement in how we think, feel and act towards others. As Valerie Walkerdine[13] and others have pointed out, it is not a simple matter of explaining to students the oppressive nature of racist or sexist texts but of exploring the role texts play in the formations of our own personal identities. Mr T. in television's *The 'A' Team* may seeem like a racist stereotype to some adults but many children identify with him because he represents an unarticulated refusal of injustice and how this can be expressed as benevolent power.

Chris Richards suggests that teachers should open up their own views and attitudes, to examine how these have been formed, to make these areas of private or personal subjectivity available for public examination in order to demonstrate what cultural factors shape them:

> Anti-racist teaching means intervention in the formation of ourselves and others; it is an attempt to redefine the subject and can be resisted as an intrusion of class and institutional power into the personal space of those without, or with less, of that power . . . . The knowledge position from which we read, from which we negotiate, is what we need to recognise and interrogate as a particular historical formation.[14]

English

The aims of much English teaching overlap with those of media education. The NEA GCSE syllabus sees an aim of English language 'to evaluate information in reading material and in other media and select what is relevant to specific purposes'. An aim in English Literature is 'to explore through Literature the cultures of their own and other societies'.

The notion of Literature here could easily be extended to include all forms of fiction and all media texts. Literature is after all a medium, a signifying practice, even though it has tended to be limited to the study of a narrow range of print forms and genres. Study objects for English Literature are distinguished mainly by association with products of a 'high' culture that might just include soap operas but certainly not quiz shows or sports programmes. Media Studies could add two important dimensions to this study. The first would be attention to publishing institutions, the ways in which literature is written, circulated and marketed, as well as the relationship between these institutions and established notions of literary value. The second dimension would be a study of readers and reading, looking at who reads what and how different groups of readers interpret texts. In this way, questions about the relative status of different literary genres could be addressed: why, for example, crime thillers or melodramas are rarely recognized, by 'A' Level Literature syllabuses. English teachers and Media Studies teachers alike are involved in developing skills of textual analysis across literary representations, but whereas Literature validates certain forms of the literary and certain responses to them, Media Studies is cautious about judgements. Indeed, the whole sense of a search for value that characterizes many of the assumptions in Arts and Humanities practices can be dealt with more circumspectly through media education's concern to investigate meaning and understanding.

Art and Design

In the NEA GCSE Art and Design syllabus, it is specified that 'the course should stimulate, encourage and develop; (i) intuitive and analytical faculties; and (ii) the understanding of economic considerations which might become limiting factors in the inventive use of materials and techniques'.

While Media Studies might wish to challenge some of these formulations (perhaps, 'cultural experience' rather than 'intuitive faculties'), it is clear that here again there are considerable connections. Art and Design teachers are becoming increasingly aware of the importance of 'audio-visual communication' and its relevance to their own practice.

With Photography, for example, the Art teacher is likely to describe and assess work on the basis of 'personal expression' and 'creativity' and will apply criteria such as texture, tone and composition to the text. A Media Studies teacher reformulates this approach by analysing photographs in terms of signs and meanings, locating not only where 'value' might be discerned, but also which groups might ascribe different values for quite locatable reasons. A whole series of questions would usefully pose the issue: why are certain subjects deemed photographic? why have certain photographic practices become associated with the high culture of Art? Media Studies looks to examine the social, historical and cultural claims made by specific audiences and interest groups on behalf of certain modes of photographic practice. For learners, too, the response to visual texts is never only 'individual' since it relies on understanding *codes* of visual language, some of which are shared while others are not. As John Berger has written about the history of landscape painting, the 'naive' or 'natural' viewer is not just uncommon but impossible.[15]

Mathematics

How can this approach to understanding culture be applied to the domains of science and mathematics teaching? Let me take mathematics first of all, whilst acknowledging the tentative nature of my views as a non-specialist.

Mathematics is a sign system with a language comparable to that of the media. It operates using a system of rules that organize signs into meaningful patterns. The figure '2' is a sign that represents a unit of number. The pattern '2 + 2' is a narrative that implies closure in accord with mathematical rules: '2 + 2 = 4'.

The test of whether the rule is learned that $x + y = z$ is the insertion of other values in the equation and the prediction of the correct outcome. This depends upon grasping the relationships between the signs; not just the numbers two and four, but also plus and equals. Once children can manage this they have mastered simple arithmetical principles and can begin to extend and elaborate upon them. In higher mathematics, such signifiers become increasingly ambivalent and the rules of combination become more complex, underlining how *language* and *representation* are the two key aspects of mathematical learning.

If we also apply the concepts of *institution* and *audience* to the teaching of mathematics we can begin to contextualize what happens to children learning it and possibly account for the significant gender differences in success rates past the age of fourteen. Young children learn maths initially through games, mostly counting games. Early experiences provide reason to grasp aspects of measurement and money which are acquired in a variety of institutional contexts. These can range from shopping to watching televised snooker, activities for which a full understanding of a preferred reading demands mastery of mathematical concepts like sorting and matching. Relating work in mathematics to familiar institutional contexts and experiences is a well-tried way of motivating learning. But it can also raise questions about who wants what problems solved and why, questions which encourage students to develop a critique of institutional practices around finance and commerce.

There is also the institution of mathematics itself, closely tied to economic and scientific establishments. That these are very male-centred is too simple an explanation for the often-remarked gender differences in achievement in maths in schools, but, as Walkerdine and Walden have pointed out,[16] girls' struggle for femininity may involve a resistance to the academic or intellectual, particularly to disciplines thought of as masculine, like mathematics and the sciences. They argue that the different treatment of males and females and their development of a sexual identity need careful scrutiny by teachers in their routine practices.

There are also useful questions to raise about how the media represent mathematics as in taken-for-granted assumptions about the value and use of statistics – how the fall and rise of the pound becomes a kind of magical factor in economic success or in the creation of a permanent sense of crisis.

The Sciences

Trends in post-14 science teaching are transforming the subject. The emphasis is on integrating the sciences, reducing content to encourage active learning and locating science in a social context. The implication of this direction is that how science is understood is as important an object of study as the internal language of the discipline itself. This allows for study of subjects such as the politics of science, how 'science' is often equated with 'progress', and controversial matters such as the nuclear and arms industries. In the London and East Anglian Board's Science syllabus, we read that one of its aims is 'to equip pupils with an appropriate body of scientific knowledge to appreciate developments in the modern world'. In Physics we find the aim 'to provide a basic knowledge and understanding of the principles and applications of Physics which contribute to the quality of life in a technically-based society'. And in Biology the aim is to develop 'an ability to identify and solve biological problems'.

These concerns with knowledge and principles refer to institutional questions about the authority of scientific knowledge, and contexts for scientific investigation and funding of scientific research. The study of the sense students make of representations of science in textbooks and TV programmes, etc. is also a part of problem-solving activities. Teachers can investigate the under-standing of science their students already possess, much of which is likely to have been gained from advertising, science fiction and documentary television.

The popularity of animal fiction and the natural world is a good place to start. There are obvious differences between the cartoon and performing animals of Disney films and the animals of natural habitats in natural history television programmes. But there are similarities, too, in the tendency to anthropomorphize and balance the sentiment of pet ownership against the cruelties of 'nature in the raw' in a regular pattern of narratives.

Ideas about science are popularized through forms of science fiction and the various treatments of 'science fact'. *The Fantastic Voyage* is a 1960s science fiction film in which a group of scientists in a submarine are miniaturized in order to travel through the bloodstream to perform an operation on a fellow scientist's brain. *The Miracle of Life* is a 1980s documentary in which optic fibre technology takes us inside the human body to examine the process of reproduction and gestation. Despite their differences, the treat-ment of the subject is similar in its use of fictional devices to 'tell' the story of a journey through the body. The organs of the body are introduced like characters in a fiction whose performances lead to the denouement of fertilization. Both contrast with magazine programmes like *Tomorrow's World* with their 'gee-whizz' view of science and technology. The spectacular fantasy of *The Miracle of Life* is worth considering further for the way it exemplifies how cultural attitudes infuse representations of science. In this documentary, the journey through a female and male body is accompanied by electronic music. The quality of the music is ethereal in the Freudian odyssey back to the womb, but the music becomes more resonant when the male body is explored and particularly dramatic as the penis is entered. The tone of voice of the male narrating the journey betrays no difference in attitude but different attitudes to the male and female body are being expressed by the music. How do students react to such differences? Males often respond with a mixture of awe and squeamishness as the camera enters the penis, girls with studied inquisitiveness. Both responses can be understood as overriding the musical cues, their social positions exceeding the positions they are being encouraged to adopt by the formal make-up of the programme.

The relationship between popular fictional forms and serious 'factual' television, e.g. science fiction and documentary science, can be explored as a way of gaining access to the understandings students bring to many subjects on the curriculum. Such methods of analysis can be applied to science programmes too so that they become not just a *means* of scientific investigation but *objects* of enquiry in themselves. When using films or programmes for study in this way, it is worth spending time situating them in their formal contexts. Conventions of natural history filming, for instance, reproduce certain narrative techniques and representations that enable us to see which views about natural history tend to be repeated and when something different is being said.

Many natural history programmes are implicitly conservationist and sometimes explicitly so. *This Fragile Earth*, for instance, is dedicated to a conservation organization, Earthlife, which protects rain forests. In the early travelogues of Armand and Michaela Dennis, and Hans and Lottie Haas, in television's *Zoo Time* and with more recent figures like Peter Scott and David Attenborough, two trends are discernible. The first is to present through the eyes of First World 'explorers' a natural world very different from our own. The second is to make it seem that the product of scientific labour and study is somehow 'naturally' available to us through the cinema or television institution. The recording of a barn owl's night-time movements or the slow motion recording of a cheetah, the result of long-term scientific labour, are transformed into spectacle and the bizarre.

Natural history is a relatively minor part of science and the school curriculum but a considerable part of science on television.[17] There are a number of reasons why certain kinds of scientific practices are under-represented in the media and why certain images of science recur with great frequency. These include the widespread belief that abstract scientific concepts on television will not communicate well or be understood. The phenomenon of the eccentric scientist – David Bellamy, Patrick Moore, Magnus Pike *et al.* – has developed so that we might find sufficient interest in the (invariably male) presenter to distract us from the apparent difficulty of the subject. The media tendency to trivialize or marginalize complex approaches to science and technology can disguise important political questions. The classroom is a good place to study the process and seek answers to the questions.

The vocational curriculum

The Technical and Vocational Educational Initiative provides much-needed resources for schools and its modular approach offers a diversity of subjects and knowledge. TVEI has undoubtedly had a marked effect on the curriculum, providing a major thrust for the development of Media Studies through resources and encouraging curriculum reorganization on the core/options model. With its technological aspects, its vocational links as well as the opportunities it provides for active experiential learning, Media Studies (and in particular video production) has been an attractive proposition for many secondary schools. TVEI has been concerned to offer a breadth of educational experiences and has in part at least encouraged cross-curricular approaches in the development of a modular curriculum.

Media Studies very often finds itself linked with Art, Music and Drama as part of a Creative Arts option. Groupings like this can encourage integration whilst offering protection for minority subject areas which are at risk under the pressure of a core curriculum at 14+. Media Studies may be taught in a modular fashion in which the major concepts of media language, institutions, representation and audience are explored separately or, more usually, in combination through the vehicle of media production. Students can be encouraged to reflect on the context of their work and the decisions they have made.

CONCLUSION

In *Teaching the Media*, Len Masterman argues forcibly that media education

> ... is one of the few instruments which teachers and students possess for beginning to challenge the great inequalities in knowledge and power which exist between those who manufacture information in their own interests and those who consume it innocently as news and entertainment.[18]

Certainly media education can play an important role in revealing the ideological functions of the media, but it would be misleading to perceive media audiences simply as innocent consumers. As David Morley points out in *Family Television*,[19] television viewing is an irrevocably active and social process. Accordingly, teachers need to be as involved with how things are learned as with what is being offered for learning. The same goes for our understanding of media texts: we must distinguish between the ways criticism understands them and the ways people in different social groups and formations understand them.

Media Studies provides the concepts and procedures to enable students to analyse their own knowledge and, importantly, their pleasures. It encourages ways of thinking about culture that deserve to be promoted across the widest possible range of disciplines and 'areas of experience'.

Media education is a means of extending Media Studies across the curriculum, negotiating and transforming its concepts and procedures as it gains greater purchase. For this to happen effectively, some sharp strategic planning will be required. Certainly, the failure of the 'Language across the Curriculum' initiative to extend language awareness from the English classroom to all the classrooms of schools offers a warning. If even such a well-supported initiative as this, with the weight of an official report[20] behind it, has little curriculum effect, the possibilities for other cross-curricular initiatives may seem even slighter. Yet, media education can strengthen its identity as an educational initiative through notions of language that extend beyond that of the Bullock Report. It has many attractions to other subject specialists – and, indeed, to general educationalists such as primary school teachers – most of whom use media technology and products in many forms. In addition to these points of appeal, media education finds itself in a climate of educational change when cross-curriculum initiatives are better understood than at the time of Bullock and have more chance of succeeding.

In this chapter I have tried to identify some of the features of Media Studies which can be located on the curriculum map. I have examined the curriculum in very general terms looking mainly at the aims of a number of GCSE subjects and how they overlap with the field of Media Studies.

The next phase is to encourage schools to offer forms of Media Studies as part of a GCSE programme in order to integrate and consolidate learning about the media in the Lower School. In selecting options at 14 it is to be hoped that Media Studies GCSE will be on offer (though the position of GCSE must now be uncertain) but curriculum managers will need to ensure that even if it does not appear as a named subject on the timetable, learning about the media will take place in post-14 schooling.

As the potential of media education becomes more widely understood and gains greater purchase on curriculum planning, so its influence will extend. The task of media educationists now is to develop a programme of work in the politics of education that creates and maximizes opportunities for it to happen.

NOTES

This chapter was written in 1986 and updated in 1989.

1 See, for instance, *National Curriculum: From Policy to Practice* (London: DES, HMSO, 1989); *The Report of the Records of Achievement National Steering Committee* (London: DES, HMSO, 1989); *The National Curriculum Council Interim Report to the Secretary of State on Cross-Curricular Issues* (London: DES, HMSO, 1989).
2 *The Curriculum from 5–16, Curriculum Matters 2*, an HMI series, (London: HMSO, 1985).
3 *Picture Stories* (London: BFI, 1987).
4 *English for Ages 5–11* (London: DES, HMSO, 1988).
5 These include: the simulations *The Front Page* and *Radio Covingham* from *Nine Graded Simulations*, vol. 1; the photoplay *Teachers' Protest* and the simulation *Choosing the News*; the exercise 'Television News' from Len Masterman, *Teaching about Television* (London: Macmillan, 1980); the simulation about reporting on events in the Third World, *Crisis in Sandagua*, from the Development Education Project; *Making the News* from the Save the Children Fund; *Front Page News* from the English and Media Centre, and the recently published package which includes crime stories, advertising and censorship called *Writing the News* from the Glasgow Media Group.
6 'History in the Primary and Secondary Years – an HMI view', (London: HMSO, 1985).
7 This idea is explored by Patrick Wright in 'A blue plaque for the Labour Movement? Some political meanings of the "National Past"', in *Formations of Nation* (London: Routledge & Kegan Paul, 1984).
8 *Popular Culture*, Open University Second Level Course (0203), Block One, Units 1/2, 1982.
9 Len Masterman, *Teaching the Media* (London: Comedia, 1985), Chapter 8, pp. 243–51.
10 M. J. Young, 'The ante-bellum south as an image religion', Discussion Paper, *Geography*, no. 12, Oxford Polytechnic, 1980, quoted in Masterman, ibid., p. 246.
11 Philip Schlesinger, Graham Murdoch and Philip Elliott, *Televising 'Terrorism': Political Violence in Popular Culture* (London: Comedia, 1983).
12 *Films and TV Drama on Offer* (London: BFI annual publication).
13 Valerie Walkerdine, 'Video replay: family, film and fantasy' in James Donald *et al.* (eds), *Formations of Fantasy* (London: Methuen, 1985).

14 Chris Richards, 'Anti-racist initiatives', in *Screen*, vol. 27, no. 5, September–October 1986.
15 John Berger, *Ways of Seeing* (London: BBC/Penguin, 1972).
16 Valerie Walkerdine and Rosie Walden, *Girls and Mathematics: From Primary to Secondary Schooling*, Bedford Way Papers 24 (London: University of London Institute of Education, 1985).
17 See Roger Silverstone, *Framing Science: The Making of a BBC Documentary* (London: BFI, 1985); and Carl Gardner and Richard Young, 'Science on TV: a critique' in Tony Bennett *et al., Popular Television and Film* (London: BFI/OU, 1981).
18 Masterman, op. cit. p. 24.
19 David Morley, *Family Television: Cultural Power and Domestic Leisure* (London: Comedia, 1986).
20 *A Language for Life*, Report of the Committee of Inquiry (The Bullock Report) (London: HMSO, 1975).

Chapter 9

Listings

Tim Blanchard

HOW TO USE THE LISTINGS

Decisions about what to include and how to organize a mass of entries are difficult for any compiler of bibliographies. Here, there is an added task in that much of the material for media education is in more than one medium. More than a bibliography, this collection of publications, resources and services for media education takes the shape of a catalogue or listings. The listings have been organized as follows in order to make access to the widest of selections as simple as possible.

Section 1 is a list of *introductory* book titles which are both accessible and authoritative in the various areas of media education. The section is sub-divided into titles concerned with teaching about the media and titles covering specific media (eg. news, cinema, the music business, etc.)

Section 2 is a *reference* section which includes other listings and bibliographies, as well as surveys of courses.

Section 3 concentrates on *teaching the media*. It includes books, articles and even a cartoon which explore issues concerning classroom practice and media education. There is a great variety here including studies of single issues such as race or television, accounts of classroom practice, surveys of attitudes to the media by teachers and pupils, and the role of educational broadcasting in schools. This section deals with the politics and pedagogy of media education.

Section 4 on *media criticism* is academic work on specific media. In researching this section, care has been taken to ensure reference is made to a range of media in listings of the most accessible writing available.

Section 5 lists *teaching materials*. These are difficult to categorize and there are a number of cross-references. Section (a) lists materials which are predominantly print-based (i.e. textbooks and teaching packs) although those with important accompanying videos or slides are cross-referenced in Section (c). Section (b) lists television programmes made for educational purposes. Each entry gives details of availability for hire or purchase. Section (c) lists packs with mainly visual material in slide, film or video form and some supporting print-material. Section (d) lists only a small sample of the many films and videos available from the independent sector, chosen either because they were made with education in mind or have been recommended by teachers. Section (e) lists exhibitions, including the two museums of most relevance to media education. Section (f) briefly lists the desk top publishing software most widely used in educational institutions.

Section 6 lists *sources* of the listed material at the time of publication. Readers are advised to check that the services and material listed here remain as described by contacting the source direct.

Thoroughness and precision has been a primary objective but, as any good media educationalist should, I acknowledge my authorship by noting that selection and comments are ultimately based on my own prejudice/ judgement/experience.

1   INTRODUCTORY READING

(a) Teaching the media

These titles are selected for the accessibility of their general introductions to teaching about the media.

Manuel Alvarado, Robin Gutch and Tana Wollen, *Learning the Media* (London: Macmillan, 1987). Gives detailed accounts of the key concepts in media education and offers an overall theoretical strategy for teaching and learning about the media.

Mike Clarke, *Teaching Popular Television* (London: Heinemann Educational Books in association with the BFI, 1987). Covers the range of popular television programming and offers practical teaching strategies and activities.

David Lusted and Phillip Drummond (eds), *TV and Schooling* (London: BFI/ Institute of Education, 1985). A useful collection of essays following up the issues raised by the DES Report *Popular TV and Schoolchildren* published in 1983 and reprinted here. More a series of statements about why teach about the media than how to.

Len Masterman, *Teaching the Media* (London: Comedia, 1985). Wide-ranging critical analysis of media teaching with a full annotated bibliography.

James Watson, *What is Communication Studies?* (London: Edward Arnold, 1985). An introductory book explaining the aims and scope of Communication Studies.

(b) Media criticism

Each of these books offers a good introduction to a specific medium or an approach to all the media.

Pam Cook (ed.), *The Cinema Book* (London: BFI, 1985). A comprehensive guide to debates in Film Studies over the last fifteen years, including genre, authorship, narrative and structuralism.

Andrew Crisell, *Understanding Radio* (London: Methuen, 1986). The most considered analysis of broadcast radio and its institutions, programmes and audiences.

James Curran and Jane Seaton, *Power Without Responsibility: The Press and Broadcasting* (London: Methuen, 1985, 2nd revised edn). Provides a very thorough critical account of broadcasting and press history.

Gillian Dyer, *Advertising As Communication* (London: Methuen, 1982). Contains chapters on the history, economics and ideology of advertising as well as suggestions for analysis of social and cultural meanings in advertising.

Terry Eagleton, *Literary Theory: An Introduction* (Oxford: Blackwell, 1983). A witty and readable account of the rise of English as an academic discipline, the various recent theoretical challenges to 'English' as an institution and an explosive conclusion.

John Ellis, *Visible Fictions* (London: Routledge & Kegan Paul, 1984). A readable and thought-provoking study of cinema and television, and how they relate to their audiences.

Simon Frith, *Sound Effects: Youth, Leisure and the Politics of Rock'n'roll* (London: Constable, 1983). A revised version of *The Sociology of Rock*, this is a good – though perhaps too generalized – introduction for teachers into an under-developed area of media education. Combines a history of popular music with analysis of the tensions between the music industry and the youth market.

Richard Greenhill, Margaret Murray and Jo Spence, *Photography* (London: Macmillan, 1977). A good introduction not only to the technical processes of photography but also to the various uses of photography in advertising, art and photojournalism.

John Hartley, *Understanding News* (London: Methuen, 1982). Analyses how news is constructed as a 'language' of meanings, values, codes and conventions, and indicates how these messages can be decoded without simply reproducing their underlying assumptions.

Dave Morley and Brian Whitaker (eds), *The Press, Radio and Television: An Introduction to the Media* (London: Comedia, 1983). Brief introduction to the structures of ownership in the British media, with sections on the press, radio, TV and new technology. A large-format book used by some schools as a textbook.

Jane Root, *Pictures of Women*, (London: Pandora Press/Channel Four, 1984). A readable, illustrated account of the ways women are represented across a range of media.

——, *Open the Box* (London: Comedia, 1986). Accompanying the Channel Four series of the same name, this book provides a series of essays summarizing critical debates about television.

2   REFERENCE

This includes bibliographies, catalogues and listings.

BFI Education Catalogue (London: BFI, annual). Contains information on all BFI educational services, publications and teaching materials.

BFI Film and Video Library Catalogue (London: BFI, 1987). The library holds over 400 film and video study extracts and compilations, listed in a catalogue and supplements.

Black and Asian Film/Video List, June Givanni (London: BFI, 1988). Contains sections on independent film and video material which is available in the UK with extensive information on distributors, black workshops and production companies.

Guide to Film Studies in Secondary and Further Education, David Lusted (ed.) (London: BFI, 1983). Introduces the main areas of work in Film Studies from conventional approaches such as authorship and genre to more recently developed notions such as institution and representation. Each area has an annotated bibliography including teaching materials.

The English Curriculum: Gender (London: English and Media Centre, 1984).

The English Curriculum: Race (London: English and Media Centre, 1984).

Media Studies: A Selective Bibliography (London: English and Media Centre, 1986). Excellent resource listings for English teachers.

Films on Offer (London: BFI, 1987/8). Publication from the Distribution Division of the BFI, listing all available 16 mm prints and video tapes of feature films, selected shorts and TV programmes for hire.

Media Studies: A Selective Bibliography (London: English and Media Centre, 1988). An excellent annotated selection intended for English teachers.

Media Studies at 16+, Tim Blanchard (London: BFI, 1989). Critical account and listings of all syllabuses; biennially updated.

Media Studies Bibliography, Lez Cooke (London: BFI, 1986). Lists useful introductory reading, writing around the 'mass culture' debate, studies about the media themselves and a listing of books and articles about media education and available teaching materials.

Media Studies for Adults, Andrew Goodwin (London: BFI, 1988). Offers an imaginative range of exercises and teaching strategies, not just for adults; especially good at dealing with news and current affairs.

Teaching Media Studies: An Introduction to Methods and Resources, compiled by Eddie Dick and Kevin Cowle (Glasgow: Scottish Film Council, 1985). Partly an extensive and annotated guide to media education resources, partly an introduction to some of the main ideas and developments in classroom practice (in the form of questions and answers).

Television Studies Bibliography, Andrew Goodwin (London: BFI, 1987). The most recent edition contains annotated sections on institutions, programme studies, audiences, teaching television and relevant journals.

Women's Film List, Jane Root (London: BFI, 1986). Provides details of films directed by women which are currently available for hire in the UK. Specialist sections include: animation, experimental films and TV material.

Women and Film Bibliography, Prudence Smith (London: BFI, 1984). Categorizes films, film-makers and feminist criticism.

3   TEACHING THE MEDIA

Manuel Alvarado, 'Television studies and pedagogy' in *Screen Education*, vol. 38, Spring 1981. Important essay about the kinds of knowledge, teaching and learning media studies should be promoting.

Beginning Media Studies in the Primary School, BFI Advisory Document, 1983. Perhaps the first substantial writing on teaching about media in this sector.

BFI Advisory Documents, BFI. The BFI produces a number of duplicated papers called Advisory Documents. These offer general introductions to various areas of media education. Write to BFI Education for free listing.

Tim Blanchard, *Media Studies and the CPVE* (London: Institute of Education Media Analysis Papers, 1985). Argues that the CPVE offers a rich area for Media Studies development which is illustrated by a possible course framework.

——, *Media Studies and the GCSE* (London: SEFT, 1986). Discusses Media Studies syllabuses within the context of GCSE. Suggests a number of possible strategies for establishing GCSE Media Studies. A supplement (January 1987) describes and comments upon the 4 Mode 1 Media Studies syllabuses which are now available.

Julian Bowker, *Media Education in Primary Schools (Papers 1 and 2)*, Occasional Papers for Teachers of English in West Sussex (available from Professional Centre, Clarence Road, Horsham, West Sussex or (Paper 2 only) BFI Education). Papers from an INSET Working Group of primary teachers which describes a variety of experiences in teaching the media in the primary classroom.

David Buckingham, '*Viewpoint 2*: a study of audience response to schools television' in *Journal of Educational Television*, vol. 9, no. 3, 1983. Small-scale action research which questions whether programme makers' intentions – in this case, to introduce anti-racist ideas into the classroom – are likely to meet with success.

David Buckingham (ed.), *Teaching through Television: Critical Approaches to Educational TV* (London: ILEA, 1983). A collection of papers arising out of the ILEA conference held in 1982 on the place of educational TV in schools. Raises fundamental questions about the skills which pupils might need to be able to learn from TV, how teachers might help develop these skills and about the 'hidden curriculum' of some ETV (Education TV) output.

David Buckingham, 'Against demystification – teaching the media' in *Screen*, vol. 27, no. 5, 1987. Part of an important debate about the limitation of Media Studies if it is primarily concerned with demystification and does not seek to engage pupils and teachers in a more fundamental critical way.

David Butts, *Media Education in Scottish Secondary Schools* (Stirling: University of Stirling, 1987). A report which is the result of a three-year study into Media Studies teaching in Scottish schools and colleges. Through a series of case studies, illustrates particularly well the institutional issues involved in establishing a Media Studies course.

Clwyd Media Studies Unit, *Working Papers at 16+* (Mold: Clwyd Media Studies Unit, Shire Hall, 1988). Produced in association with the Centre for Contemporary Cultural Studies. A collection of essays, for the most part by and for Media Studies teachers. The theoretical papers on teaching strategies are more useful than the accounts of classroom practice. A set of slides is available to accompany the booklet.

Ian Connell, 'Progressive pedagogy' in *Screen*, vol. 24, no. 3, 1983. Argues that media studies should enable students to explore their own readings and experience of the media, rather than the roles ascribed to them either by the media or (perhaps unconsciously) by teachers.

Jim Cook and Jim Hillier, *The Growth of Film and TV Studies 1960–1975*, BFI Advisory Document. Clear account of how film and TV studies grew and were redefined during the period in question.

Andrew Dewdney and Martin Lister, *Youth and Photography* (London: Macmillan, 1987). Essentially a practical guide to the use of photography in schools and in the youth service. Contains many examples of the work of young people.

Eddie Dick, *Signs of Success: Report of the Media Education Development Project* (Glasgow: Scottish Film Council, 1988). A description and analysis of the work of a project which has been of central importance to the development of media education in Scotland.

Umberto Eco, 'Can television teach?' in *Screen Education*, vol. 31, Summer 1979. A key essay which argues that if teachers expect children to learn from television they must first teach them the skills necessary to use it.

Terry Edwards, *The Youth Training Scheme: A New Curriculum?* Episode One (Basingstoke: Falmer Press, 1984). Raises basic issues about the politics of YTS and other new vocational curriculum initiatives. Useful for teachers involved in new curriculum developments.

Bob Ferguson, 'Race and the media: some problems in teaching' in *Multiracial Education*, vol. 9, no. 2, Spring 1981. Part of a double issue devoted to race and the media, suggesting an approach to teaching about race via the notions of myth and ideology.

John Fiske, *Introduction to Communication Studies* (London: Methuen, 1982). An excellent critique of the concepts and methods of communications studies gives way to an account of media studies, almost as an implied replacement framework.

John Fiske and John Hartley, *Reading Television* (London: Methuen, 1978). Difficult book, occasionally bordering on the obscure, which none the less contains valuable analyses of some popular TV programmes and genres, notably *Come Dancing*, *Top of the Pops* and *The Sweeney*.

GCSE Media Studies: There are four Mode 1 GCSE Media Studies Courses now available (NEA, SEG, LEAG and WJEC). Each examining group has produced helpful and supportive teachers' guides which usually include suggestions about classroom practice, advice on assessment and recommended resources/reading lists.

Christine Gledhill (ed.), *Film and Media Studies in Higher Education* (London: BFI, 1979). Revised papers from BFI Higher Education Conference surveying ten years of Film and Media Studies and questioning future developments.

Patricia Marks Greenfield, *Mind and Media – The Effects of Television, Computers and Video Games* (London: Fontana, 1984). Interesting and refreshing account of the educational implications of new technology (including video games). Argues that educationalists are generally resistant to these new literacies and fail to recognize the learning potential (both cognitive and conceptual) of the new technology.

Bob Hodge and David Tripp, *Children and Television* (London: Polity Press, 1986). Challenging and vigorous account of Australian research into children's viewing of cartoons and packed with provocative insights.

Jim Hornsby, *The Case for Practical Studies in Media Education*, BFI Advisory Document. Makes a brief but precise argument.

David Lusted, 'The field of Media Studies' in *English Magazine*, vol. 16, Spring 1986. A witty cartoon, drawn by Gary Kennard, with an article summarizing the main features of media teaching.

Aileen Macintyre *et al.*, *School Broadcasting in Scottish Schools*, Report of the Inter-college Research Project on School Broadcasting, Jordanhill College of Education, 1981. Part of an extensive and impressive array of reports and research carried out in Scotland to investigate the use of school broadcasting in schools. Makes some sensible comments about the use and abuse of current ETV output.

Len Masterman, *Teaching About Television* (London: Macmillan, 1980). A standard work which combines a theoretical framework for media education with a wealth of ideas about classroom practice. Includes an extensive bibliography.

Media Analysis Papers, Institute of Education, University of London. A series of occasional pamphlets concerning the development of media education as well as media analysis. Tim Blanchard's *Media Studies and the CPVE* and David Buckingham's *Educational Television: Institution and Ideology* are titles most closely related to classroom practice.

Media Education (UNESCO, 1984). International collection of essays describing media education developments.

Media Education Conference 1981: A Report, BFI and University of London Goldsmith's College. Contains conference reports and overviews of media education in the 1970s by David Lusted and in the 1980s by Len Masterman.

Media Education Curriculum Guidelines (Glasgow: Scottish Film Council, 1987). A proposal for a national framework for media education in Scotland.

Media Education – Guidelines, County of Avon Education Service, 1988. A four-part publication by the first LEA to attempt to establish LEA-wide media education policy. Titles include:

1 *Media Education in the Primary School* – a mixture of classroom ideas, formulating school policy and the exploration of certain key concepts;
2 *Media Education 11–13* – a detailed teachers' guide to classroom activities including recommended resources;
3 *Media Education in Practice: Documentary* – accounts of classroom practice on and around this topic;
4 *Media Studies GCSE* a teachers' guide to support the Mode 3 GCSE in Media Studies which the Avon Media Teachers Group has developed.

Media Education in Scotland, Outline Proposals for a Curriculum, Scottish Council for Educational Technology and Scottish Film Council, 1979. Particularly valuable rationale for why media education should be an essential part of the school curriculum, with an outline of what a media education curriculum might look like in primary, early and later secondary, further and community education and teacher education.

Graham Murdock and Guy Phelps, *Mass Media and the Secondary School* (London: Macmillan, 1973). Important study of the attitudes of teachers and pupils to studying the mass media in schools. Identifies four approaches which teachers have to the use of popular cultural texts in the classroom. Interesting social class dimension in pupils' responses.

Jo Murray (ed.), *Television Studies in Scottish Schools* (Edinburgh: Scottish Council for Educational Technology, 1980). Interesting collection of essays from practising teachers which describe media work in a variety of subject and school contexts.

Tim O'Sullivan *et al.*, *Key Concepts in Communication* (London: Methuen, 1983). A glossary of key terms in media, communications and cultural studies.

Papers from the Bradford Media Education Conference (London: SEFT, 1985). Collection of papers from the SEFT National Media Education Conference held in 1985. Some valuable ideas.

Primary Media Education: A Curriculum Statement, BFI/DES National Working Party for Primary Media Education (London: BFI, 1989). A valuable contribution to the relatively small bibliography covering the role and potential of media education in the primary school. A guide for teachers and a contribution to the National Curriculum debate.

Screen Education, SEFT.
Generally excellent journal, incorporated into *Screen* in 1982. Particularly valuable editions are:
Screen Education:
No. 21 on practical work in TV and Media Studies.
No. 34 on popular culture and Cultural Studies.
No. 38 valuable articles on media pedagogies.
Screen incorporating *Screen Education*:
Vol. 24, no. 3 on Teaching Film and TV.
Vol. 27, no. 5 on Pedagogy.

Roy Twitchin, *Primetime – Evaluating INSET in Primary Media Education* NFER and Clwyd Media Studies Unit, 1988). As the title suggests, a detailed evaluation of a primary media education INSET course which took place between 1987/88.

Judith Williamson, 'How does Girl No. 20 understand ideology' in *Screen Education*, vol. 40, Autumn/Winter 1981. Crucial essay. Describes a particular class which gave teacher the (anti-sexist) answers they thought she wanted but did not in any way shift their frame of thought. Argues that Media Studies must be concerned with connecting issues of a student's personal identity with their cultural studies.

4   MEDIA CRITICISM

A select list, organized alphabetically according to author, of writing on the media referenced in this book or recommended for teachers.

Robert Allen (ed.), *Channels of Discourse: Television and Contemporary Criticism* (London: Methuen, 1987). A series of essays exploring issues in commercial television.

Manuel Alvarado and Ed Buscombe, *Hazell: The Making of a TV Series* (London: BFI, 1978). Detailed account of how a particular series was put together. Useful material for teachers wanting information on TV programme production and the TV institution. Also part of integrated teaching materials from BFI.

Ien Ang, *Watching 'Dallas'* (London: Methuen, 1985). Very accessible account of relationships between soap opera, fantasy and women audiences.

Martin Barker (ed.), *The Video Nasties: Freedom and Censorship in the Media* (London: Pluto Press, 1984). Collection of essays illustrating just how easily broadcasting freedom and civil liberties are discarded in the face of moral panics and how strong a hold the 'direct effects' audience model has on the public and parliamentary imagination. An essay by Geoffrey Pearson places the video nasty 'panic' in an historical context.

———, *A Haunt of Fears: The Strange History of the British Horror Comics Campaign* (London: Pluto Press, 1984). Useful historical account of how a campaign was mounted in the 1950s against the American horror comic which had the support of both the 'moral Right' and the Left (in this instance, the Communist Party). Interesting parallels with more recent debates on censorship.

Roland Barthes, *Mythologies* (London: Jonathan Cape, 1972). Essential reading. Contains the essay 'Myth today' which sets out a theoretical framework for image analysis, later used in some marvellous short analyses on different aspects of our cultural life such as wrestling, soap powder, etc.

Tony Bates, *Broadcasting in Education: An Evaluation* (London: Constable, 1984). Well-researched 'school report' on ETV. Describes the different forms which educational broadcasting can take and draws on a wide range of (international) examples. Valuable section on new technology and the future of ETV in a deregulated broadcasting context.

Catherine Belsey, *Critical Practice* (London: Methuen, 1980). An investigation of critical approaches underlying new developments in media and cultural studies from literary theory.

Tony Bennett *et al.*, *Popular Television and Film* (London: BFI/OU, 1981). Open University set book/reader for the Popular Culture course covering issues such as genre, the discourse of television, realism and narrative. Particular essays cited elsewhere in this section.

John Berger, *Ways of Seeing* (London: BBC/Penguin, 1972). Classic analysis of painting, art history and contemporary visual representation. Draws from the work of Walter Benjamin to examine ideas on mechanical reproduction, the female body, oil painting and private property, and the politics of representation.

David Bordwell and Kristin Thompson, *Film Art: An Introduction* (Wokingham: Addison-Wesley, 1979). A basic text on film with chapters on film production, form, narrative, *mise-en-scène* and editing. Particularly valuable section on film criticism with detailed analyses of film sequences.

Oliver Boyd-Barrett, *The International News Agencies* (London: Constable, 1980). Study of how the big four international news agencies (AP, AFP, Reuters and UPI) work. Useful particularly in the absence of work in this area.

Simon Broadbent (ed.), *Twenty Advertising Case Histories* (London: Holt, Rinehart & Winston, 1988). Interesting accounts of twenty advertising campaigns, giving useful information about how particular decisions were taken.

Charlotte Brunsdon and David Morley, *Everyday Television: 'Nationwide'* (London: BFI, 1978). Excellent textual and audience analysis of the magazine programme *Nationwide*. Particularly useful for teachers as it offers an analytical framework which can be applied to many other programmes.

David Buckingham, *Public Secrets* (London: BFI, 1987). Account of *EastEnders* and empirical research responses to this popular TV soap.

Tom Burns, *The BBC: Public Institution and Private World* (London: Macmillan, 1977). Provides insights into the nature of a media institution and the values which are attached to particular forms of production.

Ed Buscombe (ed.), *Football on Television*, BFI Monograph no. 5, 1975. One of the few studies of how sport is treated on television. Includes analyses of sport and ethno-centricism, sport as spectacle, the role of 'experts', etc.

Mary Cadogan, 'Horse sense, heroes and hero-worship' in *The D. C. Thompson Bumper Fun Book* (Edinburgh: Paul Harris, 1977). Essay about Beryl the Peril, Nancy the Little Nurse and many more comic characters. One of the very few accounts of the comic heroine to analyse her historical development.

Allan Clarke, 'TV police series and law and order' in *Politics, Ideology and Popular Culture*, Unit 22, Popular Culture Course (Milton Keynes: Open University, 1982). Very lucid essay about how the development of the TV police series has mirrored contemporary panics and concerns from *Dixon of Dock Green* days onwards. One of the excellent OU Popular Culture course booklets.

Jeffrey Clarke and Tom Jefferson, 'Working class youth cultures' in *British Working Class Youth Culture*, Mungham and Pearson (eds) (London: Routledge & Kegan Paul, 1976). An overview of youth studies which sets out the main issues from a mid-1970s standpoint.

Michael Cockerell *et al.*, *Sources Close to the Prime Minister* (London: Macmillan, 1984). Interesting account of how the state's news management machinery works, with section on the lobbying system, the role of the PM's Press Secretary, etc.

Bernard Cohen, *The Press and Foreign Policy* (Princeton, NJ: Princeton University Press, 1963). An analysis of how the American press works, with particular reference to foreign policy. Based partly on interviews with journalists, editors, etc. Suggests that the mutual hostility between reporters and diplomats makes for garbled and over-simplified news coverage.

Phil Cohen, *No Kidding Project Papers*, Institute of Education, University of London, 1983–6. A thought-provoking series of publications which investigate issues around youth, (un)employment and education. Asks intriguing questions about the effectiveness of some recent anti-racist initiatives in education

Stan Cohen, *Folk Devils and Moral Panics* (Oxford: Martin Robinson 1980) (second edn). A study of the mods and rockers phenomenon in the early 1960s which explodes a few of the myths prevalent at the time. The introduction to the 1980 edition is an invaluable survey and critique of what Cohen sees as the excesses of some Youth Studies work.

Jim Cook (ed.), *Television Sitcom*, BFI Dossier 17 (London: BFI, 1982). A collection of essays looking at the formal and ideological characteristics of sitcom. Useful in conjuction with *Teaching TV Sitcom* teaching pack.

Ros Coward, *Female Desire* (London: Paladin, 1984). Collection of essays which explore the concepts of femininity and femaleness. Topics include agony aunts and the Royals.

James Curran *et al.* (eds), *Mass Communication and Society* (London: Edward Arnold, 1977). An Open University set book containing sections on the organizational structure of the media, the transmission of culture and meaning via the media and some general perspectives about the relationship betwen society and the media.

Melvin De Fleur and Shearon Lowery, *Milestones in Mass Communication Research* (Harlow: Longmans, 1983). Very comprehensive and readable account of the ways in which mass communication research has evolved since the early part of the century. A good starting-point for teachers unfamiliar with the field.

Nicholas Dorn and Nigel South, *Of Males and Markets: A Critical Review of Youth Culture Theory*, Research Paper 1, Middlesex Polytechnic Centre for Occupational and Community Research, 1984. A critique of earlier youth culture theory and research, particularly the work of the Centre for Contemporary Cultural Studies in the 1970s, which it accuses of ignoring non-white and female youth experience.

Chris Dunkley, *Television, Today and Tomorrow (Wall to Wall 'Dallas'?)* (Harmondsworth: Penguin, 1985). Very readable account of the likely implications for broadcasting when deregulation and the new technologies (DBS and cable) are in place. Although beginning to look rather dated and ducking issues concerned with what is 'quality TV', a good introduction to the issues and jargon of the new technology.

Kevin Durkin, *Television, Sex Roles and Children* (Milton Keynes: Open University, 1985). Questions received wisdom about sex stereotyping and the effect of 'alternative images'. Essential reading for teachers concerned with stereotyping and representation.

Richard Dyer *et al.*, *Coronation Street*, BFI Television Monograph no. 13, 1981. As much about the conventions of the soap opera (or the continuous serial) as about *Coronation Street* itself. An invaluable collection of short essays which deal with narrative, realism, ideology, the production process and character type. Recommended.

Owen Dudley Edwards, 'Cow pie and all that' in *The D. C. Thompson Bumper Fun Book* (Edinburgh: Paul Harris 1977). Essay on *The Dandy* and *The Beano* which sets out some of the comics' motifs and mores which have hardly changed since the 1930s and yet continue to attract a large readership.

Graham Faulkner, 'Media and identity: the Asian adolescent's dilemma' in Charles Husband (ed.) *White Media and Black Britain: A Critical Look at the Role of the Media in Race Relations Today* (London: Arrow, 1975). The result of research into the role of television in the lives of young Asians and their families.

Marjorie Ferguson, *Forever Feminine: Women's Magazines and the Cult of Femininity* (London: Heinemann, 1983). Account of how women's magazines have evolved from the 1950s to the 1980s.

Simon Garfield, *Expensive Habits: The Dark Side of the Music Industry* (London: Faber & Faber, 1986). Interesting account of how some of the biggest names in the pop world have been swindled out of fortunes by unscrupulous managers, record and publishing companies.

Glasgow University Media Group, *Really Bad News* (Glasgow: Readers and Writers, 1982). Part of a(n) (in)famous series of research studies on television news coverage, with particular reference to industrial relations, arguing that TV coverage is biased against trade unions.

Barry Gunter, *Television and Sex Role Stereotyping* (London: John Libbey/IBA, 1986). A research paper which covers four areas: how the sexes are generally portrayed on TV; viewers' perceptions of such portrayals; a review of research carried out into the effect of TV's sex role portrayals; and the potential of TV for countering sex stereotyping.

Stuart Hall, 'Encoding/decoding' in Stuart Hall *et al.* (eds) *Culture, Media, Language* (London: Hutchinson, 1980). Important essay on the text/audience relationship which explores a variety of ways in which a 'reader' might respond to a particular text.

——, 'Culture, media and the "ideological" effect' in James Curran *et al.* (eds) *Mass Communication and Society* (London: Edward Arnold, 1977). Wide-ranging seminal essay which identifies three key functions of the mass media: to offer, to reflect upon and to suggest ways of making sense of 'social knowledge'.

—— and Paddy Whannel, *The Popular Arts* (London: Hutchinson, 1964). A classic book which argues that media education should discriminate between different kinds and different qualities of popular culture and not against them.

—— and Tom Jefferson (eds), *Resistance Through Rituals: Youth Subcultures in Post-war Britain* (London: Hutchinson, 1976). An early collection of essays analysing the significance of youth culture. Contributions from Hebdige, McRobbie, Willis, Corrigan, etc., many of which have since become more extensive studies.

Martin Harrison, *TV News: Whose Bias? A Casebook Analysis of Strikes, Television and Media Studies* (London: Policy Journals, 1986). An antidote to the Glasgow University Media Group which criticizes *Bad News* by alleging a lack of academic rigour and honesty in research findings. Extremely detailed case studies of ITN's coverage of industrial disputes.

Paul Hartmann and Charles Husband, *Racism and the Mass Media* (London:

Davis-Poynter, 1974). Excellent study of how the press constructed the 'immigrant' issue as a 'black' and not a 'white' problem in the early 1970s. Makes clear the agenda-setting function of the media.

Dick Hebdige, *Cut and Mix: Culture, Identity and Caribbean Music* (London: Comedia/Methuen, 1987). An investigation into West Indian popular music and its impact on British popular and youth culture, including a chapter on hip-hop. Accessible to upper secondary school students.

——, *Subculture: The Meaning of Style* (London: Methuen, 1979). Important study into the way in which youth subcultures attempt to appropriate space for themselves via fashion and music. Details the tensions between the consumer industries and subcultures.

Dorothy Hobson, 'Housewives and the mass media' in Stuart Hall *et al.* (eds) *Culture, Media, Language*, (London: Hutchinson, 1980). Excellent research paper based on a series of interviews with housewives which stresses the gender specificity of most media output. Recommended as a way into the concept of audience.

——, *'Crossroads': The Drama of a Soap Opera* (London: Methuen, 1981). Concentrates particularly on the interaction between the programme and its elderly audience. Interesting contrast between the attitudes of the viewer and the broadcaster.

Paul Hoggart, 'Comic and magazines for school children' in Paul Hoggart (ed.), *Eccentric Propositions* (London: Routledge, 1984). A short essay on the comics and magazines read by children in a London school. Begins to suggest ways to approaching the topic in the classroom.

Tim Hollins, *Beyond Broadcasting: Into the Cable Age* (London: BFI, 1984). Very detailed account of the development of cable abroad and its likely direction in the UK. Examples of social access and education cable channels abroad are particularly useful.

Stuart Hood, *On Television* (London: Pluto Press, 1980). A detailed account of broadcast television's inner regulation systems and relation to the state.

Rosemary Jackson, *Fantasy: The Literature of Subversion* (London: Methuen, 1981). Clear and relatively brief exposition of fantasy and realism in literature. Helps to clear the fog in a very complex area.

Geoffrey Lealand, *American Television Programmes on British Screens*, Broadcasting Research Unit Working Papers (London: BFI, 1984). Excellent taster into a hitherto under-researched area. Contains some interesting remarks and statistics about the marketing of US programmes.

Angela McRobbie, 'Settling accounts with subcultures: a feminist critique' in *Screen Education*, Spring 1980: also in Tony Bennett *et al.* (eds) *Culture, Ideology and Social Process: A Reader* (Milton Keynes: Open University, 1981). Particularly welcome essay which attempts to counter the tendency of male researchers to produce youth studies of exclusively white, male and working-class youth.

——, *'Jackie': An Ideology of Adolescent Femininity*, Women Series no. 53 (University of Birmingham, Centre for Contemporary Cultural Studies, 1978); also in Brian Waites *et al.* (eds) *Popular Culture: Past and Present* (Milton Keynes: Open University, 1982). One of the few detailed accounts of a girls' magazine offering insights into the world which it offers its readers. Useful as a starting-point for teachers interested in textual analysis or in raising questions about representation but does not deal with issues of audience or pleasure.

Len Masterman (ed.), *Television Mythologies: Stars, Shows and Signs* (London: Comedia/MK Media Press, 1984). A mixed bag of, for the most part, very short essays focusing primarily on television light entertainment, comedy, game shows and music. Ian Connell's polemic against assumptions about the influence of the media is recommended.

David Morley, *Family Television: Cultural Power and Domestic Leisure* (London: Comedia, 1986). One of the growing number of studies stressing the home context of TV viewing in order to theorize about audience and the meanings which specific programmes might generate.

——, *The 'Nationwide' Audience* (London: BFI, 1980). Very influential study of the text/audience relationship based on the responses to the *Nationwide* programme by twenty-eight different groups. Constructs a complex and sophisticated model for accounting for audience response not based on mechanistic definitions of class or gender.

Leslie Morphy, *Sexuality – Pictures of Women: A Study Guide* (London: Channel Four Television, 1988). A study guide to accompany the series of the same name.

Steve Neale, *Genre* (London: BFI, 1980). A brief but illuminating theoretical work which inflects genre study into studies of narrative.

Grant Noble, *Children in Front of the Small Screen* (London: Constable, 1975). A broad behavioural study of the effects of TV on children.

Dave Pirie, *Anatomy of the Movies* (London: Macmillan, 1981). Comprehensive and entertaining look at the inner workings of the cinema industry. Particularly good on the financial side, with many examples. Accessible to secondary school students.

George Pumphrey, *What Children Think of their Comics*, (London: Epworth Press 1964). Although an attempt to confirm fears about links between reading comics and a range of society's ills, this is one of the few studies about the comics children read. Based on comparative studies of grammar, secondary modern and primary schools in the Midlands.

Dave Rimmer, *Like Punk Never Happened: Culture Club and the New Pop* (London: Faber & Faber, 1985). Wonderfully readable journalistic account of the music industry in the early 1980s. Combines salacious gossip and anecdote with occasional sharp insight into the pop business. A good starting-point for issues of institution and audience.

Sue Steward and Sheryl Garratt, *Signed Sealed Delivered: True Life Stories of Women in Pop* (London: Pluto Press, 1984). About how women have been traditionally under-represented/exploited in the pop industry and how this is slowly beginning to change. A fascinating chapter about fans of the Bay City Rollers argues that girl fans are not necessarily the dupes of pop music's big business but in the process of discovering their own collective strength.

Alan Tomlinson, *Consumption, Identity and Style* (London: Routledge, 1989). Explores the role of the consumer in the contemporary political economy through a wide-ranging series of studies such as popular music, fashion and holidays.

Barrie Troyna, 'The product being sold is racial harmony: a case study in social advertising and race relations' in *Multiracial Education*, vol. 12, no. 2, 1984. Fascinating case study about how a local authority poster campaign intent on improving race relations had the opposite effect. Interesting points made about audience.

Jeremy Tunstall, *The Media are American* (London: Constable, 1977). A description of the international media markets and the omnipresence of American companies.

Brian Waites *et al.* (eds), *Popular Culture: Past and Present* (Milton Keynes: Open University/Croom Helm, 1982). An Open University set book consisting of essay in two sections. The first part deals with the historical development of some popular culture forms between the nineteenth century and the Second World War. The second part offers accounts of popular cultural phenomena such as motor-cycle gangs and football.

Valerie Walkerdine, 'Some day my prince will come' in Angela McRobbie and Mica Nava (eds) *Gender and Generation*, (London: Macmillan, 1984). Important essay which raises questions about relevance and fantasy in girls' comics and books. Argues that young readers can make meaning of stories which seem to have little class or cultural relevance to their own lives – which might throw a few spanners in the works of some contemporary educational thinking.

Frank Webster, *The New Photography* (London: John Calder, 1980). Argues that photography should be much more than a technical learning process and that account should be taken of its social and political function.

Raymond Williams, *The Long Revolution* (Harmondsworth: Pelican, 1965). Extremely influential in establishing cultural studies as an important academic area. Discusses a theory of culture which traditionally espouses the creative mind and applies this to a number of our institutions, including the popular press.

——, *Television: Technology and Cultural Form* (London: Fontana, 1974). Analyses television in terms of its flow rather than discrete programmes.

Judith Williamson, *Decoding Advertisements: Ideology and Meaning in Advertising* (London: Marion Boyars, 1978). Intelligent and particularly thorough analysis of a large number of adverts within a framework drawn largely from semiology and psychoanalysis. Useful as an introduction to detailed and structured image analysis.

Paul Willis, *Learning to Labour* (Farnborough: Saxon House, 1978). Classic study of boys in secondary schools and how the resistance of some self-styled 'lads' to school can be understood.

Janet Woollacott, 'Class, sex and the family in situation comedy', Unit 23, Block 5, Popular Culture course (Milton Keynes: Open University, 1981). Particularly lucid analysis of the way in which specific social mores about the family can be safely contained within the sitcom.

5   TEACHING MATERIALS

Listed alphabetically by title.

(a) Print-based materials

These materials are mainly teaching packs and occasionally textbooks or other forms of documentation. Where they include or relate to slides, a video tape, film extracts or other visual materials they are cross-referenced in subsequent sections. Addresses of sources mentioned more than once are listed under 6(f) Media Education Organizations.

Baxters: The Magic of Advertising, Scottish Film Council. Made with the co-operation of Baxters and Geers Gross (the advertising agency concerned), the pack offers an insight into the process by which a particular Baxters ad about soup was produced. The accompanying video includes the marketing which Geer Gross used to sell the idea to Baxters. Probably more appropriate with the upper secondary pupil and beyond.

The Brand X Game, Scottish Film Council. A simulation exercise on creating an advertising campaign. Students have to select their product, target audience and, from a range of prepared photographic material, produce their own campaign. A useful starting-place for teachers wishing to concentrate on advertising. Easily adapted.

The British Media, Moyra Grant, Comedia, 1984. The nearest Media Studies has to Coles notes. In addition to a section on media constraints, and specific issues such as nuclear arms and the Falklands, contains a useful appendix with past 'O' and 'A' Level questions, examiners' comments and possible approaches to answers.

Coast to Coast, East Sussex LEA or TVS Community Unit, Southampton. Still in pilot form, the result of a teacher secondment to TVS, the pack consists of a video which contains *Coast to Coast* (the early evening regional magazine programme from TVS) and a series of interviews on the day with reporters, news editor and producer.

Choosing the News, English and Media Centre. Simulation which asks students to produce the front page of a local newspaper from prepared copy and photographs. Good for raising issues about editorial decisions and assumptions about readership.

Clwyd Media Materials, Clwyd Media Studies Unit, Mold. A series of booklets for secondary school pupils. Titles include *The News*, *Coronation Street*, *The Western*, *The Press*, *Early Cinema*, *Hitchcock*, *Teenage Magazines*, *Film Narrative*. Some are available on slides or video tape (see Section 5(c), pp. 215–18).

Comics and Magazines, Leggett and Hemming, English and Media Centre. One of the few teaching materials which takes comics and magazines seriously. Primarily an activity booklet for students, it raises a number of key questions about representation and stereotyping. Grapples with the concept of 'alternative'.

Communicate, Foster, Carter and O'Shea, Macmillan Education, 1981. First published in association with BBC Schools programme of the same name. A number of useful sections on journalism, advertising, TV news and documentaries. Tends towards an explanation rather than a critical examination of how the production process works. Some interesting source material. Good for older students.

Criminal Records, Teaching TV Crime Series, Jenny Grahame and Netia Mayman, BFI. An excellent pack containing an imaginative range of classroom exercises and teaching strategies dealing with the TV crime series. Particularly suitable for GCSE courses. Can be used in connection with video tapes on hire from the BFI Film and Video Library (e.g. *Z Cars, Law and Order, The Gentle Touch, Juliet Bravo*).

Crisis in Sandagua, Development Education Project. Simulation about British press coverage of Third World issues, suitable for older students.

Death of a Gangster, Steve Jenkins, BFI. Booklet for use with a compilation of film extracts available from the BFI Film and Video Library. Contains detailed analyses of the extracts together with a discussion of the gangster film in relation to one specific element, the death of the gangster character. Could do with detailed teachers' notes and possible classroom activity sheets.

The Dumb Blonde Stereotype, Richard Dyer, BFI. For use with a compilation of film extracts available from the BFI, the booklet gives dialogue scripts of the extracts and a set of slides, and also contains an account of how the dumb blonde stereotype has developed in the cinema. Teachers' notes and a reference list are also included.

Every Picture Tells A Story, Media Studies and Communication Series no. 1, Visual Literacy, O'Brien Educational, Ireland. Primarily an image analysis pack with a workbook with assignments, questions and discussion points.

Eye-Openers (Books One and Two), Andrew Bethell, Cambridge University Press. Excellent booklets designed for secondary school pupils but adaptable to other age-groups. Contains many good exercises which focus attention on the image and how meaning can be made. *Eye-Openers 1* concentrates more on visual codes and conventions, while *Eye-Openers 2* deals with the image in specific contexts of news, documentary and advertising. Extremely useful as an introduction to Media Studies.

The Facts about a Feature Film – Featuring Hammer Films, Marjorie Bilbow, G. Whizzard, André Deutsch Ltd. Very much in the tradition of 'how a film is made' with details of the different roles on the film set and beyond. Though not intended as such, a useful companion to the BFI *Hammer Horror Pack* (see p. 208).

The Fairground, English and Media Centre. Exercise which asks students to construct a story from a series of photographs.

Film Education Study Guides, Film Education. The study guides are work booklets for pupils which ask questions and set exercises about various aspects of particular films. The activities range from questions about issues raised by particular films to analysis of a film's characters or publicity poster. Quality varies and titles often go out of print. Some of the most useful have been/are: *Local Hero, Another Country, Bigfoot and the Hendersons, Peggy Sue Got Married, Platoon, Stand By Me, Cry Freedom, The Last Emperor, Empire of the Sun, Little Dorrit, Tess, The French Lieutenant's Woman, The Color Purple*.

Film Education Teacher Guides, Film Education. A series of pamphlets on various aspects of film analysis and film study. Although differing widely in approach and style, the Guides suggest practical ways of introducing particular issues into the classroom and some usefully offer further reading. The following are available: *Film Narrative* (Annette Kuhn), *Film Genre* (Phillip Drummond), *Film and the Star System* (Stephen Kruger), *Film and Audiences* (Tana Wollen), *Film and Gender* (Gill Branston), *Film in the Primary School* (Fiona Wright), *Reading a Film* (Ian Wall and Stephen Kruger), *Film and Literature* (Philip Simpson), *Film Studies* (David Lusted), *Film and Race* (Chris Vieler-Porter), *Film and Music* (Peter Hayward), *Film and History* (Barry Jones).

The Film Industry, Trish Jenkins and Dave Stewart, The Media Centre, South Hill Park, Bracknell. A simulation game about the film industry in which a production company makes proposals for new films and the battle over distribution begins. A breakdown of the production and promotional costs of *Star Wars* is provided in order to give some comparison on costings. One of the few of its type.

Finding Out About Advertising, produced by the Advertising Association and available from Careers Research and Advisory Centre (CRAC), Hobson's Ltd, Bateman Street, Cambridge CB2 1L2 or Sheriton House, Castle Park, Cambridge CB3 0AX. A glossily-produced, if uncritical, booklet containing useful material on various campaigns.

The Football Game, Scottish Film Council. Using a Celtic–Aberdeen football match as a starting-point, the pack consists of video material, forty slides (with accompanying sets of the same photographs for pupils) and encourages editing and captioning activities. Useful if not avoiding sexism.

The Front Page, in *Nine Graded Simulations* (vol. 1), Ken Jones, Blackwell, or from European Schoolbooks Ltd, Craft Street, Cheltenham GL63 0HX. A simulated local paper exercise provides pupils with news material from which to make editorial decisions.

Front Page News, English and Media Centre. Well-produced students' booklet which deals with ownership, bias and stereotyping in the press. Particularly useful on aspects of race relations. Teachers' notes are excellent.

The Gangster Film: Teachers' Study Guide 2, Tom Ryall, BFI. Useful general introduction to the concept of genre and some of its problems. Includes notes on teaching strategies and a guide to resources. Upper secondary and above. Can be used with *Death of a Gangster* (see p. 207).

Gone Fishing, English and Media Centre. Similar to *The Fairground*; students are asked to produce a story from a series of photographs.

Hammer Horror: A Cinema Case Study, Dave Pirie, BFI. The pack consists of a well-illustrated booklet about Hammer Studios and the films it produced within the context of British society and culture in the 1950s plus 79 separate study cards which are facsimiles of documents discussed in the booklet (such as actors' contracts, publicity ideas, etc.). Useful for studying institution, stars, narrative and, in conjunction with film extracts available from the BFI Film and Video Library, the horror film.

Introducing Media Studies, David Butts (series editor), Hodder & Stoughton, 1988. A series of very useful (and low–priced) booklets about different aspects of the media designed for 12 to 16-year-olds. Each booklet suggests practical activities. Titles include: *On Your Radio* (John Wood), *Thinking About Images* (Keith Thomson), *Planning the Schedules* (Cameron Slater), *Looking into Advertising* (Carol Niven and Colin Youngson), *Advertising in Action* (Carol Niven and Colin Youngson), *Newspapers* (Nancy Butler), *Teenage Magazines* (Margaret Hubbard).

Introduction to the Mass Media 1: Pupil Text, David Owens and Pat Hunt, Veritas Publications. Includes 'What is Communication?'; the roles of news, TV, radio, newspapers, advertising and popular music. Teachers' notes available separately. Companion volume to *Understanding the Mass Media*.

'*Hazell Meets the First Eleven*', David Lusted, BFI. A set of slides, teachers' notes and a range of other documentation on one episode of the 1978 Thames TV series 'Hazell' arising from the book *Hazell: The Making of a TV Series*. The episode is available for hire from the BFI Film and Video Library.

In Concert: Educational Exercises in Pop Music and the Record Industry, T. Attwood, from System Publishing Company, 12–14 Hill Rise, Richmond, Surrey. A large loose-leaf folder which covers various aspects of the music industry. Needs additional material from the teacher.

King's Royal, Scottish Film Council. About how one episode of the programme *King's Royal* (BBC Scotland TV Drama) was made. Compares the book and the teleplay; has interviews with the actors and crew. Teachers' notes and a video tape available.

Looking at Newspapers, The Newspaper Society. A ten-lesson set of teachers' notes focusing on how newspapers are produced with numerous suggestions for follow-up work (e.g. what difficulties might a reporter have in sending back a story from the Himalayas). Heady stuff.

Making Sense of the Media, John Hartley, Holly Goulden and Tim O'Sullivan, Comedia. Consists of ten separate booklets divided into three blocks: the world of images, the industry of images and images of the audience, plus a general introduction to the course. Rather uneven and seems uncertain whether it is intended for teachers or pupils but nevertheless has some useful ideas.

The Market, English and Media Centre. Primarily a cropping exercise. Pupils are able to highlight different detail from a single photograph (of a busy market scene). Variety of possible activities (e.g. story-telling, captioning, etc.). Photo itself is now rather dated but the idea is capable of adaptation.

Media, Paul Moss, Harrap Education. Wonderfully illustrated but poorly organized pamphlet for students. No teachers' notes or index.

The Media, Wayland Publishers, 61 Western Road, Hove, East Sussex

BN3 1JD. A new series of eight booklets (series consultant, Philip Hayward) described as offering support rather than textbooks for GCSE Media Studies courses. Titles include *Newspapers* (Brenda Mann), *Television and Video* (Manuel Alvarado), *Advertising* (David Lusted), *Radio* (Rebecca Coyle), *The Pop Music Business* (Philip Hayward), *Comics and Magazines* (Kim Walden), *Cinema* (Andrew Higson) and *Book Publishing* (Julia Knight).

The Media Manual: A Teachers Guide to Media Studies, Stephen Kruger and Ian Wall, Mary Glasgow Publications, 1988. A hasty guide for teachers.

The Media Pack, Ian Wall and Stephen Kruger, Macmillan, 1987. A folder-style pack containing sections on film, TV, the news, advertising, teenage magazines and popular music. Useful one-off lesson ideas.

Media Resources Pack, available from Southampton Media Education Group, c/o Andrew Hart, Southampton University. A loose-leaf folder with a range of teaching ideas for a wide range of age groups. Covers topics such as Television News-Bulletins, Reading Cartoons, Storyboard, etc.

Moving On – A Photopack on Travellers in Britain, Lynne Gerlach, Stella Hillier, Julia Bennett and Danny Hearty, Minority Rights Group Education Project, 29 Craven Street, London WC2N 5NT. Contains a series of photos of travellers as well as an informative booklet about them.

The Music Business: A Teaching Pack, Tim Blanchard, Julian Sefton-Green and Simon Greenleaf, Hodder & Stoughton, 1989. Made with the co-operation of EMI and RCA, the pack contains three detailed case studies on the marketing of three different record releases and also an extensive simulation which takes students via role-play through various activities from signing a band, deciding on a first release to developing a marketing policy. One of the few detailed teaching packs on the music business available. Comes with a cassette featuring transcripts of the case studies and three 'demo' songs.

The Nature of News, Newspaper Society. Aimed at 14 to 16-year-olds, it encourages pupils to analyse the use of language in the press.

The Newspaper Activity Book, Newspaper Society. As the title suggests, this is an activity book asking pupils to find, among other things, words which rhyme with each other and to analyse the obituary columns to find the median age of death.

Pictures on a Page: Photo-journalism, Graphics and Picture Editing, Harold Evans, Heinemann, 1978. Part of a five-volume work on journalistic techniques (others in the series are: *Newsman's English*, *Handling Newspaper Texts*, *News Headlines* and *Newspaper Design*). Hang the expense – this is one of the best sources on news photography around.

Picture Stories (Starting-points for media education in primary schools), Yvonne Davies, BFI. One of the few media resources specifically designed for primary pupils, this is an introduction to image analysis and covers issues such as dominant/alternative codes, narrative and sequencing. Very good teachers' notes, slides and photoplays.

Radio Covingham, in *Nine Graded Simulations* (vol. 1), Ken Jones, Blackwell, or from European Schoolbooks Ltd, Craft Street, Cheltenham, Glos.

GL63 0HX. A simulated radio news programme exercise providing pupils with news material to make editorial decisions and produce a brief news programme. It has been adapted by many teachers to suit local conditions and facilities.

Reading Pictures, BFI. Three different exercises on image analysis. Useful starting-point for students (of all ages) in making problematic codes and conventions which we take for granted. With slides and multiple copies of student material.

Rock Bizz: Managing a Rock Band, Chris Lent, Open College course CO501A. A package of workbooks, audio cassette and boardgame designed to help young musicians through the various pitfalls of the music business. Can be used to gain a BTEC qualification.

Selling Pictures, BFI. A teaching pack which offers an introduction to representation and stereotyping for the upper secondary school and above. Concentrates on commercially-produced images. Consists of booklet *The Companies You Keep* which looks at the question of ownership and product 'integration', a broadsheet of women's magazine covers, accompanying slides and multiple copies of photosheets for student use. Excellent teachers' notes.

The Semiology of the Image, Guy Gauthier, BFI. One of the first slide packs available for image analysis and still one of the best. The teachers' notes are excellent.

Star Dossiers, BFI. A series of resource packs for teachers on individual stars, each containing a teachers' booklet and a range of materials (slide and facsimile format) such as studio promotion, stills, press coverage and fan magazine articles. Series includes: *Star Dossier One: Marilyn Monroe*; *Star Dossier Two: John Wayne*; *Star Dossier Three: Robert Redford*. Teachers using these materials may also find *Teachers' Study Guide 1: The Stars*, Richard Dyer, BFI, of particular assistance. Details the main conceptual areas involved in the star system, and includes teaching notes and further resources.

Starters: Teaching Television Title Sequences, Roy Twitchin and Julian Birkett, BFI. Analysis of seven title sequences of TV programmes with a variety of worksheets for students (with slides). Good way of setting up practical work. A video of the seven sequences is available for hire from the BFI Film and Video Library.

The Station, English and Media Centre. Students are required to create a particular mood using a series of photographs featuring a boy and a railway station.

Swallow Your Leader, English and Media Centre. Pack consisting of slides and notes focusing on this television documentary.

Talking Pictures, Mike Clarke and Peter Baker, Mary Glasgow Publications. Tape-slide and teacher's booklet. Designed as an introduction to image analysis, the sixty slides provide a thorough grounding.

Teachers' Protest, Mike Simons, Cary Bazalgette, Andrew Bethell, English and Media Centre. Consists of a series of stills about a teachers demonstration, from which students can develop news items and/or documentary work. Now rather dated, but an excellent teaching model. Slides are also available.

Teaching 'Coronation Street', BFI. Useful pack which offers some ground-work for studying soap opera. Contains student exercises on character and narrative in the continuing serial, together with synopses, slides and teachers' notes. A number of episodes of *Coronation Street* are available for hire from the BFI Film and Video Library.

Teaching Television: The Real World, Andrew Hart, Cambridge University Press, 1988. The result of the work of a group of teachers. An extremely detailed pack about one programme from the popular science series *The Real World* (made with the co-operation of TVS). Contains sections on representation, presentation and viewing, as well as extremely useful information about programme costs. Accompanying video contains the programme itself, interviews with the presenters, editor, researcher and producer as well as a number of silent extracts for voice-over and other exercises. Teacher- rather than pupil-oriented; designed for GCSE Media Studies. A paperback entitled *Making the Real World* is available separately.

Teaching TV Drama-Documentary, Andrew Goodwin, BFI. A three-part teaching pack which contains an introduction to the key issues about TV drama-documentary, student exercises on codes and conventions associ-ated with 'fact' and 'fiction' on TV, and possible areas of discussion (particularly related to a number of drama-documentaries available for hire from the BFI Film and Video Library).

Teaching TV Sitcom, BFI. Offers a great deal of material, background information (including brief surveys of theories of comedy and the history of the sitcom) and possible classroom activities in an area which is often ignored or derided. The examples used in the pack can be used in conjunction with videotapes available for hire from the BFI Film and Video Library, including *George and Mildred*, *Porridge*, *Hi-de-Hi!* and a compilation tape.

Television Sitcom, Netia Mayman, The English and Media Centre, 1988. Covers issues such as genre, audience, representation and narrative through reference to particular programmes (e.g. *Porridge*, *Hi-De-Hi!*) which are available from the BFI Film and Video Library. Suitable for upper secondary school.

Television Studies, Sue and Wink Hackman, Hodder & Stoughton, 1988. A practical look at television which includes video work, how a TV studio is run and looking behind the scenes.

Understanding Breakfast Television, Len Masterman and Paul Kiddey, MK Media Press. Pack which gives information on the origins of Breakfast TV as well as ideas for classroom activities.

Understanding Television, Julian Birkett and Roy Twitchin, Thames Television. Designed to accompany Thames TV's *Understanding Television* series, but equally useful as a textbook on its own. Contains sections on the constructed nature of TV, how and why programmes are made, politics and TV, audience and Dutch TV. Each section has a lot of ideas for 'activities'.

Understanding the Mass Media 1: Pupil Text, David Owens and Pat Hunt, Veritas Publications. Covers TV, newspapers, advertising and radio. Companion volume to *Introduction to the Mass Media 1* (see above). Teachers' notes available separately.

Viewpoint 2, Andrew Bethell, Thames TV. Well-produced booklet to accompany the Thames TV *Viewpoint 2* series. Concentrates on the concept of representation with particular reference to youth, race, workers and welfare. Some useful exercises.

The Visit, Andrew Bethell, English and Media Centre. A classic Media Studies photoplay pack. Using a series of stills about a man in a flat and two visitors, students are asked to create a suspense narrative.

Watching the World: Media and Development Education, Development Education Project, 1988/9. An excellent series of materials investigating relations between the media and Third World systems and representations. There are five titles so far: *Investigating Images, News from Nicaragua, Aspects of Africa, Picturing People,* and *Whose News?*

Wham! Wrapping: Teaching the Music Industry, Lilie Ferrari and Christine James (eds) BFI, 1989. A detailed case study on the pop group Wham! highlighting the production, distribution and marketing of the band. Contains student worksheets and interviews with people working in the business.

Who is this Woman?, Resources for Learning Development Unit, Avon LEA. A pack of photographs designed to help students to develop the skills of image analysis: to observe the effects of caption and context; and to examine stereotyping and narrative. Consists of a series of photographs of the same woman in different locations, costumes, moods and from different angles. With teachers' notes.

(b) Broadcast television programmes

English File: *Media Studies*, BBC, 1984. Broadcast in 1984, the series included a number of programmes about the media which concentrated more on how things were done than why. Not available for hire or purchase.

The English Programme, Thames TV. Thames TV has the most comprehensive range of Media Studies programmes and accompanying materials of all the TV companies. Since 1975, four major series of programmes for media teaching have been produced under these titles:

(1) *Viewpoint 1* (1975) and *Viewpoint 1 Revised* (1977). The 1975 series consist of ten programmes divided into three parts: Communication in Society; Mediation; Structures (programme titles included *Believe Me, News Story, Love Story,* and *No Way*). The 1977 series updated four of these programmes and also includes *Viewpoints on Viewpoint* in which Gwen Dunn and Gillian Skirrow discuss the 1975 series. Although the 'direct' presentation and the polemic of the series now seem a little dated, it contains some interesting material. The accompanying teachers' notes are particularly useful. Programmes are available for hire or purchase from Guild Learning.

(2) *Viewpoint 2* (1979). Consists of four programmes investigating representations of youth, black people, workers and social security claimants. The programmes are full of film clips, newsreels and interesting archive material. Very demanding. Useful pupils' booklet

written by Andrew Bethell available from Cambridge University Press entitled *Viewpoint*. Programmes available for hire or purchase from Guild Learning.

(3) *Understanding Television 1* (1983). Each of five programmes concentrates on a particular medium. Titles are: *How did that get on the box?*; *Three days to transmission*; *Setting up a service*; *'Minder' and its audience*; *Television in Holland*. Well illustrated and attractive pupils' book 'Understanding Television' accompanies the series written by Julian Birkett and Roy Twitchin which is available from local ITV companies. Only *How did that get on the box?* and *Minder* are available (for sale only) from Thames TV International.

(4) *Understanding Television 2* (1987). Four programmes intended to develop the issues raised in the first series. Titles are: *Television as construction*; *Genre*; *Guidelines*; *Audience*. Programme 1 may be available for sale from Thames TV International.

Other Thames TV programmes of interest to media teachers are:

Language 1 (1977) *Language 2* (1983). A programme in the 1977 series *True Stories* spoofs narrative conventions (Guild Learning).

Culture (1979). Three programmes offer views on representation of British Culture, Women and Images of America. Available for hire or purchase from Guild Learning.

One World Documentaries (1981). Describes approaches to current affairs documentaries about the Third World. Available for hire or purchase from Guild Learning under the title *Jonathan Dimbleby in South America*.

Middle English (for 9 to 13-year olds). *Dennis and Friends* (1981) and *'Eagle' Boys and 'Girl' Girls* (1983) deal with comics. Other programmes of interest include: *News Story* (1982), *Cashing in on Chips* (1983), about launching a new game; *News of War* (1984). (All available from Guild Learning.)

The Marketing Mix, Yorkshire TV/Channel Four/Institute of Marketing/ BTEC. The first of its kind, a series of ten 25-minute videos forming part of an open learning programme. The course it comprises is based on case studies of large organizations which help to identify key marketing concepts. Students following the course will be able to enter the BTEC 'Making Sense of Marketing' examination.

Open the Box, Channel Four and BFI Education, 1986. Not strictly ETV output but nevertheless a challenging series of six programmes which pose intriguing and central questions about TV production, construction and consumption. A booklet (available from Channel Four) accompanies the series as does a book of the same name by Jane Root (see entry in section 1, p. 193). Available from TEAM Video.

Time to Think, Scottish Television (Yorkshire TV Enterprises, TV Centre Leeds LS3 1JS). A series of ten programmes on Media Studies first broadcast in Spring Term 1985. Topics include 'Images of Scotland', 'In with the Incrowd' (about the record industry) among five programmes dealing with the media industries and five on how they produce messages.

Zig Zag, BBC. Two series, one on photography and animation (Autumn 1985) and the other on topics such as newspapers, reporting and the use of images to tell a story (Autumn 1986). Emphasis on practical follow-up activities. Not available for hire or purchase.

(c) Slide packs, video tapes and films

BFI slide packs

The following slide packs of images taken from the frames of feature films are available from the BFI Education Department but for copyright reasons are only available to teachers working in the formal education system in the UK. All packs are sold with accompanying documentation.

In colour: *All the President's Men, Black Narcissus, Bonnie and Clyde, Calamity Jane, Chariots of Fire, Dirty Harry, Don't Look Now, A Fistful of Dollars, Gregory's Girl, Klute, Rear Window, Rebel Without a Cause, The Way We Were.*

In black and white: *The Bad and the Beautiful, Battleship Potemkin, The Big Heat, Citizen Kane, History of Narrative Codes in Film, Psycho, Psycho —* analysis of a sequence, *Raging Bull, Triumph of the Will, Some Visual Motifs of Film Noir.*

Behind the Screen, Clywd Media Studies Unit. Videotape which decribes the production of a family quiz show at HTV's studio in Mold, with accompanying booklet and classroom assignments.

Children Behind the Camera: A study in the creative use of television in the primary classroom, Focus in Education, 65 High St, Hampden Hill, Middlesex. A videotape in which Vincent McGrath talks about his television work with primary school children, illustrated by the programmes which the children themselves made. The tape is accompanied by a series of handbooks written for teachers who might consider doing similar work.

Coast to Coast, available from East Sussex LEA or TVS Community Unit. Teaching pack includes video of the TVS programme *Coast to Coast* with additional assorted interviews with TVS personnel. (See also section 5(a), p. 206.)

Controversy: An Action Video Pack, Team Video. Via a series of video clips, this pack examines how the mass media tends to approach issues of gender and political controversy (e.g. strikes, Northern Ireland).

Death of a Gangster, BFI (56 mins). Extracts from eleven films from *Little Caesar* (1930) to *Le Samourai* (1967). Accompanied by a teachers' introductory booklet by Steve Jenkins. (See also section 5 (a), p. 207.)

Domestic Labour and Visual Representation, Hackney Flashers. A set of twenty-four slides showing women in a variety of contexts, domestic and working, glamorous and political. Few suggestions for classroom activities.

The Dumb Blonde Stereotype, BFI (58 mins). Extracts from twelve films including appearances from Lillian Gish, Jean Harlow and Marilyn Monroe. To be used in connection with the booklet which comes with a set of slides. (See entry in Section 5, p. 194.)

Film Noir Pack, BFI. Features slides from six examples of *film noir* (including *Crossfire*, *Mildred Pierce* and *Deadlier than the Male*) in addition to a set entitled *Some Visual Motifs of Film Noir*. All come with separate notes. Particularly useful in teaching about genre.

Genre Teaching Pack, BFI. Contains slide sets and notes on genre recognition, *The Outlaw Josey Wales* and *Coma*. In addition there is an introduction to genre, teaching notes and possible student activities which have been used as the basis for a six-week BFI/ILEA course for sixth-formers.

Hammer Horror: A Cinema Case Study, BFI. A number of horror film extracts are available from the BFI Film and Video Library to accompany this teaching pack. (See also Section 5 (a), p. 207.)

Images of the Developing World: An Action Video Pack, Team Video. Raises issues about the images of the Third World as represented by the mass media, concentrating on charity adverts and news disaster items.

King's Royal, Scottish Film Council. Video tape available of an episode of *King's Royal*, with teaching notes. (See also Section 5 (a), p. 209.)

Learning Through Journalism, Portsmouth Teachers Resource Centre, Olinda Street, Portsmouth, PO1 5HP. A video with accompanying materials based on the production of a day's news at The News Centre in Portsmouth.

Media Kids OK, Paul Merrison, Leicestershire Centre for Educational Technology, Herrick Road, Leicester. Tape of children's media education activities in the primary school with a first half offering useful introductions for all teachers to the potential of media education

Media Studies within English, a Year 3 Scheme, Clwyd Media Studies Unit. A pack consisting of six sections (Introductory, TV, Radio, Teenage Magazines, The Press, and Film). The Introductory section consists of 34 slides and a workbook, and the Film section (about narrative in film) consists of a videotape of *Bugsy Malone*.

The Media Tapes, Andrew Bethell, Placebo/Methuen. The first of its kind: 4 videotapes offering a structured series of exercises which encourage students 'to interrogate the text'. Tapes are entitled: *Messages and Meaning*; *Friday the 14th*; *Selling the System*; and *Fun and Games* (investigating image analysis, news, advertising and entertainment, respectively).

Narrative Teaching Pack, BFI. Contains slide sets and notes on *Strangers on a Train*, *The Taking of Pelham 123* and *Mildred Pierce*, with additional slides to introduce image study. Used in the ILEA/BFI Sixth Form Film Study Course from which teachers' notes and students worksheets are included.

Opening the Black Box, Media Education Centre, 5 Llandaff Road, Canton, Cardiff CF1 9NF. Concentrates on the issue of race covering a wide range of genres. Some accompanying documentation.

Open the Box, Meridian Video Productions, 22 Bardsley Lane, London SE10. A three-part video programme with study notes which tells the story of how a music programme, *Live from London* (screened by Sky Channel) was made. Sections concentrate on Production, The Company and People. Rather skimpy and some of the follow-up activities such as 'colouring in' do not inspire confidence.

Presenters, Soaps and Sport: An Action Video Pack, Team Video. Drawing on the series *Open the Box*, this looks at the way TV presenters gain authority, how a new character is introduced into a soap opera, and how TV might change the course of a particular event.

Representation and Blacks in the American Cinema, BFI Film and Video Library (70 mins). A compilation on video of extracts from five films spanning *The Littlest Rebel* (1936) to *Killer of Sheep* (1977), with notes.

Representation and Blacks in the British Cinema, BFI Film and Video Library (90 mins). A video compilation of extracts from seven films spanning *Sapphire* (1959) to *Burning an Illusion* (1981), with notes.

Semiology of the Image, BFI. Excellent slide pack introducing basic approaches to semiotic analysis of visual images.

Starters: Teaching Television Title Sequences, BFI. Slides come with the pack. Video available from BFI Video and Film Library (see also Section 5 (a), p. 211).

The Super-soft Quick-Mix After-Eight Woman, Women in Media, 12 St John's Wood Rd, London NW8 (15 mins). Using a mixture of parody, interviews and clips raises issues about stereotyping of women in advertising. Interesting material from an advertising agency which produced different versions of a food commercial.

Swallow your Leader, English and Media Centre. Slides accompany the pack (see also Section 5 (a), p. 211).

Talking Pictures, Mary Glasgow, London. Tape-slide set introducing basic strategies in approaches to media analysis (see also Section 5 (a)).

Teachers' Protest, English and Media Centre, London. Set of slides available (see also Section 5 (a), p. 211).

Teaching 'Coronation Street', BFI. Slides available in pack; episodes available from BFI Film and Video Library (see also Section 5 (a), p. 212).

Teaching Media Matters, available from The Media Centre, Bracknell (25 mins). Intended for teachers and parents. Raises the question of whether media education should be an integral part of a primary school curriculum. Based on the experience of a project in a Berkshire primary school.

Teaching Television: The Real World, available from Department of Education, Southampton University or TVS Community Unit. Video-tape included in teaching pack (see also Section 5 (a), p. 212).

Viewing, Appearing and Participating on TV: An Action Video Pack, Team Video. One of a series of Action Video Packs from Team Video, contains a series of short video clips (taken from the *Open the Box* series) with teachers' notes and student activity sheets. Would need to be supplemented by teachers' own material.

Visually Speaking, distributed by Educational Media International, 25 Boileau Road, London W5 3AL. Made in Canada, a series of six short videos about how we understand and communicate with the world through visual images.

Western Project, BFI. Comprises six separate sets of slides and notes which can be purchased separately. They include *Genre Recognition* (see Genre Teaching Pack entry, p. 216); *Western Genre Recognition*; *Changing Face of the Western Hero; Inflections of the Genre; Real West/Painter's West;* and *The Searchers.*

(d) Independent films and videos

This is not a comprehensive list but suggests some films and videos made in the independent sector appropriate for classroom use. Names in brackets refer to distributors.

Calling the Shots, Mark Wilcox (Albany Video) (13 mins). Starts off as a conventional love scene, but gradually the actors exchange their lines, step out of character and finally leave the set. A video that demonstrates and disputes some of the conventions of mainstream fictions, melo-drama and Douglas Sirk's *Imitation of Life* from which extracts are taken.

Death Valley Days, Gorilla Tapes (Albany Video) (20 mins). A clever 'scratch' video in which old and new footage is re-edited with different soundtracks and fast cutting to produce new meanings.

Girl Zone, Birmingham Film and Video Workshop (37 mins). The product of collaboration between eight secondary school girls and the BFVW in which the girls explore the things they like to do and some of the problems they face. Ask for teaching notes when booking.

Give Us A Smile, Leeds Animation Workshop (Albany Video) (13 mins). Very witty cartoon which explores the effect of sexual harassment on a woman who, in the end, shows how women are fighting back. Useful for dealing with issues of representation.

Handsworth Songs, Black Audio Film Collective. Eloquent film essay which links the Handsworth experience with a history of racial oppression. Impressive cutting between archive material and recent footage. For older students.

It Ain't Half Racist, Mum, Campaign Against Racism in the Media (Team Video) (30 mins). Using a selection of clips from comedy shows, documentaries and current affairs programmes, argues that a great deal of TV is subtly, and occasionally overtly, racist.

Making News, Triple Vision Productions (available from the Campaign for Press and Broadcasting Freedom, 9 Poland Street, London W1). A critical look at how newspapers and television covered the 1982 dispute between health workers and management. Offers an alternative view of the news.

MsTaken/Mistaken Identity, Albany Video. Witty series of sketches and songs about growing up by teenage women.

A Plague on You, Lesbian and Gay Media Group/BBC Open Space (Albany Video) (28 mins). A montage of press and TV images which raises issues about how anti-gay sentiments are all-pervasive, particularly within the media's AIDS coverage.

Race Against Prime Time, David Shulman (Albany Video). A case study on the media coverage of racial conflict in Miami in 1980 dealing with questions of news selection, news footage and who gets to speak and who doesn't.

Street Warriors, Ceddo. A video about the street hockey players of London.

What They Telling Us It's Illegal For? Birmingham Film and Video Workshop (40 mins). About hometaping but more about the way in which young people search out and gain access to information which affects their lives. Ask for teaching notes when booking.

Why Their News is Bad News (Team Video) (30 mins). Scrutinizes television coverage of a series of political and industrial events and challenges the way in which issues are presented (or rather what's left in and what's left out).

(e) Exhibitions and museums

BFI exhibitions

The BFI Education Department has, over the years, produced, a series of exhibitions which were available for hire. *The Melodramatic Imagination* (shows the developmental link between the melodramatic tradition of Victorian literature and film, particularly Hollywood).

Museum of the Moving Image, South Bank, London. A fascinating place which tells the story of the moving image in a very lively way. Lots of hands-on stuff as well as roving 'actors' to guide visitors through the exhibitions. There is also an education section well worth contacting.

National Museum of Photography, Film and Television, Princes View, Bradford. Tells the story of these three media giving space to technical as well as cultural and aesthetic issues. Has an education department. The Museum's screenings on the massive IMAX screen are impressive.

(f) Desk top publishing

There are a number of desk top publishing software packages now available. The two which are most commonly found in schools and colleges are: *Fleet Street Editor* (from Mirrorsoft, Maxwell House, 74 Worship Street, London EC2A 2EN) and *AMX Pagemaker* (from Advanced Memory Systems Ltd, Green Lane, Appleton, Warrington, W4A 5NG).

6 SOURCES

(a) Trade directories

Advertising Standards Authority Case Reports, Advertising Standards Authority. Fascinating series of reports which list the complaints received from the public about specific ads and the verdict which the ASA has reached about whether they are 'honest, legal, decent and truthful'. The ASA also publish a pack specifically aimed at primary schools about the code of practice for toy advertisements.

Broadcasters Audience Research Board (BARB) by Audits of Great Britain (AGB). Jointly funded by BBC and IBA, BARB produce a whole series of media-related research data including weekly programme-by-programme viewing figures with regional variations. Other regular data includes viewing by audience type (e.g. by social class, age, gender and the expansive category of housewife – which includes men) but not by ethnicity.

BBC Audience Research Findings, BBC. Occasional series which gives details of audience size and reactions. Past publications have dealt with children's TV, educational broadcasting, etc. Invaluable.

BBC Annual Report and Handbook, BBC. An annual publication which gives an overview of the BBC's myriad activities. Fascinating reading.

Benn's Press Dictionary, available from Benn Business Information Services Ltd. Annual directory which gives details of the majority of newspapers and magazines and in particular who owns them and how many people read them.

BFI Film and Television Yearbook, BFI. An essential read which covers much more than what the BFI is up to. Gives an annual update on what is happening in various parts of the country, and some useful financial data. Extensive reference sections.

British Phonographic Industry Yearbook, BPI. Annual publication containing a vast array of statistics and comments about the music industry.

British Rate and Data (BRAD), available from 76 Oxford St, London. Gives advertising rates for any size of ad for every publication in the country as well as rates for TV commercials. Some of the abbreviations might be difficult to understand and calculators are needed to work out the TV rates, but an essential source for any detailed project work on advertising.

IBA TV and RADIO, IBA. Annual report on the state of the IBA. Contains valuable factual information.

IBA, A Children's View: National Survey. The IBA undertake a bi-monthly survey of children's viewing habits which includes a remarkable research instrument called an appreciation index (on a 1 to 6 scale). In addition the IBA have published occasional studies such as *Children Are People* (1981), and *Television and Teenagers* (1980), which give a wide range of information about patterns of viewing.

Media World Yearbook, Mediatel. Fascinating annual review of the nation's viewing and reading habits (including the newer media such as video, teletext, cable and satellite). Magazine/newspaper information gives circulation figures which cover a ten-year period.

Trade newspapers, magazines and journals

Broadcast, weekly magazine for the broadcasting industry.

Campaign, weekly magazine for the advertising industry. Particularly useful on current and forthcoming campaigns.

Free Press, the monthly journal of the Campaign for Press and Broadcasting Freedom, the campaigning pressure group.

The *Guardian*, a media page appears every Monday.

Media Week, a glossy weekly 'for the media by the media'.

Music Week, the weekly magazine for the music industry. Contains

valuable information about technical developments, forthcoming releases and who's doing what.

Screen International, weekly film trade journal.

Sight & Sound, recently re-launched cinema and TV monthly from the
BFI.

Television, a weekly on all aspects of the televisual industries including
cable and satellite.

(c) Courses, conferences and schools

Association for Media Education in Scotland (AMES) Annual Conference.
Event for Scotland's media educationists.

British Film Institute (BFI) Easter School. An annual five/six day event
particularly designed for teachers relatively new to the area. Location
varies.

BFI Summer School. An annual feature which lasts a week and is intended
for anyone interested in furthering their critical understanding of film
and television. Tends to be held at the University of Stirling.

Conferences. There are a number of conferences held every year which
have specific relevance for media education. AMES and BFI hold many
events including national conferences. See sections (pp. 221 and 223) on
Newsletters and Media Organizations for the best sources of information on forthcoming events.

Directions. Occasional publication from BFI Funding and Development
listing training courses available, especially regionally in the film and
video workshops.

Film and Television Training, BFI. A guide to colleges, polytechnics and
workshops offering courses which involve film and video production.

International Television Studies Conference. A biennial event held at the
Institute of Education, University of London, which brings together
media researchers, academics, teachers and broadcasters. Papers from
the 1986 conference are available from the Institute (for guide to 1986 see
Media Analysis Papers nos 9 and 10), while a number of the 1984 papers
are available in *Television in Transition*, Phillip Drummond and Richard
Paterson (eds) (London: BFI, 1986).

Studying Film and Television, BFI. A comprehensive guide to courses in
higher education, of which there are a growing number.

(d) Newsletters

AMES Newsletter, the termly newsletter of the Association for Media
Education in Scotland.

Fast Forward, newsletter of the International Broadcasting Trust. A
quarterly newsletter which includes articles, features and reviews on a
range of development issues. Occasional features on media education.

Fast Forward, newsletter of the Media Initiative Group (North West).
Contains reviews and news of forthcoming events.

Initiatives, until 1989, the termly newsletter from SEFT which combines
articles with reviews and news. Each of the termly newsletters was

edited by one of the many groups in the network of media education initiatives (MEI).

In the Picture, Northern/Yorkshire Arts. Focusing on a different media topic with each issue, this occasional magazine is addressed to media educationists.

Media Education, newsletter of the Media Centre, South Hill Park, Bracknell. A termly newsletter for media teachers in the Southern Arts region. Combines short articles, reviews and forthcoming events listing.

Medialog, a termly newsletter for West London media teachers.

(e) Media education journals and magazines

The Media Education Journal (formerly *The AMES Journal*) published by Comedia for the Scottish Curriculum Development Service, Moray House College of Education, Holyrood House, Edinburgh. Excellently produced journal which includes shorter theoretical issues, accounts of classroom practice and curricular developments. Each issue is edited by a different regional group of the Association for Media Education in Scotland (AMES).

English in Education (49 Broomgrove Road, Sheffield). Journal of the National Association of the Teaching of English, carries occasional articles on media education.

The English Magazine (English and Media Centre, Sutherland St, Ebury Bridge, London SW1). Primarily for English teachers and frequently carrying articles about media education of interest to teachers outside as well as inside London.

Independent Media (Documentary Video Associates Ltd, 16 Fernhill Road, Farnborough, Hants GU14 9RX). A monthly publication with critical articles on independent productions and a small education sector. Was *Independent Video* until November 1986.

Independent Video, see *Independent Media*.

Journal of Educational Television (80 Micklegate, York). The quarterly journal of the Educational Television Association which includes reports of recent research, information on new media and occasional articles on media education.

Media, Culture and Society (School of Communication, Polytechnic of Central London, 18–22 Riding House St, London W1). More recent issues have included topics of relevance to media teachers.

Screen (incorporating *Screen Education*). Quarterly journal dealing with theoretical issues about film and television. Central but often difficult reading. Occasional issues devoted entirely to media education.

Screen Education. The major journal for media education during the 1970s until its incorporation into *Screen* in 1982.

Teaching English (Scottish Curriculum Development Service, Moray House College of Education, Holyrood House, Edinburgh). Journal of English teachers in Scotland with occasional articles and even issues on media education.

Teaching London Kids (40 Hamilton Road, London SW19). Radical 'grass–roots' educational magazine with frequent articles on English and Media Studies.

Ten-8 (60 Holt Street, Aston, Birmingham). A quarterly photographic magazine which raises issues of relevance to media teachers.

(f) Media education organizations

This is by no means a comprehensive list but attempts to highlight organizations most closely involved with media education. For more information see the appropriate listing in the *BFI Film and Television Yearbook*, the monthly *Independent Media* or contact the IFPVA (p. 224).

Albany Video (Battersea Studios, Television Centre, Thackeray Road, London SW8 3TW). Produces a catalogue which lists over 100 tapes for use with education, youth and community groups.

Association for Media Education in Scotland (AMES, c/o Department of Film and Television Studies, University of Stirling, Stirling). The national organization for Scotland, organizing an annual conference, occasional events and *The Media Education Journal* published by Comedia.

Birmingham Film and Video Workshop (60 Holt St, Birmingham). In addition to their film and video production the workshop has produced a West Midlands film and video handbook which details the film and video activity in the West Midlands Arts region.

Black Audio Film Collective (89 Ridley Road, London E8). One of the leading black independent film and video workshops. Producers and distributors of the film *Handsworth Songs* and tape/slide *Signs of Empire*.

British Film Institute (BFI, 21 Stephen Street, London W1P 1PL). Central agency for film and television culture. Most relevant sections are: *BFI Education*, offering an extensive range of teaching materials, publications and exhibition materials and educational services including advisory and INSET. Organizes the annual Paddy Whannel Award established to recognize educational initiatives in film, television and video; the *Museum of the Moving Image*, opened in 1988 and located on London's South Bank offers an accessible history of film and television and is particularly suited for school trips; *BFI Film and Video Library* houses the most substantial library of films, videos, extracts and compilations for media education; the *Library* houses the most comprehensive print collection for research and reference.

Campaign for Press and Broadcasting Freedom (9 Poland Street, London W1V 3DG). A campaigning group which lobbies on a wide range of media and censorship issues. Issues a regular newspaper, *Free Press*.

Ceddo Film and Video Workshop (South Tottenham Education Training Workshop, Braemar Road, London N15 5EU). Produces films, videos and courses for media education.

Clwyd Media Studies Unit (Shire Hall, Mold). The media resource centre for North Wales, producing slim, well–designed, attractive and simple teaching materials.

Cockpit Cultural Studies Centre (Gateforth Street, London NW8 8EH). Exhibitions and a major source of material including publications, especially useful for photography.

Circles, Women's Work in Distribution (113 Roman Road, London E2). One of several distributors of films and videos about and by women.

Development Education Project (Manchester Polytechnic, 801 Wilmslow Road, Didsbury, Manchester M20 8RG). Through its Media Project, INSET courses and teaching materials like *Crisis in Sandagua* (see section 5 (a), p. 207), this agency provides a service to media educationists interested in how the media represents Third World issues.

The English and Media Centre (Sutherland Street, Ebury Bridge, London SW1). Perhaps the most influential agency for English teaching in the past decade. Produces publications and a journal, *The English Magazine*; also teaching materials, many of which are excellent for media education.

Film Education (37/39 Oxford Street, London W1V 1RE). Established during British Film Year in 1986 and funded by the film industry, this organization produces study guides on films and film debates free on request, has lectures and study days and a regular newsletter.

Guild Learning (6 Royce Road, Peterborough PE1 5YB). The main film and video distributor of media education videos of broadcast TV programmes.

Independent Film, Video and Photography Association (IFVPA, 79 Wardour Street, London W1V 3PH). Representing film, video and photography practitioners in the independent sector.

The Irish Film Institute (65 Harcourt Street, Dublin 2). A small education section bravely seeks to provide services in Ireland similar to BFI Education on substantially less resources.

Leigh Media Education Centre (Railway Road, Leigh). Provides video production facilities, courses and materials for schools, colleges and community groups.

Let's Make a Film and Video Festival (CRS Ltd, Members Relations Department, 78–102 The Broadway, Stratford, London E15 1NL). Not a competition but an annual project which encourages young people in film and video work. The project culminates in a week-long exhibition of materials in addition to a day of screenings and discussions. Awards are made in a wide range of categories.

Media Education Centre (MEC, 5 Llandaff Road, Canton, Cardiff CF1 9NF). Team of educationalists and producers with extensive INSET and resources servicing an area of South Wales.

Media Education Development Project/Scottish Film Council (74 Victoria Crescent Road, Dowanhill, Glasgow G12). The central Scottish agency for media education and producer of teaching materials like *The Brand X Game* and *The Football Game*.

National Association of Teacher Educators and Advisers in Media Education (TEAME, c/o Dept of English and Media Studies, University of London Institute of Education, 20 Bedford Way, London, WC1H 0AL). This association has organized events by and for these educational interests.

National Media Education Archive (c/o the Film and Video Officer, Portsmouth College of Art, Design and FE, Winston Churchill Avenue, Portsmouth, PO1 2DJ). Established in association with the British Film Institute to house materials and documents relating to media education. Aims to create a comprehensive record of how media education is developing.

Newspaper Society (74–7 Great Russell Street, London WC1B 3DA, tel: 071 636 7014). The association of publishers of regional and local press promoting the study and use of newspapers in the classroom. It has an education officer, publishes teaching materials and has a 'Newspapers in Education' scheme.

Open University (Learning Materials Service Office, Centre for Continuing Education, PO Box 188, Milton Keynes ME7 6DH). Two courses, *Mass Communications and Society* and *Popular Culture*, produce an outstanding series of teaching booklets containing essays which offer overviews of aspects of media and cultural studies.

Oxfam Education (189 Dyke Road, Hove, BN3 1TL). Oxfam Education has produced a number of publications which deal directly with Third World issues. The most relevant for media education include: *Disasters in the Classroom*, containing ideas on how to counter Third World stereotypes in the classroom; *The News Behind the News*, which concentrates on how the news media dealt with Ethiopia; *Deadlines*, a role play focusing on news coverage of crop failure in Africa.

Resources for Learning Development Unit (Bishop Road, Bristol). Resource centre for Avon LEA which produces teaching pack *Who is this Woman?* (see Section 5 (a), p. 213) and plans further packs on the development and use of photography, how newspapers use photographs, photographs as icons, and war photography from the Crimea to Vietnam. (All produced as a result of a joint project by the Arts Council, Avon LEA and the Royal Photographic Society.)

Scottish Film Council (74 Victoria Crescent Road, Dowanhill, Glasgow G12 9JN). See Media Education Development Project.

Society for Education in Film and Television (SEFT) Between the 1950s and 1989, SEFT campaigned initially for film education and then television and media criticism and education. It produced *Screen* magazine from 1970, incorporating *Screen Education* journal from the early 1980s, and *Initiatives*, a termly newsletter for media teachers. It organized events and listed the regional Media Initiative Groups (MEI's), many of which continue since SEFT's demise in 1989.

Sheffield Media Unit (Central Library, Surrey Street, Sheffield). A joint initiative by the Council and a voluntary association which offers training, resources and services to schools, colleges and other groups.

Thames TV International (149 Tottenham Court Road, London W1P 9LL). A commercial company offering some Thames broadcast programmes useful for media teaching for sale on video. Write to *The English Programme* at the same address for a full catalogue of programmes 1977–88.

Team Video (2 Ridgemount, Ridge Road, London N12). Distributors of broadcast and independent media education videos.

Bookshops

Compendium Books (Camden High Street, London). Has a very wide selection of books about the media, including many American titles.

Dillons (Gower Street, London). Has quite a large section on the media, primarily from a sociological perspective.

First of May Bookshop (Candlemaker Row, Edinburgh). A good selection with a large catalogue.

The Media Bookshop (P.O. Box 1057, Quinton, Birmingham B17 8EZ). Has a huge catalogue containing more than 2,000 titles.

NOTE

This section was written in 1989 and updated at the beginning of 1990.

Index